Catalog of the Unusual

Catalog of the Unusual

Harold H. Hart
Designed by Gary Saylor

Hart Publishing Co., Inc.   719 Broadway   New York City

To Martin Gerson, who went through life with a discerning eye that could readily distinguish the beautiful and the unusual from the tawdry and the commonplace.

How to Use This Book

Every item in this book is accompanied by a picture and a descriptive writeup which presents prime information—size, color, material, weight (where that factor is important), and price. In almost all cases, shipping charges are given.

The name of the company from which the article can be purchased appears in italics at the very end of the writeup. If you turn to the back of the book, in the section marked SOURCES, you will find an alphabetical listing of every supplier, along with the full address of the company. Names are alphabetized exactly as listed in the writeups, that is, under the very first initial.

Notes to Buyers

In normal times, prices of articles undergo some change, up or down. Today, with inflation in full cry throughout the world, and with the devaluation of the dollar, prices are uncommonly unstable.

We have made every effort to verify the current price of every article in this book. But we cannot guarantee the prices listed, since changes are so rapid. We believe the reader will find that most prices listed in these pages are pretty close to what he can expect to pay. However, to be on the safe side, the prospective buyer might verify the price by writing to the source of supply.

The more than 1,000 possessions in this book derive from over 300 sources located in many different cities and countries. If you should decide to order any of these things by mail, keep in mind that shipping will take at least 10 to 12 weeks from Africa or Asia, 8 to 9 weeks from South America, and 6 to 7 weeks from Europe. Orders from firms in the United States may take anywhere from two to four weeks to deliver.

Buyers from overseas sources should also bear in mind that goods they purchase might be subject to duty. It would be prudent before purchase to consult the U.S. Customs Department.

Where goods are shipped parcel post, the postage stated in these pages is only approximate. Obviously, postage for a parcel shipped from California to Oregon is bound to be much less than if shipped to New Jersey. The reader is advised to use his judgment in this matter. It is our belief that if you have included a substantial overpayment of postage with your order, most reliable firms will reimburse you.

Also, please note that no postage is stated for small articles found in lists, such as a package of spices, or a pound of coffee, or a half-pound of tea, or a jar of preserves. We have consulted with a number of suppliers of such articles, and find that, generally speaking, adding 60¢ to the price is sufficient to cover postage and handling of any such items.

Although we cannot guarantee to answer all letters from readers, we would be happy and grateful to hear from any reader who has either been immensely pleased or immensely displeased with his experience in using this catalog. Such information would help us enormously in any future compilation of a CATALOG OF THE UNUSUAL.

Introduction

Much as he would have liked to, the author has not examined most of the articles listed in this book; this would have been a physical impossibility.

However, it is confidently believed that the buyer may order with assurance, since the sources for these items are, for the most part, firms of reputation that have been in business for a considerable length of time. Yet we wish to make it clear that we cannot accept responsibility for the quality of anything ordered, or for the kind of service that might be rendered on any order.

None of the items in this book have been included because they are bargains. They may be, but this has not been a reason for selection. Nor has any item been included because it represents unusually fine workmanship, although that might well be the case. The reason for inclusion is simply that in its genre, the article has been deemed to be unusual.

What is unusual? To start with, one must admit that what is unusual to one person may not be unusual to another. A man who operates the pro shop of a golf club may have been solicited, at one time or another, with every kind of golf gadget that has ever been manufactured. To such a person, there is hardly any golf item that would seem unusual, no matter what it was. But there are probably many gadgets in this book that are unknown to the most enthusiastic of Sunday golfers.

As a pragmatic definition, we would say that we would class as unusual any item not known to four out of five people. In poring over scores and scores of items in no less than 1,000 catalogs, the author was obliged, almost as a rule of thumb, to discard any item which appeared in as many as three or four catalogs.

Obviously, categories such as original paintings or antiques, of which there is only one of a kind, or wallpapers or posters, of which there is simply an endless array, or women's clothing, and other unmanageable categories have had, perforce, to be excluded. On the other hand, objects which may not be of great practical value, but which were particularly off-beat or wildly surprising have been included, even though their main interest may be as reading matter rather than as practical commodities.

Nevertheless, if the author is typical, one could well spend a small fortune on the items in this book, which intrigue through description. The author admits to having succumbed to some fifty such blandishments.

The gamut of offerings in this volume might well represent a compendium of the best material offerings of our affluent society. Whether or not you want, need, or admire these items, they are likely to engage your interest; and they are likely to be of even greater interest, let us say, some ten or twenty years hence. This is a book to hold on to.

Harold H. Hart

Contents

It's about Time

Does time pass us by, or do we pass it by? Is it an omnipresent fact of life, or an arbitrary order imposed on a chaotic and confusing universe? Whatever the case, man has sought to measure time ever more accurately, as if in finally capturing it he could make time stand still.

All methods of measuring time have been based on some recurring natural phenomenon—the daily course of the sun, the phases of the moon, the change of the seasons. Perhaps the earliest of man's time-measuring devices was the upright pole or stone, which functioned in the same way as its successor, the sundial. The Egyptians, for instance, used their pyramids and obelisks to measure time. Other early methods were the hourglass and the clepsydra, or water clock.

Invention of the first mechanical clock—a clock with an escapement—has been attributed to I'Hsing and Liang Ling-tsan of China, circa 725 A.D. An escapement is a device that controls the motion of the train of wheelwork, and permits a tooth to escape from a pallet at regular intervals. In the next century, Pacificus, the archdeacon of Verona, invented the first weight-driven clock.

Between 1150 and 1400, many great cathedral and tower clocks were constructed. Among the most famous of these were the clock of the Cathedral of Strasbourg and that of St. Paul's Cathedral in London. Built in 1286, the St. Paul's clock contained mechanical figures which would strike a bell on the hour. A dial was added in the following century.

The advent of the coiled spring, circa 1500, made possible the construction of lighter and smaller clocks. Weight or pendulum clocks, forerunners of the grandfather clock, could now be used in the home, and watches could be borne by the individual.

The first portable timepiece was made in Nuremberg in 1504 by Peter Henlein. Because of their shape and heft, these early watches were called "Nuremberg live eggs." The first wrist-watch appeared as early as 1790. It was made by Jacquet-Droz and Leschot of Geneva.

Swiss watch-making continued to be the finest in the world in succeeding years. All work and construction were done by hand, until the introduction in the 1850s of machine-made parts in the United States. Soon afterward came the innovation of the attached stem, which replaced the bother of a separate key for winding.

Modern timepieces are electric, self-winding, magnetic, solar-cell-powered, etc. The most accurate time-measuring device of all is the system of twin atomic hydrogen masers installed at the U.S. Naval Research Laboratory in 1964. It is accurate to within one second per 1,700,000 years.

Undoubtedly, man will push on until he has perfectly synchronized his timepieces with nature. But even then, he will have come no closer to capturing the essence of time, not to speak of solving the mystery of the beginning and end of time.

Renaissance Watch

The rosy-cheeked Renaissance lady is made of fired porcelain enamel, and is surrounded by handcrafted metallic lacework. The watch is 2" in diameter. $167.00 postpaid. *Arnex.*

How did the term o'clock originate? Unquestionably, the original form was *of the clock;* *o'clock* is merely a contraction. Both phrases mean to say, *according to the clock.* In Chaucer's day, the term *of the clock* was used. Chaucer's language was *ten of the clokke.* Many writers of the 16th and 17th centuries said *ten of clock* or *ten a clock.* In the early 18th century, the form *o'clock* began to appear.

Tide Clock

Designed for use in any semidiurnal tide area, this brass clock indicates the stage of your tide accurately and at a glance. A 13-jewel movement operates on a long-life transistor battery. 5¼" diameter. $96.00. Postage $1.00. *Orvis.*

Squashed Clock

Projecting a rather interesting image of time, this lucite clock is battery-operated. Its 8" square face comes in white, red, blue and yellow. $17.50. Postage $1.00. *Ever-Lite.*

Foliot Wall Clock

The foliot, the earliest form of mechanical-clock escapement, was mentioned by Dante in 1320 in his *Divine Comedy.* This clock measures 14" by 30"; but because of its stone-weighted pendulum, requires hanging room of six feet. $249.50. Shipped express collect. *J. Kenneth Zahn.*

It's about Time

Tide Timer

Timed to the tides instead of to the sun or to the moon, this clock accurately tells the stage the tide is in: high, low, rising, falling. And it also reveals the amount of time till the next tide change. Usable wherever there are two complete tidal cycles daily. The 6" square face has an indicator hand legible from a distance. Made of acrylic and aluminum. Can be hung on a wall, or set to stand on a table. $29.50. Postage 75¢. *Chris Craft.*

La Menerbes Sundial and La Dijon Sundial

French artist, Maurice Djian, makes each sundial to order so that it is mathematically oriented and accurate for your particular latitude. Hand-carved from limestone, the sundial can be left in its natural white so that it can develop its own gray patina, or fixed white, or treated to have a century-old look. The gnomons are wrought iron. 16" x 20". When ordering, note latitude and the compass reading of exactly the direction the dial will face (preferably south). Since the dial comes from France, allow eight weeks for delivery. $200.00 postpaid. *Sundials and More.*

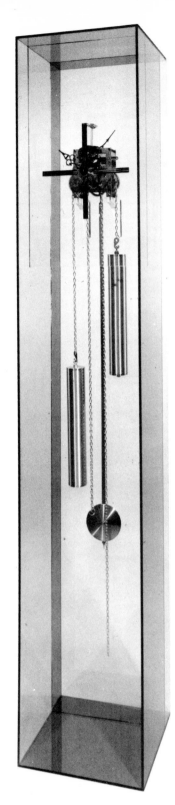

Carriage Clock

A reproduction of a 17th century timepiece, this clock measures 5" high from the bottom of its four, finely turned bun-feet to the tip of the bell-turret at the top of its five finials. The dial frames the image of a blazing sun whose rays reach outward to a ring of the 12 zodiac signs. Baroque gold-finish filigree adorns the sides of the case. Tarnish-resistant. 15-jewel eight-day Swiss alarm movement. $120.00 postpaid. *Arnex.*

Grandmother Clock

Bronze Plexiglas encases the weight-driven movement of this ultra-modern see-through clock. Chimes on the hour and half hour. 56" high, 10" wide, 10" deep. $400.00 postpaid. *1984 Store.*

Locomotive Clock

This replica of an old woodburning steam locomotive is 11½" high by 6½" wide. The face is chrome trimmed on black plastic. Runs by electricity. $12.95 postpaid. *Eastland.*

It's about Time

The Nude Maiden

Goya's "Maja Desnuda" is depicted in fired porcelain enamel on the back of this conversation piece. The painting is set within a circle of 18K solid gold. The front of the watch is decorated with porcelain enamel around the dial. Has a 17-jewel Swiss shock-protected movement. 1½" diameter. $660.00 postpaid. *Arnex.*

Lantern Alarm Clock

Constructed in the style of the late 19th century, this clock (according to the manufacturer) uses the most successful eight-day movement in horological history. The escapement balance oscillates visibly. The porcelain enamel dial is decorated with gold flower spangles; ornate gilt filigreed hands point to dial numbers, each set in a raised cartouche. Four turned-brass legs with four matching finials. 15-jewel Swiss movement. 3" high. $153.00 postpaid. *Arnex.*

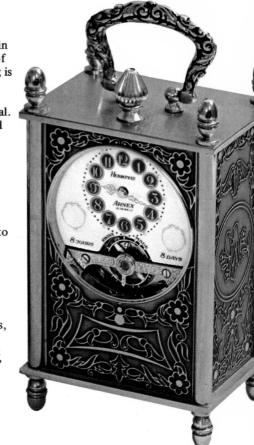

World Clock

A time zone dial lets you find out what time it is in any of the world's 124 time zones and major cities depicted on a map. The time appears lit at the top. Another light indicates a.m. or p.m. The clock communicates by electronic digital readout. Hand-finished walnut case. 7-3/4" x 7-1/2" x 4-3/8". AC only. $200.00. Postage $2.00. *Hammacher Schlemmer.*

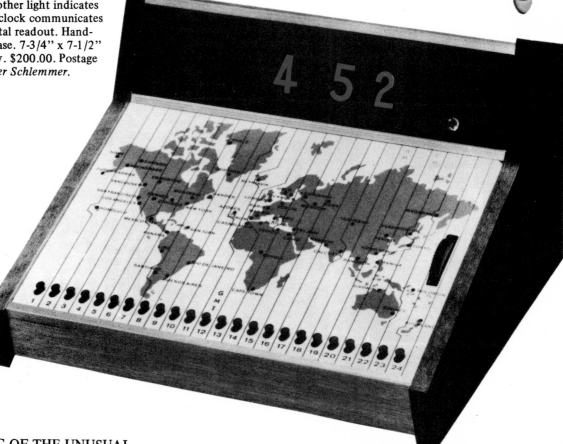

Wall Clock

A transistor battery operates this 12" round clock. White hands on black face. Spun aluminum case. $25.00. Postage $1.00. *Patio.*

Table Clock

This mantel, or table, clock is in clear Plexiglas with a butcher block base. Movement is an eight-day key wind. 18½" high, 8½" wide, and 6" deep at base. $65.00 postpaid. *1984 Store.*

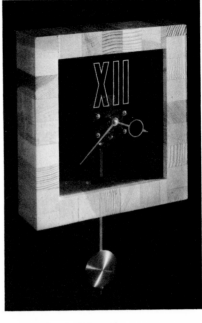

See-Thru Clock

This ultra-modern wall clock is featured by a Plexiglas face framed by butcher block wood. The clock itself appears to be a wraith-like mechanism hanging in space. A pendulum operated by an eight-day key-wound movement keeps the clock going. 10½" high, 9" wide, and 3" deep. $66.00 postpaid. *1984 Store.*

Solunagraph

In addition to being a highly accurate time-piece, this wrist watch is equipped with a moon-time dial, showing tides and animal feeding periods, and a waterproof stop watch. Directions included. $169.00. Postage $1.00. *Orvis.*

It's about Time

Counter-Clockwise Clock

You must have a certain kind of innate perverseness to want to have this sort of thing around the house. This crazy electric clock which is about 7½" in diameter runs backwards. $9.95. Postage $1.00. *Aristera.*

Man cannot call the brimming instant back;
Time's an affair of instants spun to days.
John Masefield (1875-1967),
THE WIDOW IN THE BYE STREET

Gather ye Rose-buds while ye may,
Old Time is still a flying:
And this same flower that smiles today,
Tomorrow will be dying.
Robert Herrick (1591-1674),
TO THE VIRGINS, TO MAKE MUCH OF TIME

Catch then, oh catch the transient hour;
Improve each moment as it flies!
Life's a short Summer, man a flower;
He dies—alas! how soon he dies!
Samuel Johnson (1709-1784), WINTER: AN ODE

Does thou love life? Then do not squander time,
for that is the stuff life is made of.
Benjamin Franklin (1706-1790),
POOR RICHARD'S ALMANACK, 1757

Exeter Sundial

This equatorial timepiece will prove to be accurate in any latitude. It is cast in solid bronze, and polished to its natural brilliance. 13½" high. Base diameter, 7¼". $40.00 postpaid. *Sundials and More.*

Emperor's Court

As the hour chimes, colorfully robed figurines start on parade while heralds blow their horns. The wooden case is in the shape of an old church. The blue face is shaped like a rose window. The weights on the chains are brass. 15" tall. $129.50. Postage $4.50. *Hammacher Schlemmer.*

Spilhaus Space Clock

The blue, brass framed, illuminated dials show almost every kind of time: mean solar time, world time, Greenwich mean time, ordinary time. Also shows the position of the sun and the moon, the constellations, and the relative position of the sun, the moon, and the earth; also indicates the moon phases, the time of sunset and sunrise, moonset and moonrise, and the current highs and lows of tide. Runs by electricity. Base of wood. 15½" high, 11½" wide at base, 5" deep. $250.00. Shipped express collect. *Hammacher Schlemmer.*

Butcher Block Clock

Le dernier cri in modern design, this handsome clock is finished on all sides. Runs on batteries. 10" high, 9" wide, 5" deep. $70.00 postpaid. *1984 Store.*

Clock the World

This 3" long desk clock makes it easy to calculate the time anywhere in the world. Anti-magnetic 17-jewel Swiss movement. Gold-tone case. $40.00. Postage $1.10. *Kenton Collection.*

In the famous cathedral of Notre Dame de Dijon in France, there is the oldest gong clock in the world. Given to the town of Dijon in 1383 by Philip the Hardy, this clock has been keeping abreast of the time ever since. Constructed by Jacques Marc, the clock contains two large bronze figures which have struck the hour every hour for the last 590 years. An ambitious mathematician computed that by January 1, 1950, these bronze figures had struck the clock 32,284,980 times.

It's about Time

Tide Clock

Nautically styled, this chronometer tells at a glance whether the tide is high or low, rising or falling, how much time till low tide and high tide. Brass, $98.00; chrome, $103.00. Postage $1.25. *Adirondack Store.*

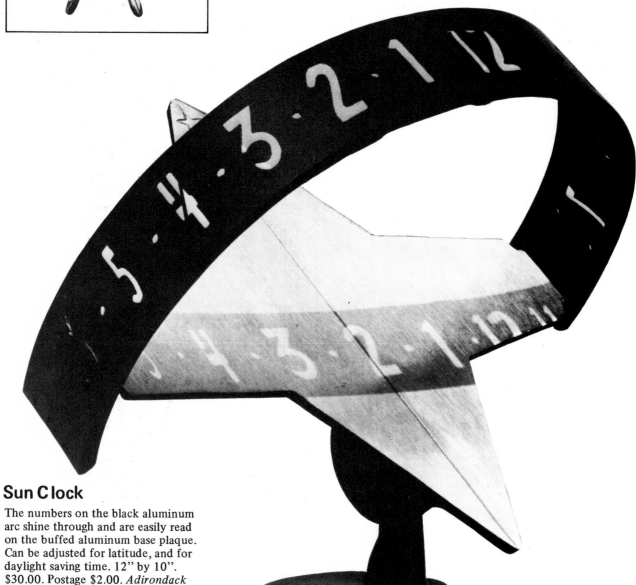

Sun Clock

The numbers on the black aluminum arc shine through and are easily read on the buffed aluminum base plaque. Can be adjusted for latitude, and for daylight saving time. 12" by 10". $30.00. Postage $2.00. *Adirondack Store.*

TIME DIFFERENCES

When it's 12:00 Noon in New York (Eastern Standard Time), the standard time in other cities is as follows:

Amsterdam	6:00 p.m.	Lima	12:00 Noon
Anchorage	7:00 a.m.	Lisbon	6:00 p.m.
Athens	7:00 p.m.	London	6:00 p.m.
Auckland	5:00 a.m.*	Los Angeles	9:00 a.m.
Azores	3:00 p.m.	Madrid	6:00 p.m.
Baghdad	8:00 p.m.	Manila	1:00 a.m.*
Bangkok	12:00 Midnight	Melbourne	3:00 a.m.*
Barcelona	6:00 p.m.	Miami	12:00 Noon
Basra	8:00 p.m.	Monrovia	4:15 p.m.
Beirut	7:00 p.m.	Montevideo	2:00 p.m.
Berlin	6:00 p.m.	Moscow	8:00 p.m.
Bermuda	1:00 p.m.	New Orleans	11:00 a.m.
Bogotá	12:00 Noon	Nome	6:00 a.m.
Bombay	10:30 p.m.	Noumea	4:00 a.m.*
Boston	12:00 Noon	Okinawa	2:00 a.m.*
Brussels	6:00 p.m.	Oslo	6:00 p.m.
Bucharest	7:00 p.m.	Paris	6:00 p.m.
Buenos Aires	1:00 p.m.	Phoenix	10:00 a.m.
Cairo	7:00 p.m.	Portland	9:00 a.m.
Calcutta	10:30 p.m.	Rangoon	11:30 p.m.
Capetown	7:00 p.m.	Recife	2:00 p.m.
Caracas	1:00 p.m.	Reykjavik	5:00 p.m.
Chicago	11:00 a.m.	Rio de Janeiro	2:00 p.m.
Copenhagen	6:00 p.m.	Rome	6:00 p.m.
Dakar	5:00 p.m.	Saigon	1:00 a.m.*
Damascus	7:00 p.m.	Salt Lake City	10:00 a.m.
Delhi	10:30 p.m.	Samoa	6:00 a.m.
Denver	10:00 a.m.	San Francisco	9:00 a.m.
Djakarta	12:00 Midnight	San Juan	1:00 p.m.
Dublin	6:00 p.m.	Santiago	1:00 p.m.
Fairbanks	7:00 a.m.	Seattle	9:00 a.m.
Frankfurt	6:00 p.m.	Seoul	2:00 a.m.*
Frobisher	1:00 p.m.	Shanghai	1:00 a.m.*
Gander	1:30 p.m.	Shannon	6:00 p.m.
Geneva	6:00 p.m.	Singapore	12:30 a.m.
Glasgow	6:00 p.m.	Stockholm	6:00 p.m.
Greenwich	6:00 p.m.	Suva	5:00 a.m.*
Guam	3:00 a.m.*	Sydney	3:00 a.m.*
Hayana	12:00 Noon	Tahiti	7:00 a.m.
Helsinki	7:00 p.m.	Teheran	8:30 p.m.
Hong Kong	1:00 a.m.*	Tokyo	2:00 a.m.*
Honolulu	7:00 a.m.	Tucson	10:00 a.m.
Istanbul	7:00 p.m.	Valparaiso	1:00 p.m.
Jerusalem	7:00 p.m.	Vancouver	9:00 a.m.
Johannesburg	7:00 p.m.	Vienna	6:00 p.m.
Juneau	9:00 a.m.	Warsaw	6:00 p.m.
Karachi	10:00 p.m.	Washington, D.C.	12:00 Noon
Keflavik	5:00 p.m.	Whitehorse	8:00 a.m.
Ketchikan	9:00 a.m.	Yokohama	2:00 a.m.*
Kinshasa	6:00 p.m.	Zurich	6:00 p.m.

*Following day.

Watertight Watch

So watertight, this watch comes packed in water. A world time indicator lists key cities of the world. It has a 24-hour face. Elapsed time indicator helps in timing situations, such as when you are using a parking meter. Shock resistant, unbreakable mainspring. Stainless steel back. The 17-jewel Swiss movement winds by arm motion; keeps running indefinitely. Day and date of month change automatically. Men's watch in black or blue dial. Women's model has blue dial and white strap. Life-time guarantee. $39.95. Postage 75¢. *Chris Craft.*

It's about Time

Open-face Watch

A fired porcelain enamel dial decorates this open-faced watch. Swiss 17-jewel shock-proof movement. 2" diameter. Available in red, blue, or black. $66.00 postpaid. *Arnex.*

Pocket Alarm Clock

At 1¼" by 1½" long, this might be the world's smallest alarm clock. Shock-proof, 17-jewel movement; battery-powered electronic buzzer. Leather case. $95.70. Postage $1.00. *Projects Unlimited, Inc.*

Ceiling Alarm Clock

This electric clock projects the exact time on the ceiling at five minute intervals. 7" high, 5" wide. Finished in French beige. Wood base, $34.95. Postage $1.99. *House of Minnel.*

When Emperor Charles V of Spain retired to the monastery of Yuste, he indulged his mechanical bent by lining up several clocks and trying to make them tick in unison. He finally gave up in despair, observing that if he could not make any two clocks run together in the same rhythm, how could he possibly have believed he was able to make thousands of men think and act alike?

However, William H. Prescott, the noted historian, refused to credit this story. In his book, *The Life of Charles the Fifth After His Abdication*, Prescott wrote: "The difficulty which he found in adjusting his clocks and watches is said to have drawn from the monarch a philosophical reflection on the absurdity of his having attempted to bring men to anything like uniformity of belief in matters of faith, when he could not make any two of his time-pieces agree with each other. But that he never reached the degree of philosophy required for such reflection is abundantly shown by more than one sentiment that fell from his pen, as well as his lips, during his residence at Yuste."

The chief companion of Charles V at his retreat was one Torriano who was reputed to be highly skilled in the manufacture of time-pieces and who had made many elaborate clocks to adorn his monastic apartments.

Road Runner Clock

This horologe features inlaid road runners, permanently fused into the Couroc phenolic resin face which is 14" in diameter. Lustrous satin black. Seven jewel. Takes C battery. $39.95. Postage $2.10. *Clymer's.*

Talking Clock

This clock, possibly the world's first to talk, announces the time anytime you touch it. Can be set to call the time automatically every hour, or to wake you by repeating the time every 10 seconds for up to three minutes. Equipped with remote control switch, so you don't even have to turn over in bed. Contains an FM/AM radio. $149.95. Postage $1.75. *Taylor Gifts.*

It's about Time

There is . . . a time to be born, and a time to die; a time to plant, and a time to pluck up that which is planted; A time to kill, and a time to heal; a time to break down, and a time to build up; A time to weep, and a time to laugh; a time to mourn, and a time to dance . . . A time to love and a time to hate.

Old Testament: ECCLESIASTES, iii, I

O Time! the beautifier of the dead,
Adorner of the ruin, comforter
and the only healer when the heart hath bled.

George Gordon, Lord Byron (1788-1824),
CHILDE HAROLD

Old Time, in whose bank we deposit our notes,
Is a miser who always wants guineas for groats;
He keeps all his customers still in arrears
By lending them minutes and charging them years.

Oliver Wendell Holmes (1809-1894),
OUR BANKER

Time is but the stream I go a-fishing in.

Henry David Thoreau (1817-1862),
JOURNAL, 1862

Flying Pendulum

Encased in a 12" by 16" crystal dome on a wood base, this old-world clock is run by a wooden gear drive mechanism first used in the 14th century. Distinguished by its flying pendulum escapement invented in Europe about 100 years ago, this clock is absolutely fascinating to watch. The flying pendulum was never commercialized, since it was not as accurate as the regular pendulum, yet it remains an original, fanciful mechanism. Choice of Gothic or Roman letters. Comes in antique red or antique gold. 7½" by 15" by 6". $185.00. Shipped express collect. *J. Kenneth Zahn.*

Sundial and Birdbath

Cast in iron and aluminum, this garden piece serves a dual function. Measures 12" in diameter. Birdbath depth is ¾". Screws and bolts for mounting. $16.50. Postage $2.60. *Clymer's.*

Edelweiss Watch

The back of this watch, ¾" in diameter, reveals a flower in enamel. Swiss 17-jewel shock-proof movement. $69.00 postpaid. *Arnex.*

Ah! the clock is always slow;
It is later than you think.

Robert William Service (1874-1958),
IT IS LATER THAN YOU THINK

As we advance in life, we acquire a keener sense of the value of time. Nothing else, indeed, seems of any consequence; and we become misers in this respect.

William Hazlitt (1778-1830)
THE FEELING OF IMMORTALITY IN YOUTH

Animated Musical Clock

The tableau, framed in the lower portion of this 5" high clock, depicts the following animated scene: a mounted huntsman, bearing a falcon, moves his extended arm up and down; a horse bobs his head as he drinks from a well; a maiden pumps the handle of the well. High-polished steel gives the illusion of water flowing from a spigot. Castles, a bridge, a stream are seen in the countryside background. Two melodies accompany the action: "Oh, What a Beautiful Morning," and "The Clean Fountain." The luminous hands are in Louis XV style. This eight-day alarm is a 15-jewel Swiss product. $385.00 postpaid. *Arnex.*

It's about Time

Flower Watch

The cover of this watch is fired procelain enamel. Choice of Arabic or Roman dial. Swiss 17-jewel shock-proof movement. 2" diameter. $195.00 postpaid. *Arnex.*

Marine Chronometer

This classic re-creation of a celebrated 18th century navigation clock has been commended for its accuracy by the Swiss Observatory. The brass-inlaid mahogany box is completely hand-crafted. All hardware is of solid brass. Twin axis gimbals keep the clock horizontal despite ship's motion. Battery powered; a single dry cell keeps this machine running accurately for a year. Brass-plate too, for boat owner's name. $435.00. Postage $2.00. *Chris Craft.*

> *There's a time for some things, and a time for all things; a time for great things, and a time for small things.*
>
> Cervantes (1547-1616), DON QUIXOTE

> *It is the wisest who grieve most at loss of time.*
> Dante Alighieri (1265-1321), PURGATORIO

> *What does not destructive time destroy?*
> Horace (65-8 B.C.), ODES

> *Go, sir, gallop, and don't forget that the world was made in six days. You can ask me for anything you like, except time.*
> Napoleon Bonaparte (1769-1821), TO ONE OF HIS AIDES, 1803

> *The small intolerable drums*
> *Of Time are like slow drops descending.*
> Edwin Arlington Robinson (1869-1935), THE POOR RELATIONS

> *Time is a sandpile we run our fingers on.*
> Carl Sandburg (1878-1967), HOTEL GIRL

> *Time is a river of passing events—aye, a rushing torrent.*
> Marcus Aurelius (121-180), MEDITATIONS

Quartz Clock

Built for accuracy, this spherical battery-operated clock is guaranteed to operate under normal room temperatures with a loss or gain of no more than five seconds a month. Sweep second hand. Approximately 5" in diameter. White case. Royal blue dial with white markings. $100.00. Shipped express collect. *Deluxe Saddlery.*

Atmos Clock

Changes in air temperature wind this perpetual motion clock. Runs accurately, silently, without batteries, electricity, or winding. Made of jeweler brass with a glass case by Le Coultre. Measures 9¼" by 8¼" by 6½" deep. $185.00. Shipped express collect. *Hammacher Schlemmer.*

Dice Clock

A face of clear lucite shows the hours in dice cubes. Made of walnut and brass. Battery-operated. 6½" by 5¾". $34.95. Postage $1.99. *House of Minnel.*

Calico Cat Clock

In the early 18th century, Russian woodcuts of cats aimed at lampooning Czar Peter were exported to the U.S. In America, these patterns were copied onto calico cotton, so called because the fabric was imported from Calicut, India. These cats became a very popular design. The pattern shown here is hand-screened on washable vinyl, and mounted on a 2" black-wood frame. It is 18" by 22". The cat is yellow. $52.00. Shipped express collect. *Patrice, Unlimited.*

Coffee

Surprisingly enough, coffee, which accounts for a staggering $2 billion a year in international trade, didn't reach Brazil until a mere 250 years ago. The coffee tree, indigenous only to Arabia and Ethiopia, was supposedly discovered by goats. They ate the wild-growing berries and began to cavort in the fields, convincing their goatherd to join them in a cup.

The Arabs were cultivating the plant as early as 600 A.D., and used the berries as medicine. It wasn't until the 13th century that it was discovered how to brew coffee into a beverage. For the next 400 years, the Arabs jealously guarded the coffee trade, exercising a monopoly by forbidding the export of fertile seeds on pain of death.

But about 1700, Dutch traders managed to smuggle out some plants, sending the embezzled botanica to the island of Java, where the growth became so prolific, the island's name became synonymous with the brew.

Equally intent on preserving their stolen monopoly, the Dutch likewise forbade taking seeds or seedlings from East Indian plantations. But a dashing young Brazilian officer won the heart of the wife of the governor of Dutch Guiana, a coffee growing colony in South America, and as a token of her affection, she gave him some of the precious beans and cuttings, anticipating Cole Porter by declaring her love thusly: "Take the beans, for you're the cream in my coffee!"

Whatever the method used to brew coffee, the prime requirements are properly roasted, freshly ground beans, boiling water, and absolute cleanliness of utensils. "Turkish" coffee, finely powdered, heavily sweetened, and unfiltered, is favored by most Eastern peoples. Westerners prefer clear coffee. The French *café au lait,* coffee plus scalded milk, is largely a breakfast drink.

Opinion differs about the moral value of coffee. Despite suppression on religious and political grounds, coffee became the universal beverage of Islam. It was then opposed by Italian churchmen as a drink of the infidel, but was Christianized by Pope Clement VIII. By 1650, coffee had reached most of Europe. Although introduced in North America about 20 years later, coffee became the staple American drink only after tea had been downgraded with the Boston Tea Party of 1773.

Cappuccino Espresso

After-dinner coffee is made quickly with this machine. Water is electrically heated in the chrome center cylinder, then forced through the grounds. Makes up to five demi-tasse cups of coffee, and puffs the milk for Espresso Cappuccino. $225.00. Shipped express collect. *Hammacher Schlemmer.*

Coffee Warmer

Designed to commemorate the forthcoming Bi-Centennial of the U.S., this beverage urn, made of earthenware, is glazed with a warm white background, decorated in cobalt blue. Holds 24 cups. Kept hot by a candle warmer. $44.95. Shipped express collect. *B. Altman.*

Half-a-Cup of Coffee

You may ask your guest if she will have another cup of coffee. The answer may well be, "Oh, just half a cup." So you trot out with this. White ceramic. 3½" high. Holds 4 oz. $1.00. Postage 49¢ *Lillian Vernon.*

Coffee Starter

Plug this gadget into the socket and you can sleep until the very, very, very last moment. Then the comforting aroma of brewing coffee will beckon you to the tribulations of the day. You fill the percolator the night before, and set the coffee starter to the desired time. 3 5/8" high; 2 3/8" wide; 2" deep. Comes in beige, white, or gold. $7.95. Postage 90¢. *Sleepy Hollow Gifts.*

UNUSUAL COFFEES

	per lb.	
Amahara Ethiopian	$1.60	*House of Yemen*
Bedouin Arabica	1.75	*House of Yemen*
Colombian Supremo	2.05	*McNulty's Tea & Coffee Co.*
Guatemala Antigua	1.79	*Vermont Country Store*
Hawaiian Kona	2.40	*H. Roth & Son*
Jamaican Blue Mountain	2.75	*McNulty's Tea & Coffee Co.*
Mocha-Java	2.05	*McNulty's Tea & Coffee Co.*
Mocha-Colombian Supremo	2.05	*McNulty's Tea & Coffee Co.*
Santos	1.79	*Vermont Country Store*
Toltec	2.00	*McNulty's Tea & Coffee Co.*
Anisette (Demitasse) (12 oz. jar)	$1.30	*Manganaro's*

Coffee

Traveling Coffeemaker

All the makings for a refreshing coffee-break come in this compact kit. The six-cup percolator comes with separate 220 and 110 volt cord sets and a dashboard safety bracket so you can brew coffee in your car or on a picnic bench. Four plastic cups, four spoons, sugar holder, creamer and coffee measure are included. Comes in black vinyl case. $21.00. Postage $1.00. *Chris Craft.*

Mr. Coffee—Coffeemaker

Pour cold water in, and hot coffee comes out. Filtered coffee is automatically brewed by this 13 1/2" high, 7 3/8" deep coffeemaker. Coffee flows from the brewing funnel into a heat-resistant, glass decanter on a thermostatically controlled warming plate, which is designed to hold the coffee at the right drinking temperature. $40.00. Postage $3.15. *Hammacher Schlemmer.*

Electric Cappuccino Machine

Operated by pushbutton, this machine has a built-in steam jet which puffs the milk for cappuccino coffee. Thermostatically heats and re-heats the coffee. Makes two demi-tasse cups every 20 seconds. The water reservoir is sufficient for 20 servings. 7" wide; 9" deep; 13" high. Stainless steel. $175.00. Shipped express collect. *Hammacher Schlemmer.*

Show Me the Way to Go Home!

Many sources credit the Chinese with the invention of the compass, but there is no hard evidence to back up this claim. The first mention of the compass in European literature does not occur until the 12th century.

The usefulness of the compass in finding direction lies in the fact that its magnetic needle points unerringly to the magnetic north, no matter that the needle turns freely on its pivot. Certain non-magnetic devices, such as the gyro-compass, can perform the same function as the compass.

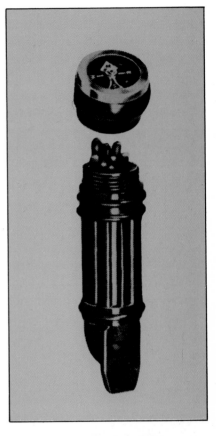

Compass Combination

The case contains three things: a compass with a luminous dial; a waterproof match case, large enough to hold a small candle; and a whistle which can be heard over a long distance. 4½" long. Weighs only 1½ oz. $3.75 postpaid. *L. L. Bean.*

Prismatic Compass

An adjustable prism eyepiece permits simultaneous viewing of the hairline, compass dial, and target. Movable inclination indicator measures both percentage and degree of inclination. Useful as a bearing compass or as a geologist's or an engineer's compass. Luminous. Leather case included. 4" by 2¼" by 1". $29.95. Postage $1.75. *Taylor Gifts.*

Self-Illuminated Compass

Designed for use in car or boat, this compass has a fingertip flash cell built into the case. Upon pressing the button, the dial lights up with a soft glow. The light goes off when the button is released. A single cell lasts for months. Replacements obtainable everywhere. Comes in black and grey case. Battery included. $7.95 postpaid. *Gokey.*

Lakeside and Seaside

The largest lake in the world is not called a lake, but is misnamed the Caspian Sea. Lying between Asia and Europe, it covers an area of over 343,000 square miles, and is approximately 760 miles long. This immense body of water is about four and one-half times as large as the next largest lake. Lake Superior, the second largest lake in the world, is 350 miles long, and is nearly four times as large as Lake Ontario, the smallest of the Great Lakes.

The saltiest lake in the world is the Dead Sea, which is so full of chemicals that it is really difficult for anyone to drown, or even remain fully submerged in it for any length of time. The chemicals make the water so heavy that it is also hard to swim. Each stroke you take makes you feel as if you're pushing away a ton of bricks. Of course, it's so easy to float in the Dead Sea that the thing to do is to get out there under an umbrella, hold a book in hand and simply lie on your back and read in comfort. But when you get out of the water, you'll find yourself covered with an oily film which is rather difficult to remove.

The deepest lake is Lake Baykal, which lies in Siberia. Its bottom is almost a mile down.

According to a very orthodox Jewish religious sect, the holiest lake in the world is Lake Tefilin.

Inflatable Sportboat

This speedster can deflate to a size small enough to stow in a car trunk. The craft, made of nylon, can support 1,250 lbs., or six people, and up to a 45 h.p. engine. It has three air compartments. Inflated, it measures 12'6" long, 5' 6" wide. It stows into two bags. $877.00. Shipped express collect. *Abercrombie and Fitch.*

John Quincy Adams, the sixth President of the United States, rose before dawn every summer morning and took a quick dip in the Potomac. Thurlow Weed gave us this description of the energetic President's activity on a hot day in June 1825:

Having heard that the President was in the habit of bathing early every morning in the Potomac, I rose before the sun, and walked down to the bank of the river, observing, as I approached it, a gentleman in nankeen pantaloons and a blue pea-jacket walking rapidly from the White House towards the river. This was John Quincy Adams, the President of the United States. I moved off to a respectful distance. The President began to disrobe before he reached a tree on the brink of the river, where he deposited his clothes, and then plunged in head first, and struck out fifteen or twenty rods, swimming rapidly and turning occasionally upon his back, seeming as much at his ease in that element as upon terra firma. Coming out, he rubbed himself thoroughly with napkins, which he had brought for that purpose in his hand. The sun had not yet risen when he had dressed himself and was returning to the Presidential mansion.

* * *

The sun gives the sea its blue color. Actually, pure sea water is colorless. The surface water absorbs all but the blue rays of the sun. But the sea reflects back the blue rays to make the ocean traveler think the water itself is blue.

* * *

Ocean waves are sometimes 80 feet high. Most so-called mountainous waves are only 30 to 40 feet high, and no ocean wave is higher than 100 feet from trough to crest. The highest wave ever scientifically measured was 80 feet tall. But mariners are sure some waves are as high as a ten-story building.

* * *

The long-distance swimming record holder must be Mihir Sen of India. In recent years, he has swum from India to Ceylon, across the Dardanelles, across the Strait of Gibraltar, and the length of the Panama Canal.

Adolf Keifer won more than 2,000 races. He won his first U.S. championship in 1935, when he was 16 years old. For eight years thereafter the great backstroker was undefeated, and won 24 indoor and outdoor championships.

In 1946, at the time of his retirement from amateur competition, Keifer held every backstroke record in the books. In a brilliant athletic career, Keifer had lost only two races out of more than 2,000!

* * *

One day in July, 1940, John V. Sigmund waded into the Mississippi River at St. Louis and started swimming south. When his friends pulled him out of the drink, a little above Memphis, Sigmund had covered 292 miles. He had been swimming continuously for 89 hours and 42 minutes!

* * *

Three thousand feet below the sea's surface, its waters are pitch black. Not even a tiny bit of the sun's light can penetrate down more than half a mile. Sea creatures living at depths below 3,000 feet have been found to be blind or to possess their own phosphorescent "lighting system."

Tyler the Turtle

Tyler has a magic tail; twist it, and he swims. Then when he hits shore he starts crawling. Battery-operated. (Batteries not included.) $5.95. Postage $1.50. *Haverhill's.*

Lakeside and Seaside

When Johnny Weissmuller retired from amateur competition in 1929, he could have taught Tarzan himself how to swim.

The handsome natator won his first National Championship in 1921. From then on, Johnny made records in every free-style distance from 100 yards to 880 yards and even held the world's record for the 150-yard backstroke.

His mark of 51 seconds flat for the 100 yards stayed on the record books for 17 years!

* * *

Helene Madison held 16 swimming records at one time. At the end of 1932, the 6-foot, 18-year-old blonde from Seattle, Washington, held every important free-style swimming record. She had smothered all Olympic competition.

She was the first woman to swim 100 yards in one minute flat. Tank experts predicted that her records would last for generations. *Sic transit records!* Today not a single one of Helene's marks stands.

* * *

Anyone can swim or float more easily in salt water than in fresh water because salt water is heavier, and thus has greater buoyancy. There is so much salt in the Great Salt Lake of Utah, that one cannot sink or completely submerge oneself in it. Nevertheless, an inexperienced swimmer can drown if he panics and loses his balance. Although his body will float on the surface, the brine will suffocate him.

* * *

The highest tides anywhere in the world are to be found in the Bay of Fundy, which separates New Brunswick from Nova Scotia. At the head of the bay, a few times each year, the tides rush in and out at a rate of 10 feet an hour—an incredible 60 feet from highest to lowest tide. The tide moves nearly as fast as the water rises in a bathtub with both taps opened full, and the rise of the tide goes on for six hours, twice a day. At no time is the water in the bay still.

The greatest mountain range lies under the sea. This is known as the Dolphin Rise and extends from the Arctic to the Antarctic. Mountain tops are so high that at points they rise above the ocean's surface. We know some of these points as the Azore Islands and the Canary Islands. The deepest valleys between these mountains are, in some places, more than five miles below the surface of the ocean. If Mt. McKinley, Alaska, the highest mountain in North America, were dropped into such a spot, it would be completely submerged!

Water Walkers

Made of polystyrene, these walkers are buoyant and can support up to 240 lbs. $29.95. Postage $3.65. *Hammacher Schlemmer.*

Hippo Boat

Gaily colored in violet with pink and black trim, this fiberglass boat will hold two youngsters or one adult and one youngster. Has a steering wheel, electric accelerator, and rudder. Runs on a rechargeable battery. 6' long, 32" wide. $950.00. Shipped express collect. *Hammacher Schlemmer.*

Packaway Leisure Chair

This full-length lounge chair of chrome tubing and sturdy canvas folds into a 27" by 5" bag with shoulder strap. Locks in any position. $29.95. Postage $3.50. *Haverhill's.*

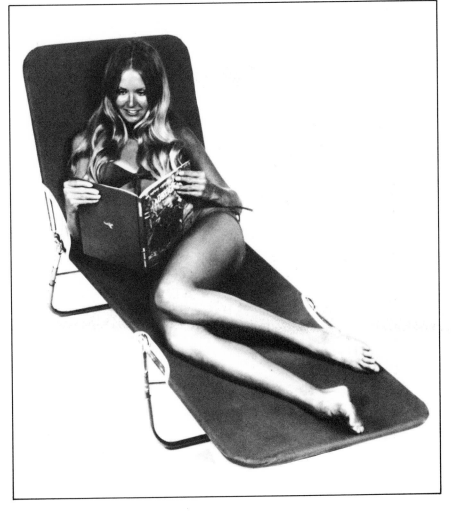

Weather or Not

The first thermometers, devised independently by Galileo and Sanctorius at the turn of the 17th century, consisted essentially of a bulb atop a stem which descended into a liquid. Heating or cooling the bulb affected the height of the column of liquid in the tube, which was marked by a scale.

About a hundred years later, in 1714, Fahrenheit of Danzig invented the mercury thermometer to measure heat. The thermometer of Reaumur, invented about 15 years later, used alcohol to measure cold. Mercury was not feasible for this thermometer because mercury solidifies at -39°C.

The centigrade thermometer, created by Celsius in 1742, is used primarily in laboratory work. It has the computational advantage of a 100-degree range between the freezing point and the boiling point.

One of the most significant uses of the thermometer is to measure body temperature. When a body temperature is above 98.6°F taken by mouth, the patient is said to have a fever. High fever indicates a bodily disturbance that requires professional attention. Persisting low-grade fever may signal a chronic infection such as tuberculosis, rheumatic fever, or mononucleosis.

Thermometer Cuff Links

These links are actually working thermometers, though accuracy is not the intention behind this decorative set of jewelry. One shows fahrenheit, the other centigrade. Gold electroplated. Black face. $10.00. Postage $2.00. *Hammacher Schlemmer.*

Electronic Thermometer

Works in both fahrenehit and centigrade. Records temperatures up to 250' from instrument. Accurate to within one degree. Housed in a wood cabinet. $39.95. Postage $1.50. *Haverhill's.*

I remember, I remember,
  Ere my childhood flitted by,
It was cold then in December,
  And was warmer in July.
In the winter there were freezings—
  In the summer there were thaws;
But the weather isn't now at all
  Like what it used to was!

Digital Desk Thermometer

Big easy-to-read numbers show the room temperature at a glance. The numbers appear, change color, and disappear almost mystically as the temperature changes. The thermometer utilizes liquid crystals sensitive to slight temperature changes developed from research by the U.S. space program; accuracy is said to be superior to normal household thermometers. The thermometer has a unique fluted tube design in soft silver finish, 8" long on a black aluminum base. $8.95. Postage 50¢. *Decor Galore.*

Jumbo Thermometer

At a full foot in diameter, with contrasting black and white dial, this temperature and humidity gauge provides maximum visibility. The top of the dial registers temperature; the bottom, humidity. Slotted on the back for wall mounting. $6.95. Postage $1.00. *Orvis.*

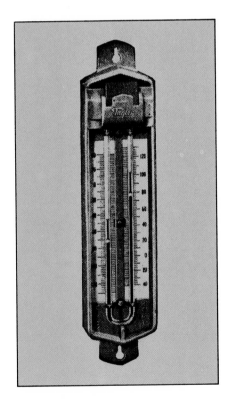

Maximum-Minimum Thermometer

Tiny steel-cored indices move to the day's highest point and to its lowest temperature point, and remain there until reset by a magnet which is supplied. The present temperature is also shown in this mercury-filled tube mounted in a grey plastic case. 10 1/2" by 2 3/8". $12.95 postpaid. *Gokey.*

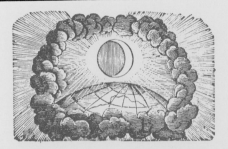

The lowest temperature ever recorded was 90 degrees below 0 Fahrenheit, in the Siberian city of Verkhoyansk. At this temperature, ice is like stone, and snow is as hard as table salt. A person who stood still outside for five minutes without proper clothing would become a stonelike corpse. Rubber would crack as easily as glass, and mercury would turn as hard as steel.

Although no one would choose Verkhoyansk for a winter vacation, the city's climate has certain unquestionable advantages. It is virtually impossible to contract a cold or a germ-caused disease, because the air is too cold for the germs to live. And food can be stored at this low a temperature for years without spoiling.

* * *

On September 13, 1922, the thermometers in Azizia, Libya were about ready to burst. On that day, the temperature in the shade soared to 136 degrees Fahrenheit.

* * *

An unconfirmed report to the United States Weather Bureau states that on July 6, 1949, a freak heat wave on the central coast of Portugal resulted in a temperature of 158 degrees, which lasted for two minutes.

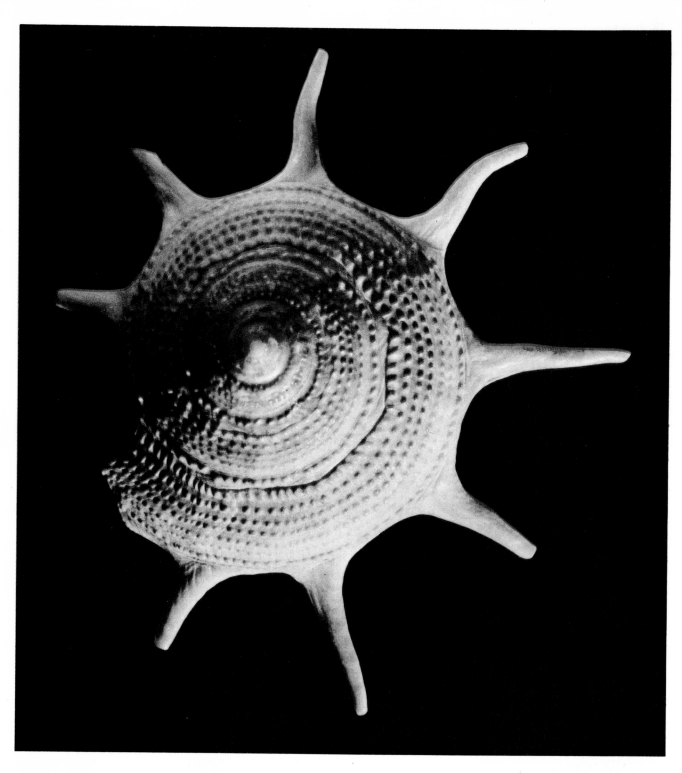

Shells

Japanese Star Shell

The triumphant star shell, known in more scientific circles as *Guildfordia triumphans*, derives from Japanese waters. About 2" in circumference. 95¢. Postage 50¢. *Dover Scientific.*

The home we first knew on this beautiful earth,
The friends of our childhood, the place of our birth,
In the heart's inner chamber sung always will be,
As the shell ever sings of its home in the sea!
        Francis Dana Gage (1808-1884), HOME

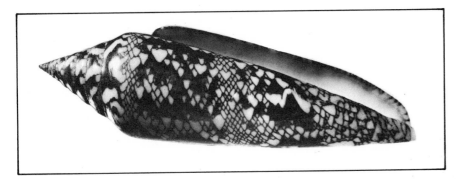

Bengal Cone

Rare and beautiful, the *Conus bengalensis* comes from the Andman Sea. Size 3½". $300.00. Postage 75¢. *Dover Scientific.*

Venus Comb

Many thin spines make this gorgeous specimen look like a comb. The *Murex triremis* derives from the Philippines. Size runs between 3.5" and 5". $6.00. Postage 75¢. *Dover Scientific.*

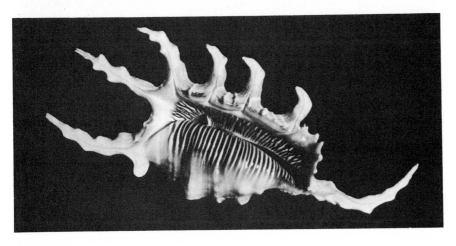

Scorpion Spider Conch

This beautiful shell (Lambis scorpius) comes from the Philippines. 4" to 5". $4.00. Postage 50¢. *Dover Scientific.*

Games People Play

The first rainy day in the history of man is the date that games were first invented to keep the kids quiet in the cave. And from that momentous time forward, diversions of one form or another have occupied much of the free time we spend.

One of the first games devised was rock tag. The object was for the one who was "it" to tag one of the other players with a rock. This could be done by touching him with the rock but most often was accomplished in a simpler manner. Of course, if you were tagged, it meant you were out of the game—sometimes permanently. Now and then, a guy was tagged with a vengeance,

and from then on, the tribe noticed, let us say, a lack of acumen. Whence the expression "rocks in his head."

The development and refinement of games continued unabated right down to our times. Baseball, football, basketball et. al. are sports that have dramatized the importance of "the big game." It's that "big game" that's responsible for that strange malady which affects millions known as "Sunday Syndrome," a disease which results in a paralysis of the body, causing it to slump all day in front of the TV, with only short bursts of movements during commercials and time-outs.

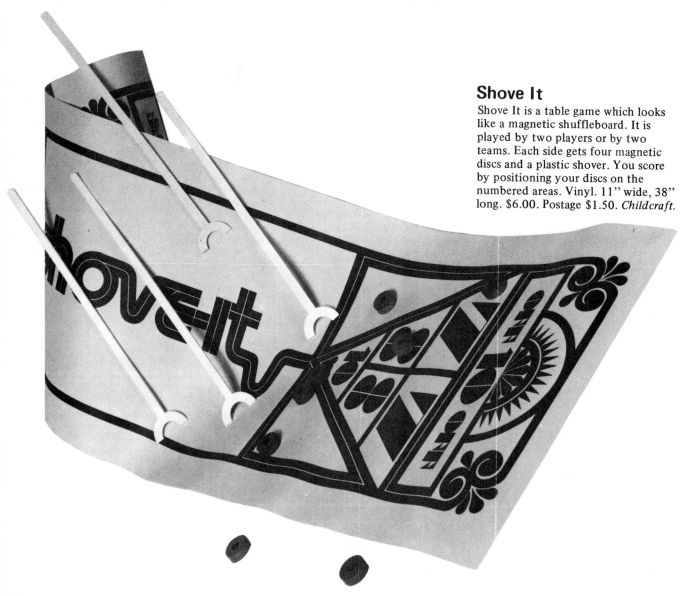

Shove It

Shove It is a table game which looks like a magnetic shuffleboard. It is played by two players or by two teams. Each side gets four magnetic discs and a plastic shover. You score by positioning your discs on the numbered areas. Vinyl. 11" wide, 38" long. $6.00. Postage $1.50. *Childcraft.*

Sockey

Two or four players, standing at opposite ends, attempt to hit a puck into their goal to score. They also try to block opponents from scoring. Plywood playing surface with solid oak edges. 29½" by 48". $34.95 postpaid. *World Wide Games.*

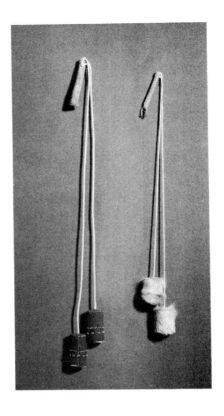

Mo-Chuck

The word "Mo-Chuck" means "fun" in Cree, but in English it might be said to mean "challenge." The object of this game, sometimes called Eskimo yo-yo, is to move the Mo-Chuck in such a way that one of the 2" x 1" cylinders at the ends of the string describes a clockwise circle while the other cylinder spins around in a counterclockwise direction. The Mo-Chuck is handmade of beads, animal skins, antlers, and other natural materials by members of the Chippewa Cree Craft Society at a Montana Indian reservation. Directions for acquiring skill are included. $2.25. Postage 75¢. *World Wide Games.*

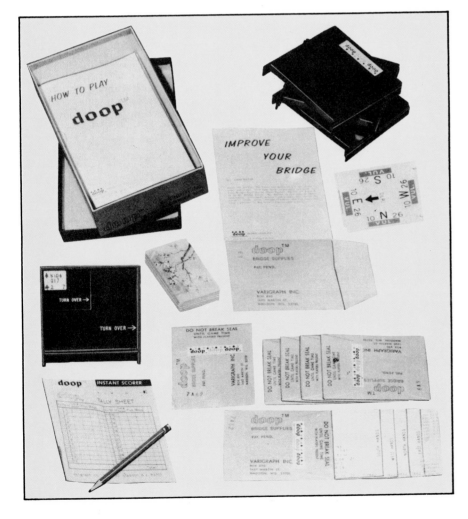

Doop
Four-Handed Duplicate

Now you can play in national tournaments at home, with your regular foursome. Doop, a great bridge game, lets you compete at duplicate, not only against your table opponents, but against some of the finest players in the game. You play specially prepared hands, and you then compare your bidding and play with the way the experts actually played the hand in a tournament. This is a game that is very instructive as well as extremely intriguing. $14.95. Postage $1.00. *Deluxe Saddlery.*

Games People Play

Folding Cribbage Table

Here's a cribbage table that, when not in use, can be hung to make a 12" by 24" wall decoration. When opened, it stands 18" high. $16.95. Postage $1.59. *House of Minnel.*

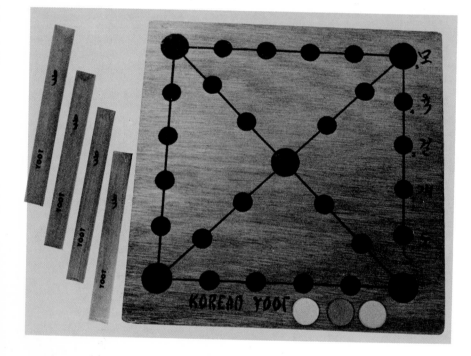

The Game of Yoot

This ancient game, the most popular in Korea, is played by rich and poor alike. According to tradition, the spots on the board represent the 29 horse-soldiers of the famous general Hiang Yu (294 B.C.) In earlier times, the gameboard was round. Discoveries of similar circular games played by Indians in the Western Hemisphere have prompted speculation about the game's migration. Equipment includes the 11½"-square playing board, men (formerly called horses), and four 7" long yoot sticks which are half-round, plain on the flat side, and decorated or marked on the round side. The game proceeds somewhat like the Hindu game of Parchesi with each player trying to get his four men around a complete circuit of the board, in spite of interference from the opponent's men. Two, three, four or six people can play at one time. The sticks serve the same purpose as dice; the combination of round and flat sides lying upward after a throw determines the number of spaces to move ahead. The gameboard is hardwood plywood; yoot sticks are made of birch wood; the men are rubberized cork. Directions are included. (Extra parts available.) $4.95 plus 75¢ handling charge. *World Wide Games.*

Flickit

Two to six players can play. The idea is to flick the loose caroms so as to hit a rubber ball into a goal. The game is fast, requires skill, and keeps everyone active all the time. Game board is made of a ¾" thick panel with heavy oak frame, measuring 39" long by 27" wide. $35.00 postpaid. *World Wide Games.*

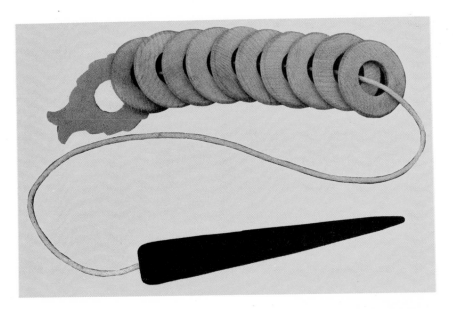

Pommawonga

The word "Pommawonga" means "spear the fish." The game itself cultivates skills in spearing and throwing. Popular among North American Indians and Eskimos from Canada to Mexico, the game developed where the food supply was dependent upon boys growing up talented in these skills. To play the game, the rings are swung up in an arc. The object is to spear as many rings as possible. You score one point for each ring you spear. Several players or teams may compete. $3.95 postpaid. *World Wide Games.*

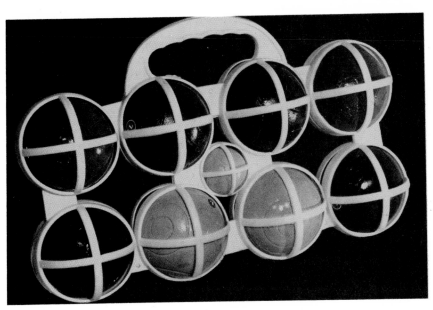

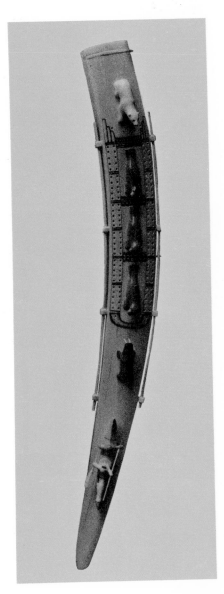

Bocci Balls

The national game of Italy is the equivalent of English Bowls. Bowls are played on a lawn; bocci is played on any kind of turf. You can play in your own backyard. A set of authentic Italian Bocci balls of wood can provide outdoor fun for the entire family. Comes in carrying case with complete instructions. $7.98. Postage $1.10. *Harriet Carter.*

Cribbage Board

Fossil ivory, etched on both sides. This is surely one of the strangest ways cribbage has ever been played. $450.00. Shipped collect plus $1.50 handling charge. *Arctic Trading Post.*

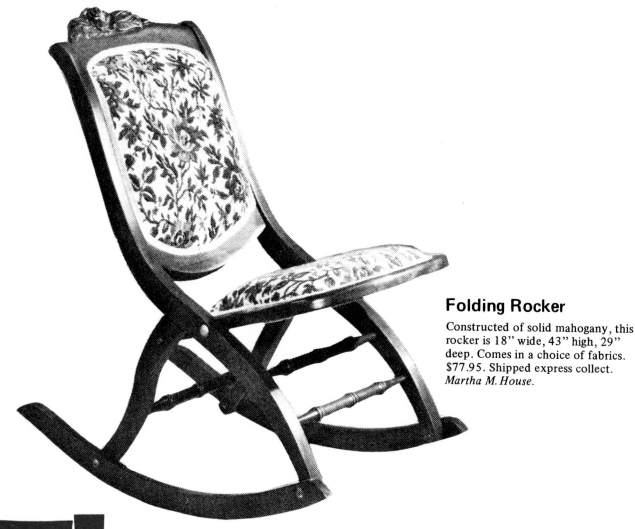

Folding Rocker

Constructed of solid mahogany, this rocker is 18" wide, 43" high, 29" deep. Comes in a choice of fabrics. $77.95. Shipped express collect. *Martha M. House.*

They All Fold

For everything that opens, there's something that's been made to fold. At its most intricate, there's Origami, the ancient Japanese art of creating sculptures from folded paper. But who'd deny that the most important artifact of all is the folding green.

There are tables that can be unpacked from a suitcase, and large corporate plans that can be unfolded at a board meeting. There are laws, however, about businesses that fold.

Where would the polka be without the accordion's folds? Or the pastor without his fold? What would the Folies Bergeres be without the folds of its fan dancers? Or Niagara without folds? *Ouch!* Enough of this folderol.

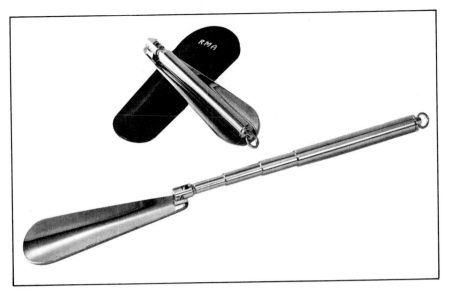

Telescoping Shoe Horn

Extended to 19½" when in use, this chrome-plated shoe horn closes to 5". Comes in cowhide case with your initials stamped in gold. $5.98. Postage 99¢. *Lillian Vernon.*

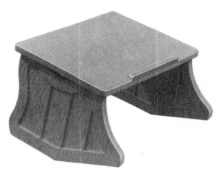

Folding Desk

Any bed, easy chair, or car seat can be turned into a working place with this portable 19½" by 13½" desk. Made of walnut-finished plastic. Folds flat for storage. $7.98. Postage 95¢. *Harriet Carter.*

Play and Work Table

Black with gold or walnut finish. Top is treated to resist stains and heat. 16" by 28" by 27" high; folds in the middle to 3½" thick. $30.00. Postage 45¢. *Lewis and Conger.*

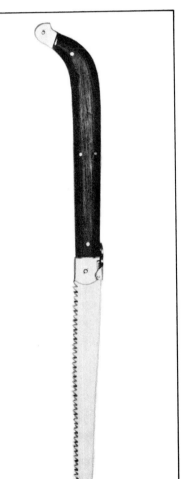

Adjustable Bed-Chair Table

The polished walnut table top adjusts to any angle, and raises and lowers from 26" to 37" high on a chrome-plated leg. Measures 14½" wide, 24" long, and 3/8" thick. A 10¼" square side tray is also provided. Both table and tray have a bracket to keep books and papers from slipping. Folds flat to 4". $75.00. Postage $6.00. *Hammacher Schlemmer.*

Folding Saw

Hunters and sportsmen might find this folding saw a real convenience. 7½" stainless steel blade locks open. Rosewood handle contained by three rivets. Brass trim. From Italy. $13.00. Postage 65¢. *Hoffritz.*

They All Fold

Monogrammed Folding Comb

Kent of London makes this tortoise comb which folds to a convenient 1" wide by 4" long size. Your choice of three initials in sterling silver. $8.50. Postage 90¢. *Sleepy Hollow Gifts.*

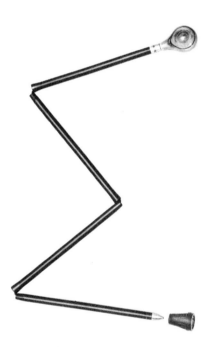

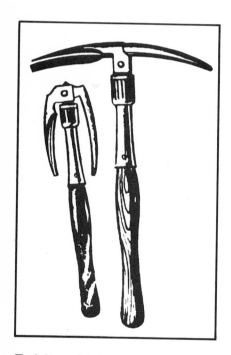

Folding Pickmattox

Use this as a pick or as a small shovel. $2.95. Postage $1.50. *Keene Engineering.*

Pruning Saw

This folding saw has a wood handle and 10" blade. Available in two types: one for green wood with deep raker teeth, 4½ per inch; one for dry wood, regular teeth, 6 per inch. Weighs 7 oz. $2.00. Postage 75¢. *Recreational Equipment Inc.*

Collapsible Cane

A 36" long cane folds up in four segments to a length of 10". Opens in an instant by means of a heavy duty cable. Made of black, rustproof aluminum, with tigerwood handle and replaceable rubber tip. Only 7 oz. $8.95. Postage $2.00. *Hammacher Schlemmer.*

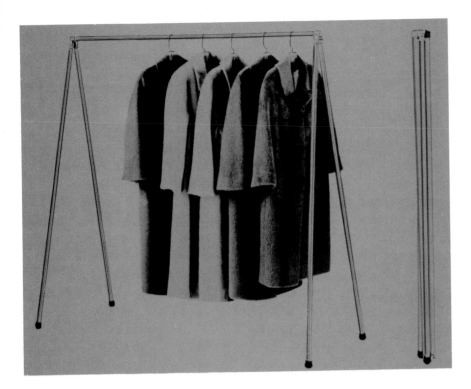

Instant-Fold Coat Rack

This rack is designed so that even when folded it is all in one piece. When the center bar is raised, the legs fall into place, and it is immediately ready for guests' coats. Disassembles just as quickly. Made of strong rust-proof aluminum tubing. In use, 58" high. Comes with carrying case. $14.95. Postage $3.00. *Hammacher Schlemmer.*

Folding Lantern

Windproof, light weight, and quickly assembled, this aluminum lantern folds to 6½" by 4" by ½". Opens to 9½" by 4" by 4". Weighs seven ounces. Comes with a citronella candle which is good for repelling insects. Size of candle, 4" by 3¼". $4.90 postpaid. *L. L. Bean.*

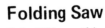

Folding Saw

Only 9" long, this saw folds neatly inside its wooden handle. The blade is a Teflon-coated alloy. The manufacturer says that the more the blade is used, the faster and smoother it becomes. Money-back guarantee, he declares, if the saw is not "the finest you ever owned." $6.50. Postage 75¢. *A Man's World.*

TEA

In 2737 B.C., says Chinese legend, leaves from a wild tea bush fell by chance into the Emperor Shen Nung's boiling drinking water. "What a delightful flavor!" said the wise Emperor, drinking the world's first cup of tea.

The Chinese poet, Lu-Yu, published the first book about tea in 780 A.D. Wait till the water boils, he tells us, and when the bubbles resemble crystal beads rolling in a fountain, it is time to pour the water over the tea leaves.

The Buddhist saint, Dengyo Daishi, crossed the sea to Japan in 805 A.D. and planted seeds in a temple garden. The tea plants flourished. In 815 A.D., the Japanese Emperor, Saga, was entertained at a monastery. He liked the tea so well he decreed that the plants be cultivated in the provinces near his capital. By the 10th century, Japan was growing her own tea instead of importing it from China.

The first European book mentioning tea was published in Venice in 1559. The first account of tea in English appeared in 1598 in the *Voyages and Travels* of Hugo van Linschooten, a Dutchman who had drunk tea in the far-away, mysterious Orient. Perhaps it was because of him that the Dutch were the first people in Europe to drink tea. During the 1660s, their ships carried most of the leaf to the West. In 1669, the East India Company began transporting tea to England from Java.

For the tea ships of 1610, sailing from the Orient to Europe was perilous. The seas swarmed with pirates and cutthroats; there were few charts to show reefs and rocks; and the frail vessels were often sunk by storms. In 1618, another method of transportation was tried—tea was brought by camel caravan from China across the deserts and mountains of Asia to Eastern Europe. The journey took 18 months.

By the 18th century, tea had become England's national beverage. Echoing its popularity, Dr. Samuel Johnson, the great lexicographer, described himself as "a hardened and shameless tea drinker."

In the middle 1700s, the sound of pistol shots by night was common along the English coast.

Tea smugglers would clash with coastguards in their effort to avoid high import taxes. Two-thirds of the tea that was drunk in England was smuggled in.

In 1721, the East India Company was granted a monopoly on the import of all tea to England. In the company's great warehouses in London, its tea was sold at auctions to the highest bidders. The monopoly ended in 1883.

In 1823, Major Robert Bruce of the British Army found tea growing wild in Northeast India. Plants were then cultivated successfully, and today India is the world's largest exporter of tea, with Ceylon second, and Indonesia third.

With all sails set, scudding along under a brisk breeze, the tea clippers of the 19th century were a thrilling sight. These ships were specially designed for the speedy transport of tea, and the ship captains and crews raced from China to London or to New York for prizes of thousands of dollars. And despite the thousands of miles they had to sail, the competing tea clippers

Icelandic Tea Server

It may be surprising to learn that a country as cold as Iceland has so many volcanoes. Some of these volcanoes are in active eruption, and from these comes a constant flow of lava. It is out of this lava that this tea server has been made. This is not a pot for brewing tea, but a server. The brewed tea is poured into the top part, which is warmed by a candle underneath. 9½" high. $37.10. Shipped express collect. *Glit.*

often arrived in England or America within minutes of each other. Excitement became intense in the ports as both tea importers and the public waited for the first of the new season's teas to arrive.

Tea played a dramatic part in the establishment of the United States of America. In 1767, the British Government put a tax on tea used by the American colonists. The settlers decided to stop buying tea and refused to allow tea ships to be unloaded. One December night in 1773, men dressed as Indians boarded British ships in Boston harbor and threw some 300 chests of tea into the sea. It was the so-called "Boston Tea Party" that sparked the American War of Independence.

It is believed the first shipment of tea to the United States arrived in New Amsterdam about 1650. At the time, tea cost from $30 to $50 a pound, and in addition to making a refreshing drink, the used leaves were sometimes salted and eaten with butter.

Tea traveled with the pioneers who explored and settled our vast land. No wagon train headed West without a good supply of tea on board. Then, as now, it was the drink for people on the go who need a lift that relaxes and refreshes.

Today the United States is the second largest consumer of tea in the world, surpassed only by Great Britain. We are the only country that prepares large quantities of tea using three different types: loose, teabags and instant.

Iced tea was invented in St. Louis, Missouri, at the World's Fair of 1904.

Unusual Teas

Alfalfa Mint	4 oz.	.75	*Shuttle Hill Herb Shop*
Althea	Pkg.	1.00	*Nichols Garden Nursery*
Aloe Cape	Pkg.	1.00	*Nichols Garden Nursery*
Bearberry	Pkg.	1.00	*Nichols Garden Nursery*
Burdock Root	Pkg.	1.00	*Nichols Garden Nursery*
Camomile	Pkg.	1.00	*Nichols Garden Nursery*
Cascara Bark	Pkg.	1.00	*Nichols Garden Nursery*
Catnip	4 oz.	.75	*Shuttle Hill Herb Shop*
Chicory Root	4 oz.	.75	*Shuttle Hill Herb Shop*
Comfrey	4 oz.	.75	*Shuttle Hill Herb Shop*
Clover Flowers	Pkg.	1.00	*Nichols Garden Nursery*
Coltsfoot	Pkg.	1.00	*Nichols Garden Nursery*
Chum Mee	16 oz.	4.00	*McNulty's Tea & Coffee Co.*
Demi-tasse	½ lb.	3.60	*Grace Rare Tea*
Dimbula	48 bags	1.50	*McNulty's Tea & Coffee Co.*
Erva Mate (toasted)	1 lb.	2.00	*McNulty's Tea & Coffee Co.*
Genma Cha (Japanese)	5 oz.	1.00	*Nichols Garden Nursery*
Connoisseur Blend	½ lb.	3.60	*Grace Rare Tea*
Lapsang Souchong	48 bags	1.50	*McNulty's Tea & Coffee Co.*
Linden	50 bags	3.00	*Maison Glass*
Lotus Root	1¾ oz.	1.25	*Nichols Garden Nursery*
Mu (Japanese)	Pkg.	1.35	*Nichols Garden Nursery*
Pouchong	16 oz.	4.00	*McNulty's Tea & Coffee Co.*
Queen's Taste	8 oz.	3.95	*Grace Rare Tea*
Rosehips	50 bags	1.75	*McNulty's Tea & Coffee Co.*
Sarsparilla	Pkg.	1.00	*Nichols Garden Nursery*
Spearmint	16 oz.	5.00	*McNulty's Tea & Coffee Co.*
Verbena	50 bags	3.00	*Maison Glass*

TEA

Tea is grown on large estates of from 300 to 3,000 acres. The best teas grow at high altitudes, sometimes at over 6,000 feet. Many of these estates in India, Ceylon, and Indonesia are completely self-contained. They provide fully equipped factories, storehouses, housing for both manager and the native workers, and even schools for the children. Large estates have their own hospitals with native doctors in charge.

New tea seedlings are carefully planted by native workers three to five feet apart in the rich, tropical soil. Fern leaves are then spread over the plantings to protect the young growth from the sun's fierce, withering heat. The soil where the tea plants grow is kept well cultivated. Hand labor and oxen are widely used, but many of the modern estates have up-to-date cultivation equipment. Chemical fertilizers are used extensively.

If left to nature, the tea plant would grow into a tree 30 feet high. The cultivated plant, however, is kept pruned to a height of three or four feet. This provides delicate growth of leaf and makes plucking easy. Usually five years must pass before a tea plant is ready for plucking. A native girl can pluck as much as 40 pounds of leaf a day.

The fresh green leaves are brought to withering lofts and spread evenly on racks. Here, currents of warm, dry air remove a great deal of the moisture from the leaves. This process takes from 12 to 24 hours. The limp, withered leaves are rolled in special machines. This breaks up the cells and hastens fermentation of the leaves. In the process, the leaves change color, and give out the fragrant aroma we associate with tea.

After rolling, the leaves are put in cool, humid fermenting rooms. They are thinly spread on racks for 20 minutes to an hour, and turn a bright copper color in that short period. In making green tea, the fermenting process is omitted.

Finally, the tea leaves are placed on trays in a drying machine. Blasts of hot, dry air are forced into a chamber through which the tea passes. The heat halts the fermentation, and completely dries the leaves.

Before packing, the tea is graded by size. Large, small, broken, and unbroken leaves are separated by sieves. The tea is then sold according to the preference of the buyer.

The tea is packed in aluminum-lined, moisture-proof plywood chests which protect the flavor. About 20 inches square, each chest is light and easy to handle, and usually holds a little more than 100 pounds.

Today, tea cargoes travel in the holds of ocean liners and tramp steamers to ports all over the world, are delivered to tea merchants for blending.

Expert tea tasters savor and smell the teas from different gardens. They decide which teas should be blended to provide the characteristics of the brand you prefer to buy in the store.

Teas to be blended are placed in large mixing drums which can hold 3,000 pounds. These revolve and thoroughly mix the tea. The blended tea then goes to the packaging department.

Machines automatically measure the exact amount of tea to go into each package and tea bag. Modern machines fill teabags at the amazing speed of nearly 300 a minute.

There are more than 3,000 varieties of tea. Like wines, teas take their names from the districts where they are grown, such as Darjeeling, Assam, Ceylon, etc.

Tea Infusion Spoon

If you like real brewed tea, this stainless steel infusion spoon, imported from West Germany, is ideal. You make a single cup of tea by putting tea leaves in the spoon, then locking it up, and placing the perforated spoon into a cup of hot water. In a couple of minutes, you'll have tea, brewed to whatever strength you want. 6" long; 1½" wide. $2.80. Postage $.60. *Downs.*

The usual tea sold in the supermarket is a blend of 20 to 30 different varieties, each chosen for a certain characteristic—color, flavor, bouquet, body.

There are three different types of tea—black, green and oolong. All three types come from the same tea bushes. It's how the leaves are processed after they are picked that makes the teas different.

Over 97 percent of all the tea consumed in the United States is black tea. In the processing, the tea is fully fermented.

Green tea is light in color when brewed. In its processing, it is not fermented at all.

Oolong tea is a compromise between black and green tea. It is semi-fermented, so that the leaves turn greenish brown.

The term *pekoe* refers only to a size of leaf—and not to a type or variety of tea. Other names of sizes are *Orange Pekoe, Souchong, Broken Pekoe, Fannings,* and *Dust.*

Teasmade

It wakes you, lights the room, tells the time, and makes up to four cups of tea or coffee. All you do is pre-set the alarm clock. At the appointed hour, a buzzer sounds. A volume control varies the sound from a whisper to a loud buzz. Bedside lights switch on; but switch off independently, should you want to sleep a while longer. A safety switch prevents you from switching on the kettle if it is dry or out of place. The kettle has an insulated handle and lid to prevent burning your fingers. Kettle is chrome on copper. Teapot is glazed earthenware. Comes complete with light, kettle, teapot or coffee pot. Available in all voltages. $79.00 postpaid and insured. *Trencherman's.*

At one time China—the land where tea drinking originated—supplied nearly all the tea used in the world. But the tea gardens of India, Ceylon, and Indonesia have long since won the race for world markets.

In 1839 eight chests of tea—the first tea ever to come from India—were sold by auction in London, England. Prices ranged as high as $8.50 per pound. From that day on, the tea industry became an important part of India's economy.

* * *

Until 1869, coffee was the chief crop of Ceylon. In that year, a terrible blight attacked the coffee trees and soon killed them all. The planters decided to start again with tea. Today, tea is the principal crop of Ceylon.

Lemon Squeezer

A stainless steel bird which efficiently squeezes and pits each wedge of lemon. The juice pours out of its beak. $2.90. Postage 86¢. *Colonial Garden Kitchens.*

Weapons

For many years, weapons changed little from the arrows, javelins, and slings of Biblical times. As late as the Persian invasion of Rome in 480 B.C., flint was used for arrow tips, and wood was used for spears. It was not until about 450 B.C. that spears, arrow tips, and swords began to be fashioned from bronze.

The famous Macedonian phalanx employed a 24-foot-long pike called the sarissa, which permitted a warrior in the sixth fighting rank to extend his arm to the first. This weapon was not subsequently employed by other peoples.

The Greek innovations in warfare were primarily the ballista and the catapult, both capable of hurling weights for hundreds of feet. The Greeks also introduced chemical warfare (Greek fire). With the Roman empire came the shift from iron to bronze in weapons and armor.

The weapons of the Middle Ages were basically refinements of those of the classical period. In particular, the armor became more elaborate, and the siege weapons—the ram, the bore, and various hurling machines—became more potent.

What really revolutionized weaponry was the invention of gunpowder, usually attributed to the Chinese firecracker-makers of the 9th century. Gunpowder was introduced into Europe in the 1300s. Field artillery and cannons were first used by the Dutch.

In the 16th century, the Spaniards introduced the musket, a firearm which enabled a marksman to hit a target 400 yards away. The intricate reloading procedure of the musket necessitated the additional defense of a pike. This drawback of the musket led to the invention of the bayonet. Rifles were introduced in the 18th century; and by the 19th century, they became the standard firearm of all infantry.

Twentieth-century developments include the submarine, the tank, the airplane, and the missile. Perhaps the ultimate in armaments has been attained since the end of World War II, with atom and hydrogen bombs capable of being delivered halfway around the globe by ballistic missiles.

Chemical Dispenser

This non-lethal chemical self-defense weapon, which includes a high-intensity flashlight, repels attack from persons or animals without causing permanent damage. Dispenses a temporarily incapacitating chemical solution in the direction that the light beam is aimed. Accurate up to 18 feet. Can be used with light off or on. Two safety switches guard against accidental chemical discharge. Includes a 20-burst chemical cartridge. Made of polyethylene. Lens is unbreakable lexan. 10½" long. Weighs about 8 oz. (Note: cannot be sold to California residents). Batteries not included. $14.95. Postage $1.25. *Gallery*.

Slingshot

Will shoot a projectile 225 yards at 233 feet per second. Made of pure gum. Deerhide leather pouch fastened by plastic grippers. $2.39. Postage 80¢. *Herter's*.

Early Indian Arrows

The points of these Indian arrows are of various types of stone, some of them obsidians found in the Yellowstone Park area. The shafts are mostly of willow. Fletchings are turkey wing quills, 6" to 9" long, with two or three feathers. The fletchings and stone heads are attached with sinew or rawhide. The overall length of the arrows ranges from 25" to 29". Availability determines stone-type, number of feathers, and length of arrow. Arrows make fine wall decorations, but are not for use on modern bows, since the arrow shafts are too brittle. $9.47. Shipped collect. *Herter's.*

Shock Rod

Purse snatchers, muggers, vicious dogs, hallway gigolos, or subway Romeos might get a real thrill from this 3000-volt shock rod, which is legal everywhere. Delivers a painful but harmless shock. Power comes from flashlight batteries. Weighs 8 oz. The 12" steel cane has a fast push-button operation. Comes with batteries. $7.95. Postage $1.25. *Joan Cook.*

Harpoon

This historical memento of the old whaling days is a toggle-head harpoon. It is designed so that after striking, it opens and becomes imbedded in the whale. 5'7" long with a 1¾" diameter handle. Head is lashed with marline to the handle. The manila lines are hand-spliced. Metal shafts and heads are steel. $29.00. Postage $2.15. *Preston's.*

Mace

The mace is a shafted weapon held in one hand. It employs a flail at the end of a chain. The flail, or spiked ball, is linked to a wooden handle by the chain. While it cannot be snapped like a whip, the mace is wielded in much the same fashion. It was possible to envelop the opponent's sword blade with the chain, and thus to pull his weapon from his hand, or to knock the enemy senseless within his armor with the mace. One could even crush his skull. In England, this weapon was called a *Morning Star.* In Spain, it was called a *mate suegra* or "mother-in-law killer." Originally a farmer's thresher, the mace became, as so many tools did, a peasant's weapon. Spikes were added to the ball to make it more effective. The length of chain made it easier to swing it about, and clear a path through a wall of armor. 46" long, 5½" round ball with spikes. $52.50 postpaid. *Excalibur.*

Weapons

Screamer

This little pocket-size whistle that sounds off with a shrieking blast might turn out to be a girl's best protector. It looks like a perfume sprayer, but at a touch, it emits an alarm that can be heard for blocks. Gold-tone metal. 4" in length. No battery. No wind-up. Ten times louder than a human scream. $1.99. Postage 60¢. *Sunset House.*

Suit of Armor

Armor evolved along with man's technological prowess. Suits of armor were designed as much for beauty as for function, and were status symbols as well as weapons. A suit was fitted to every part of the lord's body for comfortable wearing. This particular suit weighs 38 lbs., is completely articulated and wearable, and is made of durable iron plate, leather strapping, and decorative brass fittings. The large two-handed broadsword is the Talhoffer, which was used in judicial duels as an infantry man's weapon. It has a wide steel blade, iron crossbar with wavy anneau, large two-handed wooden handle, and iron pommel. Wooden stand included. 61½" long, 15" wide. $1,875.00 postpaid. *Excalibur.*

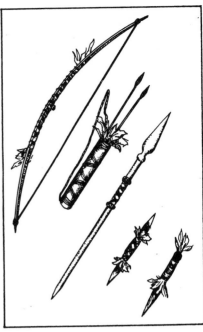

Captain General

This 15th-century cannon was particularly Spanish. Like many things Spanish, it was of Moorish origin. It has been called *paterara, paterary, patrary, pattereros, perrier, petrara, pierrier*—all indicating that the weapon originally discharged stone projectiles. The first wooden cannons of this sort were made by coopers, which is why the tube of a firearm is called a barrel, even down to the present day. By the beginning of the 15th century, the falconet was made of forged iron. The barrel of the falconet was hooped for strength, much like a wine cask. The charge was inserted in an external case or frame at the breech of the gun. A curved, tapering iron wedge was force-fitted into the slots of the iron stirrup to insure a close fit, and to thus prevent gases from escaping. To fire the thing, a slender, red hot rod was inserted in the vent. A tail projected from the rear of the stirrup to facilitate aiming. The tripod carriage, with two wheels forward, absorbed the recoil.

Falconets were the light artillery of the day, and served equally well on shipboard. Columbus had such breech-loading cannons mounted on the decks of his caravel. This falconet is called a *Captain General,* in honor of the Spanish Field Marshals who used this weapon in their conquest of the New World. For example, Ponce de Leon, who accompanied Columbus on his second voyage, used such cannon to good effect in conquering Florida. Despite the breech loader's illustrious history, it was abandoned because of its danger to the men who fired it. The bands encircling the barrel were never guaranteed to keep the barrel from bursting. Securing the breech adequately was extremely difficult. The single-cast, one-piece construction of the muzzle loader was safer, and therefore replaced the breech loader.

Iron barrel and breech. Antiqued wooden carriage with decorative iron appliques and bone inlays. 22¾" long, 12¾" wide, 23½" high. Barrel is 27" long. $315.00 postpaid. *Excalibur.*

Bow and Arrow Set

This Ecuadorian bow and arrow set, made of black ironwood, is decorated with feathers of many colors, with strings, and with jungle beans. Comes with a 39" bow, two arrows in a bamboo quiver, one spear, one knife, and one dagger. $3.00. Postage $5.00. *Akios.*

Blow Gun

Comes with quiver and 12 darts. 4' long. $10.00. Postage $5.00. *Akios.*

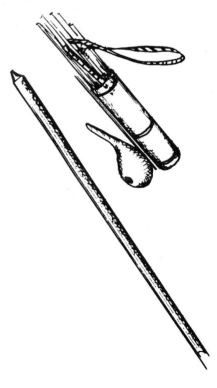

Hang It All!

Authentic Sandpaintings

Sandpaintings are used in Southwestern Indian healing rites. The paintings, made directly on the earth, are destroyed as part of the ceremonial rite. To preserve such a painting for use as a wall hanging, the sand is applied to a wooden board with an adhesive. Indian artists have created these sandpaintings, depicting subjects from their religious folklore. 6" wide by 12" high. $19.95. Postage $1.30. *Desert House.*

Musical Wall Plaque

An Israeli commemorative plaque created by Arthur Szyk. This scroll is mounted under glass in a gold and ivory wood frame. When the knob is pulled, "Hatikvah," the Israeli national anthem, is heard. Swiss movement. 9" by 7". $15.95. Postage $1.90. *Clymer's.*

Aztec Rooster

This Aztec rooster is made of cast aluminum, and is finished in black, gold, or buff white. 22" high; about ½" thick. Antique finish. $23.00 postpaid. *Home Industries.*

Embroidery Picture

This decorative piece, protected by glass, employs a 17th-century embroidery technique known as "Stump Work," so called because parts of the picture were stuffed with wadding, wool, or small pieces of wood to create a third dimension. This creation, redolent of colonial days, presents fulsome red strawberries, blossoms, and leaves on a black velvet background. The frame is made of a mellowed fine wood. 25" by 27". $70.00. Postage $2.80. *Patrice, Unlimited.*

Aztec Horse

This cast-aluminum wall plaque is a representation of an Aztec art piece. 24" high; 25" wide. Finished in antique black, gold, or white. $26.00 postpaid. *Home Industries.*

The largest painting ever painted was the mammoth "Panorama of the Mississippi," completed by John Banvard in 1846. This painting depicted the 1,200 miles of river scenery from the mouth of the Missouri to the estuary of New Orleans. For people to see the 12-foot-high and nearly 16,000-foot-long picture, the mammoth canvas had to be passed between two upright revolving cylinders on the stage of a large auditorium. It took a spectator two hours to see the painting in its entirety.

* * *

In 1642, Rembrandt painted "The Shooting Company of Captain Frans Banning Cocq," in which 29 life-sized civic guards are shown leaving their armory at high noon, with the sun shining brightly upon them. Less than 200 years later, the picture had become so dingy and dark that someone facetiously called it "The Night Watch," a nickname that has since supplanted its true title.

MIRRORS

A camera, if tilted or manipulated, might shade the truth; but a mirror has neither conscience nor grace, and doesn't lie by even a hair's breadth. Yet one sees in it what one wants to see.

Since in many of us there is more than a little Narcissus, it isn't the mirror that bears falsehood but our own I-sight.

We see time's furrows on another's brow,
And death intrenched, preparing his assault;
How few themselves in that just mirror see!
Edward Young (1683-1765), NIGHT THOUGHTS

Stars and Stripes Mirror

Perhaps you can claim that this is a reflection of your patriotism. However corny that comes off, the piece itself is quite attractive. 15¼" square. $14.00. Postage $1.00. *Yorkraft.*

Flower Mirror

This mirror, for powder room or hall, comes from Mexico. The flowered metal work is hand-enameled in vibrant combinations of pink, blue, and orange. 21" in diameter. $21.00 postpaid. *Artes Saldana.*

In 214 B.C., a powerful Roman force attacked
the island of Syracuse, the home of Archimedes,
the great mathematician and astronomer. To hold
off the Roman legions, the Greek inventor
devised one ingenious weapon after another.
Among these weapons was the catapult, which
sent a ton of stones flying as far as 600 feet.

But Archimedes' most ingenious contraption
was an arrangement of mirrors that directed the
concentrated rays of the sun on the Roman ships
and set them ablaze.

* * *

A classic Hassidic story tells about a saintly Rabbi
who was visited by one of his congregation, an
extremely wealthy man who was notoriously
stingy. The Rabbi took him over to the window,
and said to him, "My good man, look out of this
window and tell me what you see."

"People," answered the rich Jew. Then the
Rabbi escorted him to a mirror, and said to him,
"My good man, what do you see now?"

"Oh," said the man, "now I see myself."

"Aha!" the Rabbi said, "You see, the window
is made of glass and the mirror is made of glass.
Actually, they're both the same things, but when
you take a lot of silver and start to cover the
glass, then you cease to see others, and all you see
is yourself."

What's Your Bag?

If it's smaller than a breadbox or bigger than an elephant, no matter. There's a way to make it portable. But don't try to check into a hotel with an elephant unless you're a very big tipper. Taking it with you has become so highly specialized that different professions have developed their own techniques. The lawyer's open and shut case, for example.

We've all seen crowds packed like sardines, and know how easy it is to get carried away. With the aid of a multitude of devices, man is able to move mountains. Yet there are some people who can't even carry a tune.

Alphabetical Briefcase

This deluxe English case has a steel frame and is equipped with an alphabetically-indexed section. A brass lock and zipper provide access to the seven 22-carat gold-embossed compartments. The combination lock is built to watchmaker's standards. Size 19" by 13". Brass fittings. The case is available in: Morocco (black, brown), $160.50; Pendle calf (black, brown), $166.75; hide (black), $141.25; pigskin (brown), $146.10; coach hide (black, tan, brown), $148.00; ostrich skin (black, brown), $428.75. Postage $5.75. *Unicorn.*

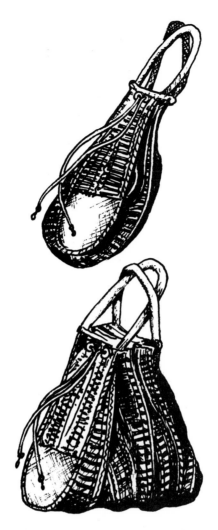

House Purse

All four sides of this purse are hand-decorated. There's a bright red roof, red doors, and yellow curtains. The brass-hinged roof lifts up to reveal a lined interior. 7" by 5" by 7". $35.00 postpaid. *Plumlea Peddler.*

Ecuadorian Shopping Bag

This large collapsible Faja wool shopping bag has a leather pocket and leather drawstrings and is cotton lined. 16" long, 12½" wide, and 5½" thick. $8.00 postpaid. *Akios.*

Wayfarer's Wallet

A chain looped to the belt secures this cowhide wallet in the back pocket. The wallet converts to a belt pouch with a back loop. Sturdy brass fittings. Five compartments. Measuring 4½" by 7", can hold passport. $12.00. Postage $1.00. *Kreeger & Son Ltd.*

Travel Kart

A personal porter for travelers, this contraption takes the "lug" out of luggage. The Kart straps on to a piece of luggage and is checked through at the terminal. Upon arrival, you fold out the rubber wheels, extend the handle, and the Kart is ready to roll, with all of your luggage on it. Made of heavy gauge steel tubing. Weighs only 6½ lbs. Can accommodate four pieces of luggage weighing 150 lbs. $34.95 postpaid. *JLM Products.*

What's Your Bag?

Racket Case

This double-walled plastic case provides space for one racket, one can of balls, plus small accessories. Designed to protect metal rackets from being scratched or bent. Available in blue, black, orange, white, or yellow. $15.25. Postage $1.59. *House of Minnel.*

Hex Handbag

Hex signs handpainted on a 19th-century Pennsylvania Dutch barn enhance this all-wood tote. 9" by 6" by 7". $28.00. Postage $1.50. *Haverhill's.*

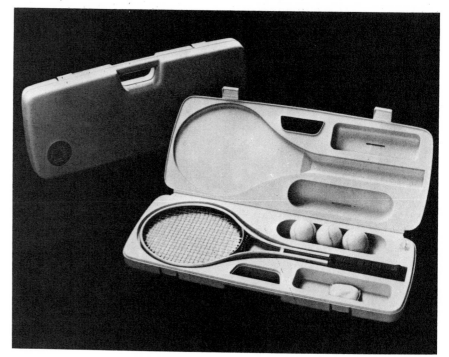

Add-a-Case

As you dash from office to plane, this piece of luggage gives you a free hand, by combining a suitcase with an attache case. The clothing carrier form-fits around your attache case to give you a clothing compartment on either side. The suit compartment is equipped with a hanger. Made of rugged dobby nylon with vinyl interior. Non-rust nylon zippers. Each side has its own lock and key. Black with tan trim. Specify size: to fit a 4" to 5" wide attache case, or to fit a 2" to 3" wide attache case. $17.95. Postage 60¢. *Chris Craft.*

Collapsible Basket

This mobile unit can hold 2½ bushels, but will fold into a thickness of only 1". Wheeling around on four casters, it performs any number of tasks: carrying the laundry, picking up toys, or holding beverages which are being iced. The galvanized wire basket is 22" in diameter and 14" deep. Washable plastic liners are available for $2.00. $11.95. Postage $1.20. *Walter Drake.*

Four-in-One Bag

Made of top-grain cowhide, this bag opens to reveal a roomy interior. A utility kit, 6" by 4", and a zipper envelope, and a garment bag are stashed away within. Measuring 21" by 12" by 7", the outer bag fits under a plane seat. Comes in Spanish moss or black. $150.00. Postage $2.75. *Abercrombie and Fitch.*

Foldaway Bag

Beige, natural-textured cotton and rayon, plastic-lined bag folds into 18" by 6" by 2" for carrying in a suitcase. Opens to 18" by 6" by 12" to supply extra carrying room for gifts, souvenirs, laundry, etc. Calf handle, brass zipper and fittings. $22.00. Postage $1.75. *Kenton Collection.*

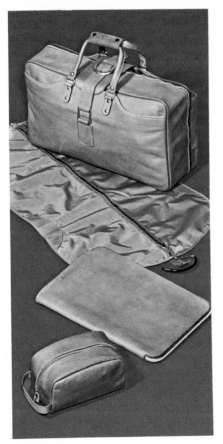

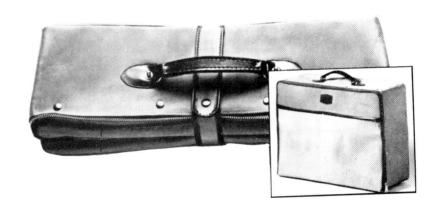

What's Your Bag?

Straw Hat Purse

When the sun waxes hot, this Ecuadorian purse can be transmuted into a broad-brimmed shade-giving hat. Made with leather drawstrings and rayon lining. $5.00 postpaid. *Akios.*

Attache Organizer

All the little items usually thrust with fine indiscrimination into the pocket of an attache case have been accorded neatly arranged places in this bag. There's a particular place for catalogs, another for reports and important papers, and even a spot for a fresh shirt. Compartments, too, for business cards, glasses, cigarettes, etc. $19.95. Postage $1.00. *Sun Gold Marketing.*

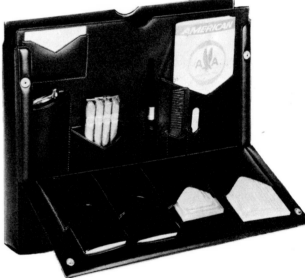

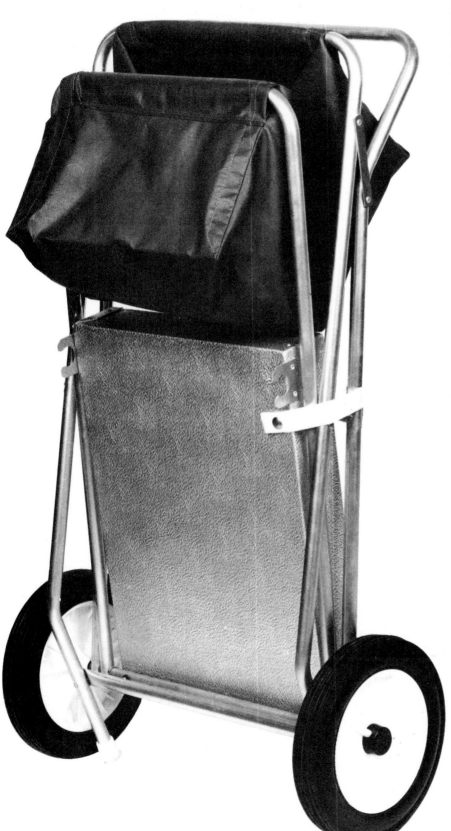

Fold-Up Bag

This bag is carry-on under-seat luggage when full; collapses flat when empty. Made of heavy duty, water repellent, navy blue canvas, trimmed in vinyl, the piece has an extra heavy center zipper which makes the 22" long, 12½" wide, and 10½" deep main compartment easy to pack. The zippered side pocket is 20" long, 9" wide, and 3" deep. Hand-grips are leather. Reinforced vinyl bottom. $18.00. Postage 80¢. *Chris Craft.*

Dock Dinghy

No need to tug and lug luggage aboard. Wheel your luggage onto the craft in this nylon basket, big enough to hold 1½ bushels. Sturdy enough to transport a 24-bottle carton or a storage battery. The 10" rubber-tired wheels will roll over any surface. Folds to 10" deep, 22" wide, and 41" long. Rust-proof aluminum-alloy tubing. Shipped unassembled. $29.95. Postage $3.00. *Chris Craft.*

Strictly for Southpaws

There are no records of the exact beginning of discrimination against lefthanders, but as far back as Rome right was right; which means to say that *dextra*, from which comes our word *dextrous* or *handy,* means right in Latin. But how did the Romans designate the other side? Anything that was left was *sinistra* (sinister). Even the Old English, who gave us the word *left,* used it to mean *weak.* Now is that fair?

Fighting a ratio of five righthanders for every lefthander, lefthanders have risen to the challenge. da Vinci worked with his left hand. A study of Einstein's brainwaves indicated that his right hemisphere—the side responsible for the responses on the left side of the body—was more highly developed than his left. In baseball, the star who holds the greatest pitching and strike-out records for both regular season hurling and World Series pitching is Sandy Koufax, a south-paw. The first pitcher to achieve the world's record of 19 strikeouts in a single game, set back in 1884—a record which is still standing—is One-Armed Dailey. Which arm? Left, of course. And the holder of the most batting records? Ty Cobb, lefthander.

One of the most influential statements ever uttered, a declaration which resulted in the expansion of the United States, was by a south-paw, Horace Greeley. Typically, he was mis-quoted by a world full of right thinkers. They say his words were, "Go West, Young Man." In fact, he said, "Go Left, Young Man."

Next time someone derisively mentions a left-handed monkey wrench, drop One-Arm Dailey's name. Or Einstein's, or da Vinci's. Lefthanders of the world, unite. If that be sinister, make the most of it.

Bread Knife for Lefties

Ordinary serrated utensils have their scalloped cutting edge ground on the wrong side for left-handed use. This piece of English cutlery is made of stainless steel with a bone-white handle, ground on the left side for proper slicing. $6.95. Postage 75¢. *Aristera.*

Left-Handed Parer

The safe and comfortable way to pare and peel food is towards the body. Danish craftsmen have combined palisanderwood and stainless steel to make a peeler and parer which is properly sized, balanced, and shaped for lefty use. $2.75. Postage 75¢. *Aristera.*

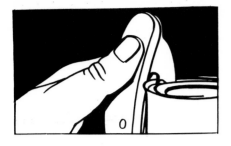

Left-Handed Can-Opener

Two-handle grip makes for extra convenient operation; produces a smooth-cut edge. $4.50 postpaid. *Anything Left Handed.*

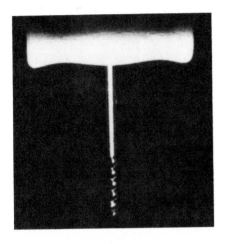

Lefty Corkscrew

The spiral is reversed on this instrument. 2" working length. Wood handle. Chrome plated shaft. $1.95. Postage 75¢. *Aristera.*

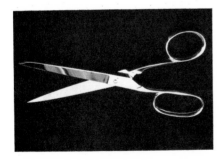

Left-Handed Scissors

A fine 7" instrument for a southpaw. $8.95. Postage 75¢. *Aristera.*

Many theories have been advanced to explain the dominance of right-handedness. One of these theories holds that the origin of this phenomenon is physiological, the result of an unequal distribution of the viscera in the abdominal cavity. A more commonly accepted view, however, is that right-handedness is primarily a product of primitive warfare. Early man was engaged in a continual struggle for survival with his fellow man. When called upon to protect himself and his family, he would instinctively protect the vital region around his heart by fending off blows with his left arm, while using his right to strike blows against his adversary. Through a long process of natural selection, those men who had powerful right arms survived to pass their hereditary characteristics on. The natural southpaws who were forced to battle with their right arms fell by the wayside.

* * *

To date, we have had only one left-handed President, James A. Garfield, and even he was subjected to the conversion attempts of his parents. Though eventually he learned how to write with his right hand, he did not abandon the use of his naturally dominant left. Legend has it that our 20th President once demonstrated his ambidextrous powers by writing Latin with one hand while he wrote in Greek with the other.

Be Chairful!

No one knows who invented the chair, but one theory is that it was stumbled upon one day by an early man who fell into a naturally formed seat in a cleft of rock that happened to be in the cave. Realizing that his feet were killing him from walking erect, the discoverer paused a moment before going back to balancing on his two feet. Pretty soon, everybody was using that spot to rest in, with some people coming from miles around to admire the new device. When they saw how comfortable and useful the chair could be, they went home to build one of their own; and in the process, they cracked up one helluva lot of rocks.

The chair has become so entwined in our lives that it even influences the way we dress. For example: designed specifically to be used with chairs, every pair of trousers has a built-in seat. From the magnificent throne to the lowly stool, the chair has served man faithfully, offering him support every step of the way.

As I was sitting in my chair
I knew the bottom wasn't there,
Nor legs nor back, but I just sat
Ignoring little things like that.

Rope Chair

This Danish ashwood chair with untreated rope back is finished in natural wood or in black. 41½" wide, 51" high. $136.65. Estimated shipping cost $77.00. *Den Permanente.*

Folding Chair

Danish designer Hans J. Wegner created this folding chair with oak legs, and rattan seat and back. $167.15. Shipped express collect. *Den Permanente.*

Swivel Rocker

Turns and rocks in just about all directions. Covered in vinyl. Available in the following colors: black, olive, gold, tangerine, or blue. Also available in animal fur-like fabrics: tiger, leopard, or zebra. Width 30", depth 32", height 42". $489.95. Shipped express collect. *Genada Imports.*

Jigsaw Chair

These big foam easy chairs come complete with footstool, which one might use for a table. Unzip one side, and the chair unfolds into a comfortable 2'6" by 6'3" bed. Chair is 30" deep, 38" wide, 20" high. In fawn or brown corduroy, $49.50; in brown cotton repp, $39.50. Shipped express collect. *Martin Sylvester.*

Scoop Chair

This snug semi-reclining chair is shaped from solid foam and is fitted with a soft reversible cushion. Each chair is 28" wide and 36" deep. Fitted together, they make a sofa. Covered in cotton repp. Zippered cover available in purple, olive green, brown, or camel, or can be covered in your own material. Seat height is 12". $39.50. Shipped express collect. *Martin Sylvester.*

Be Chairful!

Chair with Adjustable Back

The 1" leeway to tilt the back is sufficient to render this Danish chair comfortable. 29½" high, 21½" wide, 21½" deep. Four chairs made of teakwood, finished in black Naugahyde, $158.00; in rosewood and black leather, $170.00. Shipping charges $175.00 for four. *Asbjorn-Mobler.*

Child's Chair

This elephant, carved out of a solid block of rosewood, has toenails, eyes, and tusks of ivory. The piece stands 14" high and weighs 22 lbs. The leather howdah on the elephant's back makes a nice seat for a child. $49.50. Shipped express collect. *Herter's.*

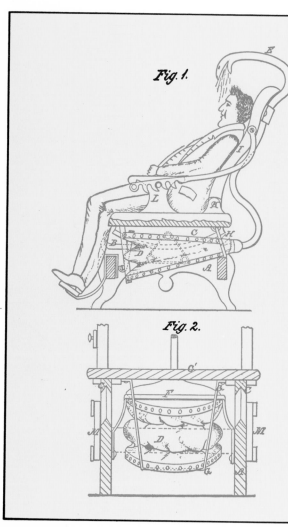

Fig. 1.

Fig. 2.

Rocking Chair.

No. 92,379.   *Patented July 6, 1869.*

UNITED STATES PATENT OFFICE

IMPROVED ROCKING-CHAIR

Letters Patent No. 92,379, dated July 6, 1869
The Schedule referred to in these Letters Patent and making part of the same.

  . . . This invention relates to improvements in the construction of rocking-chairs, with air-blowing attachments, having for its object to provide a stand or base for the support of a bellows, with tracks or rails, on which the rockers, which are fixed close to the seat, may work, instead of on the floor; also, to provide an arrangement whereby the parts may be readily detached for storage or packing in compact form; and also an improved arrangement of parts, whereby the bellows is operated, all as hereinafter specified. . . .

  This stand, with elevated rails, protects the rockers against rocking on small children crawling on the floor, or strings scattered thereon. It also provides for rocking the chair with the same ease, when sitting on the ground; and it also serves as a support for a bellows, D, whereby the occupant may, by the act of rocking, impel a current of air upon himself, through a flexible tube, E, which may be directed to any part, as required.

  The top of this bellows is connected by a bent bar, F, to the stand A, so as to be held in a fixed position, while the lower part is connected by a similar bent bar, G, to the bottom of the chair, so as to be moved up and down with it, to impel the air. . . .

Jack Daniel Barrel Chair

Made of an old hickory barrel from the Jack Daniel distillery. It was in these barrels that the whiskey was aged. The barrel has been sanded down to the natural grain of the wood. The barrels show the name Jack Daniel burned into the side, but this can be sanded down if you prefer it that way. Made completely by hand with foam cushioning. Mounted on a base that will rock or swivel. 33" high; 25½" wide. Comes in black, red, avocado, or gold Naugahyde. $135.00. Freight collect. *Lynchburg.*

Danish Armchair

A light oak frame and caned seat and back distinguish this Danish chair. 31" high, 24" wide, 20" deep. Four chairs, $368.00. Shipping charges for all, $175.00. *Asbjorn-Mobler A/S.*

Library Step Chair

A Chinese chair which converts to a stepladder when the chairback is folded forward. 21" wide, 23½" long, 35" deep. Has leather upholstering. $247.00. Shipped express collect. *Charlotte Horstmann Ltd.*

Folding Rocker

In Victorian times, longer visits were the custom, so when Aunt Millicent visited, she brought along her favorite folding rocker. This reproduction is 17" wide, 29" deep, 32½" high. The chair, made of solid mahogany, has a carved rose-and-leaf decoration. Padded back; spring-filled seat. Upholstered in grade A fabric. $89.95. Shipped collect. *Magnolia Hall.*

English Rocker

A magnificent facsimile of the first steel rocker exhibited by R.W. Winfield of Birmingham at the Great Exhibition in 1851. The flat bar steel frame is upholstered in hide to the color of your choice. $240. Shipped collect. *Ashley.*

Be Chairful!

Medallion Chair

A hand-cast replica of a 17th century masterpiece, this aluminum chair is resplendent with bas relief, scrolls, and cherub heads. Comes in white, black, bone, avocado, or pompeian green. 15" wide, 38¾" high. Seat is 15¾" high. $75.00. Postage $5.00. *Patio.*

"The Swan"

This Danish chair swivels all around and adjusts for elevation. 29½" high, 29" wide, 27" deep. Available in Naugahyde, $153.00; woolen fabric, in choice of color, $170.00; or leather, in choice of color, $299.00. Shipping charges for two chairs, $155.00. *Asbjorn-Mobler A/S.*

Hanging Rattan Swing

This egg-shaped mobile holds a comfortable seat. Woven of top-quality rattan. Heavily lacquered for weather protection. 41" high; 28" wide; 23" deep. Corduroy cushion included. $49.95. Shipped express collect. *Fran's Basket House.*

Lounge Chair and Ottoman

Weather will not deteriorate this chair and ottoman, made expressly for outdoor living in all seasons. The frames are of interlocking polyvinyl tubing which looks like bamboo. The slings are of Acrilan. Chair: 26½" wide, 30½" high; seat, 14½" high; price is $125.00. Ottoman: 26½" wide, 17½" high, 23" deep; price is $60.00. Shipped express collect. *Patio.*

Bar Stool

Constructed with materials for maintenance-free outdoor living, this bar stool will not deteriorate in the worst weather. Frames are of interlocking polyvinyl tubing, reminiscent of bamboo; the sling is Acrilan. 19½" wide, 19½" deep, and 36½" high. Seat height is 30". $65.00. Shipped express collect. *Patio.*

Monk Chair

This rosewood wide-seated chair comes from Hong Kong. 28" high, 30½" wide, and 27" deep. $164.00. Shipped freight collect. *Charlotte Horstmann Ltd.*

Spanish Chair

This cherrywood chair, hand made in Spain, has a rush seat and finely turned legs. 35" high, 19" wide, and 18" deep. $62.00. F.O.B. Madrid. *Abelardo Linares S.A.*

"The Egg"

This Danish import, made of dull aluminum, is 42" high, 34" wide, and 31" deep. The footstool is 14½" high, 22" wide, 16" deep. In Naugahyde, $298.00; in woolen fabric, $328.00; in leather, $627.00. Shipping charges, $175.00. *Asbjorn-Mobler A/S.*

Brrr!!

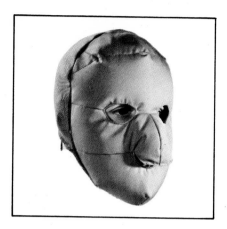

Face Mask

When the wind is howling far below zero, your face, head, and ears need protection. With this goose-down-filled mask, you may look like a zombie, but you certainly won't wind up like one. $14.95 postpaid. *Eddie Bauer.*

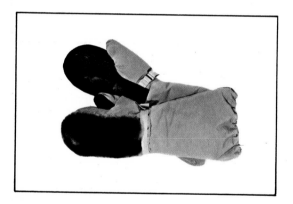

Goose Down Mitts

These are the mitts that made it to the top of Mt. Everest. Guaranteed to keep hands warm at sub-zero temperatures. Made of a tough nylon-cotton blend. Windproof. Water-repellent. Cuffs are protectively long to be worn inside or over the sleeves of a parka. Inner wristlets of stretch-knit nylon. Adjustable wrist straps. Tunneled elastic cuffs provide barrier against penetrating winds. Goatskin leather palms are abrasion-resistant. Backs are made of mouton lamb. Sizes: small, medium and large. $24.95 postpaid. *Eddie Bauer.*

The tiniest snow crystal is about 1/500th of an inch in diameter—just a pinpoint. The biggest snowflakes in the world fell in Montana in 1887; they measured 15 inches in diameter and were eight inches thick.

* * *

Some hailstones are bigger than baseballs. Most hailstones are the size of small pebbles, but occasionally some fall that are as much as 5 inches in diameter and weigh more than a pound. On July 16, 1928, in Potter, Nebraska, a huge, single hailstone fell. It tipped the scales at one and one-half pounds—the largest hailstone on record!

* * *

We say "as white as snow," but the Japanese, repeating the phrase on January 31, 1925, laughed; and, on December 6, 1926, the French thought of the expression and howled. For on the first date, snow fell on Japan and it was *gray;* and at the later date, snow fell in France and it was *black!*

Dr. Fujiwara, of Japan's Tokyo Observatory, explained that the odd event was due to a mixture of snow and ashes from nearby volcanoes. On the other hand, the French could offer no explanation. They just looked at the snow and shrugged their shoulders.

* * *

We are put to no end of trouble by a 10-inch snowfall—traffic is snarled, electricity fails, drains overflow, roofs leak. Imagine how the people of Tamarack, California must have felt in the winter of 1906-7 when 884 inches of snow fell in one heap. That's 73 feet, a world's record.

Electric Socks

A special heating element (not exposed) is activated by a small flashlight battery (not included). Completely safe. Made from a blend of 60% wool and 40% nylon. One size fits all. Grey with red. $9.80. Postage 75¢. *Casco Bay Trading Post.*

Four-Layer Underwear

Four layers—cotton, wool and nylon knit, Kodel interlining, and nylon knit tricot—keep you dry and warm in the most penetrating cold. The layers are separated by insulating air barriers. May be washed or dry cleaned. Complete suit weighs about 36 oz. Jacket has knit collar and cuffs, and full-length zipper. Pants have knit cuffs and elastic waistband. Jacket sizes 36-50; pants sizes 30-44. $30.00 postpaid. *Gokey.*

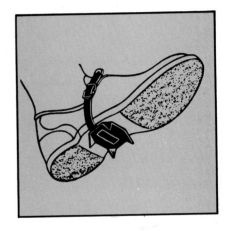

Ice Creepers

When the pavement is covered with ice, you step along carefully in fear of breaking a limb on the treacherous surface. But if you attach this gadget to the bottom of your shoes, your worries might be over. The prongs hook into the ice to give you traction. Made of cast iron with adjustable web strap. Will do for both men and women. $1.00. Postage $1.05. *Vermont Country Store.*

Buckskin Shirt

This suede finish, hand-washable buckskin will never stiffen from getting wet. It is an exact copy of the buckskin shirt worn by the frontiersmen of many generations ago. Sand colored. Sizes 38 through 46. $49.80. Postage 75¢. *Casco Bay Trading Post.*

Arctic Muff

Insulated with goose down and fitted with knit nylon cuffs, this 6" by 7" ladies' muff can double as a purse. Has zippered pocket for keys. Strap fits around neck. Made of tough nylon taffeta, fully lined. Comes in gold, powder blue, navy, dark brown. $16.95 postpaid. *Eddie Bauer.*

For Your Pooch

Some girls might opt for a diamond; some gentlemen would prefer a blonde; but most everyone has a soft spot for man's best friend, the dog.

A dog embodies all the virtues of man, and none of his vices. As Lord Byron put it, the dog possesses "Beauty without Vanity, Strength without Insolence, Courage without Ferocity."

A few years back a woman in Texas loved her dog so much she married him in a standard religious ceremony presided over by a cleric. Now this may be further than you care to go to demonstrate your affection. The items on these pages give some idea of what some people will do to render homage to the darling of their heart, even though that darling may be somewhat perplexed by the exotic largesse.

Camouflage Dog Blanket

Heavy-weave material on the outside of this fleece-lined jacket keeps your hunting dog warm in the marshes. The camouflage, of course, helps to keep him hidden from the prey. Adjustable chest and belly straps snap on and off quickly. $12.50. Postage $1.50. *Orvis.*

Dog Basket

An 8" deep seat offers protection from sudden stops and bumps. Roomy enough for most breeds. 14" long, 9" wide. Attaches to any standard bike. Washable. Trimmed in red, white, and blue with a removable carpet. $5.98. Postage $1.00. *Du Say's.*

The greatest racing dog in history was Mick the Miller, a greyhound owned by an Irish priest named Father Brophy. Mick flashed sensational speed on the English tracks, and the Father was offered $4,000 for the beast. He accepted on condition that he receive the Derby purse if the dog won the classic. The Miller came through, winning $50,000. In his three-year career on English soil, Mick never lost a race.

* * *

The most popular breed in the U.S. today is the poodle. In 1971, the American Kennel Club had 256,491 poodles on register. Compare this to 111,355 German Shepherds, the next most popular breed.

* * *

The dog who is reputed to have lived the longest was a black Labrador named "Adjutant," who died on November 30, 1963 at the age of 27 years and three months.

* * *

The smallest breed going is the Chihuahua. At maturity, this Mexican wonder generally weighs somewhere between two and four pounds, but some Chihuahuas tip the scales at no more than a pound.

* * *

The heaviest dog on record was a Wisconsin Saint Bernard who, at age five, weighed 295 pounds.

* * *

The largest litter ever thrown was 23, by a fox-hound called Lena, on February 11, 1945.

Doggie Sunglasses

These sunglasses, with adjustable temples, come in blue, yellow, or pink flame. $1.00. Postage $1.00. *Du Say's.*

Ivy League Dog Cap

Has black and white stripe with button-down peak. $2.98. Postage $1.00. *Du Say's.*

For Your Pooch

Knot Remover

Knots, mats, snarls and burrs are painlessly removed from your pet's fur. Sharp safety blades are specially designed to remove most snarls as you comb through. Contoured black handle. $6.95. Postage $1.00. *Walter Drake.*

Pet High Chair

Once your pet is put in this chair, it will stay put. Chair legs are natural wood finish; sides and back are upholstered in beige vinyl. There's a tray for feeding or for toys. 22½" high; seat is 13" by 16". $21.95. Postage $1.00. *Du Say's.*

Dog Yamulka

For the Hasidic canine. White with a blue Star of David. $2.98. Postage $1.00. *Du Say's.*

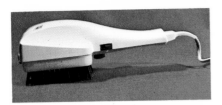

Pet Comb

Big or little, short or shaggy, every vet says nothing keeps a dog cleaner than a daily brushing. The removable bristle-pack can be rinsed under a faucet to keep it sanitary. The instrument runs on 110 to 120 volts, AC only. $10.95. Postage $1.25. *House of Minnel.*

Dog Straw Hat

Attaches at chin. $2.98. Postage $1.00. *Du Say's.*

Dog Cart

Balanced to avoid any weight on the dog's back, this cart is constructed of light tubular steel frame, reinforced 48" shafts, 16" ball bearing wheels, rubber tires and a 27" spring seat. Seats two or three children or one adult. Five sizes available to fit breed, height of dog at withers, and approximate weight. Breast type adjustable-size harness of top quality leather with 52" traces, and full breeching. $122.00. Shipped express collect. *Pearson's.*

Who loves me will love my dog also.
St. Bernard of Clairvaux (1091-1153),
SERMO PRIMUS

In the whole history of the world there is but one thing that money cannot buy—to wit, the wag of a dog's tail.

Josh Billings (1818-1885)

Oh, the saddest of sights in a world of sin
Is a little lost pup with his tail tucked in!
Arthur Guiterman (1871-1943),
LITTLE LOST PUP

He cannot be a gentleman that loveth not a dog.
Proverb

I like a bit of a mongrel myself, whether it's a man or a dog; they're the best for every day.
George Bernard Shaw (1856-1950),
MISALLIANCE

If you pick up a starving dog and make him prosperous, he will not bite you. This is the principal difference between a dog and a man.
Mark Twain (1835-1910),
PUDD'NHEAD WILSON'S CALENDAR

For Your Pooch

Mod Hat

In red corduroy, with up-down sunglasses. $3.98. Postage $1.00. *Du Say's.*

Doggie Bathrobe

Made of washable, white terry cloth with red trim. For proper fit, measure from base of collar to tail. The four-legged style has zippered back. Sizes 8 to 16: $3.98. Sizes 18 and 20: $4.98. Postage $1.00. *Du Say's.*

Of the many thousands of dogs registered by the American Kennel Club, in 1970 there were only four breeds in which there were less than five dogs registered. It appears that throughout the entire United States there were only four Sussex Spaniels of record, only three Belgian Malinois, only two Field Spaniels, and only two English Foxhounds. Compare these, for example, with 61,042 Dachshunds, or with 13,180 Great Danes, or even with 769 Irish Wolfhounds.

* * *

The fastest dog in the world is either the saluki or the greyhound, depending on whom you talk to. The greyhound has been clocked at 41.7 miles per hour.

* * *

The tallest dog extant is the Irish Wolfhound "Broadbridge Michael." Owned by a woman in Kent, England, it measures 39½ inches at the shoulder.

Dog Whistle

A knob adjusts the pitch. You set the pitch at a point where you—or anyone else, for that matter—can't hear the whistle. But your dog can. Your dog can be trained to respond to that pitch. Metal. 3½" long. $1.00. Postage 25¢. *Stadry*.

Doggie Pajamas

For cool nights or for sleeping with the kids. Pullover style is an easy on and off. Designed for complete freedom for boy or girl dogs. Made of washable cotton flannel. Comes with matching night hat. For easy fit, measure from collar to tail. Sizes 8 to 16: $3.98; sizes 18 and 20: $4.98. Postage $1.00. *Du Say's*.

Automobile Seat

This beige vinyl seat keeps a dog from disturbing the driver. Adjusts to proper height. Keeps hair off your seat. For small dogs, size 12" by 16", $12.98; for larger dogs, size 14" by 18", $14.98. Postage $1.00. *Garrett's*.

Bicycle Carrier

This wicker basket with hinged lid has an opening for your dog's head. The container will keep your pet secure so that he can't jump out. Adjustable straps fit any bicycle. Vinyl top: $14.95. Suede top, $19.95. Postage $1.00. *Catawba Trader*.

Family Hobbies

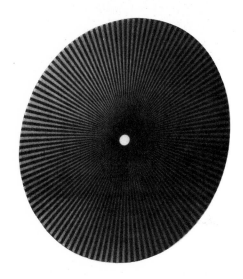

Psychedelic Disc

When the psychedelic disc is plugged into an electric socket, arachnoid shapes weave in and out. The effect is created by revolving plates which are lit with red light. White plastic case and stand. $20.00. Postage $1.50. *Haverhill's.*

Redington Theater

In the 1860s, John Redington made lithographs for his toy theater plays from copper and zinc printing plates. The present-day Theater Pack includes a color reproduction of the stage front he created, a masterpeice of mid-Victorian design, printed on strong cardboard. The stage folds flat, and can be assembled in a few seconds. The proscenium opening measures 11" long, 9" high, and 13" deep. The package also includes the curtain and scenery for two plays, "Aladdin" and "Jack the Giant Killer." printed on strong cardboard. There are also playbooks for the two plays in four languages (English, French, Italian, and German). Wire slides for moving the characters on stage are separately available. $7.50. Air freight $6.25. Surface mail $3.50. *Pollock's Toy Theatres, Ltd.*

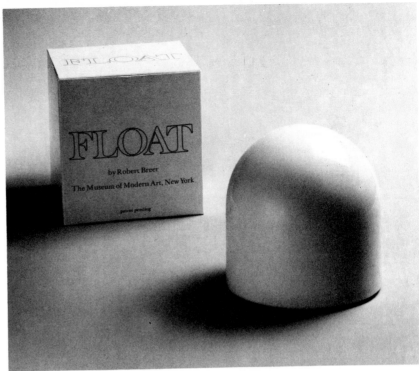

Three-Head Kaleidoscope

Each head snaps into this 9"-long kaleidoscope for intriguing spectacles. Two of the heads contain different assortments of materials; the third comes empty to provide opportunity for your own experimentation. $3.50. Postage $1.50. *Childcraft.*

Whittling Kit

The finest steel, we are told, goes into this knife, which is claimed to be perfect for whittling. The knife, guaranteed for life, comes in a kit which contains one oilstone, two sticks of Tennessee red cedar whittling wood, and an illustrated instruction sheet written by Conner Motler, one of Tennessee's greatest wood carvers. A good whittler, Motler says, is judged as much by the wood on the ground, as by the wood in his hand. An expert drops paper-thin shavings that curl into circles as soon as they leave the stick. $10.00 postpaid. *Lynchburg.*

Float

This amazing kinetic sculpture wanders at a snail's pace over any surface, backing off when it meets an obstacle. Made of durable white plastic, it is fitted with tiny wheels and a simple battery-operated motor. Uses a C battery (not included). 4" high; 3¾" in diameter. $7.95. Postage $1.50. *Childcraft.*

Family Hobbies

Space Spider

This string sculpture kit makes hundreds of stunning designs in three dimensions. The elastic string, in brilliant fluorescent colors, is threaded through the perforated black panels. Of interest to all kids, from eight to eighty. $3.95. Postage $1.50. *Childcraft.*

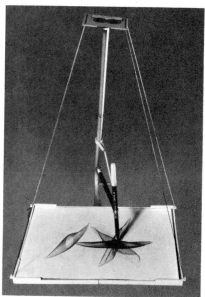

Pen Dul Art

You get an original drawing every time! This clever design-making machine, a prizewinner at the International Inventors Exhibition, is operated by setting the pen-supporting platform gently in motion. Stroke by stroke, the pen begins to form a geometric shape. For a multi-colored pattern, just switch to a pen with a different ink. To complicate the pattern, set the pen in motion in a different direction. $10.00. Postage $1.50. *Childcraft.*

Weather Station

This kit serves as a superb introduction to meteorology. The equipment assembles easily, and includes a remote-reading anemometer, a wind vane, a forecasting manual, a weather map, and a cloud chart. $15.95. Postage $1.95. *Childcraft.*

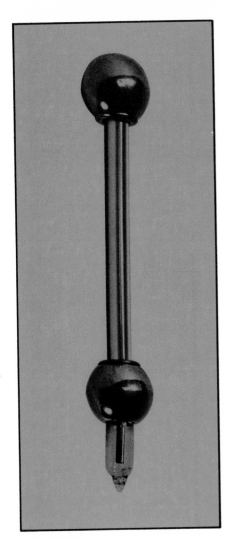

Spooky Lite

Static magic. Just hold the wand in your hand as you shuffle your feet on the rug. You create light by touching objects or people. $1.00. Postage $1.50. *Childcraft.*

Liquillusion Box

When you look through the window of this little black box, what you see looks like liquid, acts like liquid, reflects like liquid. But, somehow, you're sure it's solid. A fascinating optical puzzler! $3.00. Postage $1.50. *Childcraft.*

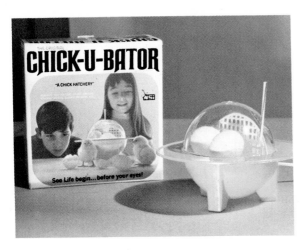

Fluids in Motion

A demonstration of ocean waves in slow motion which may have calming quality. The fluid is contained in a 13" walnut base. $26.00. Postage $1.99. *House of Minnel.*

Chick-U-Bator

The entire hatching process of a baby quail can be watched. The set includes a coupon for three fertile quail eggs which will come to you separately. The quails can be set free five weeks after birth. Instructions included. $7.95. Postage $1.65. *F.A.O. Schwarz.*

Family Hobbies

Space Bird Kite

A kite for enthusiasts, this bird is especially powerful. It requires only a whisper of a breeze to take flight. Made with a rugged wooden frame, spanned with red, white, blue, and orange checkered nylon sail cloth. Comes with yards and yards of yarn, spare parts, and instructions. 42" wing span: $6.00; 60" wing span: $8.00. Postage $1.00. *A Man's World.*

Ant Farm

Shortly after this 9" square by 2" thick windowed ant farm is delivered to you, about 25 diligent, stinging red ants will arrive by mail. You can safely watch them at all their multifarious labor. It's a fascinating occupation. The box is of solid pine construction. Instructions on how to introduce the ants to their home are part of the package. $17.00. Postage $1.30. *Kenton Collection.*

Silk Factory

One can watch the silk being reproduced by nature's clever workers in their own little factory, and observe the complete life cycle of egg to caterpillar to cocoon to silk moth. Unbreakable. Escape-proof. $5.98. Postage $1.50. *Childcraft.*

Wireless Intercom Set

These two solid state sending and receiving stations can be used on standard house current. They transmit over a distance of up to 1,500' inside a house, and constitute a wonderful babysitter. $35.00. Postage $3.50. *F.A.O. Schwarz.*

Crypto Encoder

Each rod is a lens that shows how the message is to be written in code, and then converts coded words back into plain English. Included are two rods, message pads, and printed codes. $2.00. Postage $1.50. *Childcraft.*

Radio-Controlled Yacht

The Commodore RC, a radio-controlled yacht, is designed in the classic style of the American Cup Competition. Sails into, abreast of, or with the wind, and is easy to operate. Hull, slope, weight, and balance have been carefully engineered. Over 16 lbs. of ballast has been permanently installed in the hull. Unsinkable. Sail made of spinnaker cloth. Radio control includes transmitter, receiver, and battery case. 72" tall, 48" long. Completely rigged with stand. $169.50. Postage $5.30. *Hammacher Schlemmer.*

TELESCOPES

While it is believed that early Arabian scientists knew of the magnifying power of lenses, the invention of the prototype of the telescope is credited to the great English inventor, Roger Bacon, who flourished in the 13th century. The first of the modern refracting telescopes was completed by Johannes Lippershey for the Dutch government in 1608.

In the next few years, Galileo developed the refractory telescope into a sophisticated astronomical instrument. But the refractory system caused color distortion; so later in the century, Isaac Newton invented the reflecting telescope to combat this aberration.

The refractory and the reflecting models remained the only two types of telescope in use until the 20th century, when the radio telescope was invented to study radio waves coming from outer space. Radio signals have been received from the sun, moon, and planets, and from other galaxies. It was by means of radio telescopy that the mysterious quasars and pulsars were discovered.

Today, the largest operational telescope in the world is a 236.2-inch reflecting telescope in the Caucasus Mountains of the U.S.S.R. Assembled in October 1970, it is 80 feet long, weighs 935 tons, and contains a mirror which weighs 78 tons by itself. The light-gathering power of this telescope is so great that it can detect the light of a single candle, 15,000 miles away. The range of this gargantuan instrument encompasses the entire observable universe—and scientists now believe that the universe may be a matter of "what you see is what you get." In other words, some scientists entertain the opinion that the universe is finite, and that if we could but construct a telescope strong enough we could peer into the very outer limits of space.

Pocket Scope

This four-oz. telescope will actually fit into the palm of your hand. Its coated lenses and prisms project distortion-free views. There are two quick-change front lenses: one, an 8-power, wide-view, whose 24-millimeter lens is suitable for outdoor scene or bird watching; the second, a 6-power, extra-wide 18-millimeter lens, just the thing for watching a sports spectacle or for taking to the theatre. 20-year warranty. Zippered carrying case with wrist strap. Protective lens caps. $19.95 postpaid. *Windfall.*

Pocket-Size Binocular

Small enough to fold into a breast pocket, this Zeiss instrument weighs less than 5 oz. Yet it is capable of magnifying an object eight times. The field of view is 120 meters at 1,000 meters. Comes in soft Morocco case. $147.00. Postage 80¢. *Chris Craft.*

Rangematic

This hand-held instrument accurately measures the distance to any object of landmark—from mooring buoy to ocean liner—without the need to know the target size. When the dial is turned so that the image is sharp, a scale gives the distance in yards of objects up to two miles away. An extra snap-in scale permits quick conversion of this distance into miles-per-hour. The removable six-power sighting scope is handy for buoy identification. Waterproof. Shockproof. 10½" long. $34.95. Postage 40¢. *Chris Craft.*

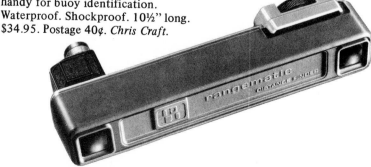

Buttons

Why do men have buttons on their coat sleeves? Well, there's no functional reason for their existence, only a historic one. Frederick the Great of Prussia was greatly put out by the grimy sleeves of his soldiers' uniforms. He inquired why the sleeves were so much dirtier than the rest of the uniform, and was told that the soldiers were in the habit of wiping the perspiration on their faces on their sleeves. To stop the practice, Frederick ordered that buttons be put on the top side of all army men's sleeves. The unmindful soldier would receive a nasty scratch on his face the next time he used his sleeve as a towel.

Eventually, the buttons found their way onto civilian sleeves—but on the lower side of the sleeve. Today, to be in vogue, men must make the weighty decision of whether to adorn their sleeves with one, two, three, or four buttons.

* * *

The rarest and most valuable button in the world is the "Morse" or "Cope" button, a magnificent work of art fashioned by Benvenuto Cellini in 1530 for Pope Clement VI. A large, round, and flat button measuring six inches in diameter, it is made of gold and encrusted with gems. Over the beautiful diamond at the center is an image of God the Father. According to his *Autobiography,* Cellini worked 18 months on this one button and employed a staff of 10 artisans to help him.

Football Button

All the members of the touchdown club might enjoy wearing this button of natural maple finish with black seams and lacing. 1 1/16" long. Set of 6, $1.10. Postage 25¢. *House of York.*

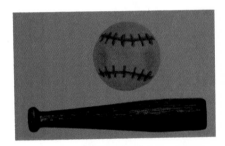

Mouse Button

These mice are 5/8" long, and have tails 1" long. The city mouse has a painted white body with light brown leather ears and tail. The country mouse has a brown body with dark leather ears and tail. Each $1.00; set of six is $5.50. Postage 25¢. *House of York.*

Baseball Button

A little leaguer might be well pleased with a sweater or jacket fastened with these buttons, made from a half-ball of finished natural hardwood with red stitching. 11/16" diameter. Each: 20¢. set of six: $1.10. Postage 25¢. *House of York.*

For Cardplayers

Porcelain buttons from Austria depict the Jack, the Queen, the King, and the Ace in gaily colored detail. Each is 7/8" by 9/16". Set of four, $3.50. Postage 20¢. *House of York.*

Padlock Button

Measuring only ¾" x ½" and gold-finished, these padlock buttons may provide just the right accent to any garment. Each 25¢; set of six, $1.30. Postage 25¢. *House of York.*

Sculpture

Most people think of sculpture as a fine art practiced in marble by such geniuses as Michelangelo and Rodin. But folk cultures the world over have produced masterpieces in stone, wood, and metal that are, in fact, more relevant to 20th-century fine art than are the works of the masters.

In the Americas, the primary folk sculpture is that of the Indian. The Aztecs of central Mexico created massive stone wheels depicting their 260-day calendar—sculptures which are strikingly beautiful and intricate.

The vitality of North American Indian sculpture is perhaps best illustrated by the totem pole. A totem is an object or being which a man regards with respect, and to which he believes himself linked by kinship or ancestry. The word *totem* itself comes from the Ojibwa Indians, who carved representations of animals on poles to represent their clan myths. These animals were also pictured in beautiful masks and on household utensils.

The folk sculpture and art of Africa has been a particular inspiration to modern artists, especially to the Cubists and the Fauves. The styles of African sculpture range from naturalism to conventionalism, from crudity to great technical refinement. Among the most highly prized of African sculptures are the bronzes and ivories of Benin, Nigeria, the best of which were created between 300 and 400 years ago.

In Europe, popular sculpture declined in the face of the industrial revolution. In the early and mid-19th century, mass-produced items increasingly dominated the market, no matter they were often insipid in conception and shoddy in execution. The beautiful works of country artisans were almost driven into extinction.

In the late 19th century, the English artist and writer William Morris fostered a new movement in arts and crafts which revived European folk art—a movement which spread across the Atlantic to sustain American folk arts as well.

Polynesian Maiden
Made of latex, then handpainted and polished, this figurehead is 33" high. Weighs 20 lbs. Includes wood bracket. $45.00. Postage $5.00. *Artistic Latex.*

American Eagle
With a 30" wingspread, this bird stands 19" high, and weighs 14 lbs. The piece is made of latex which has been handpainted to impart an interesting patina. $40.00. Postage $4.00. *Artistic Latex.*

Totem Pole
An excellent facsimile of a north-western Indian artifact, this piece made of latex and then handpainted stands 4' tall, and has a diameter of 12". It weighs 20 lbs. $45.00. Postage $5.00. *Artistic Latex.*

Indian Chief
Made of latex and then handpainted t impart authentic colors, this bust stands 2' high and weighs 10 lbs. $30.00. Postage $3.00. *Artistic Latex*

Fireman
Made of latex and handpainted, this fireman of a bygone age stands better than 4' high. Statue weighs 25 lbs. $50.00. Postage $6.00. *Artistic Latex.*

Sculpture

Brussels' best-known statue is "le Manikin Pis," a 20-inch figure of a boy responding to Nature's call, that has stood in the heart of the city for 500 years. During this time, personages such as Louis XV and Napoleon have presented the bronze lad with many medals, swords, and fancy uniforms which he has worn on appropriate occasions. Among the costumes have been the dress of a Belgian Grenadier, a French Chevalier, a British Master of Hounds, a Chinese Manchu, an Indian Chief, and an American G.I.

Uncle Sam

This pleasant figure, made out of latex, is hand-painted in bright colors. Approximately 19" high. $33.00 postpaid. *Artistic Latex*.

Assyrian Goat

The Assyrian Empire of the Tigris-Euphrates Valley in Mesopotamia reached its peak of power between 750 and 612 B.C. In strange contradiction to their warrior ways, the Assyrians developed an art form of tenderness and lifelike quality. This 14" high, 16" long goat sculpture by Austin is a reproduction of an ancient Assyrian work. Old stone finish. $30.00. Postage $5.00. *Popular Archaeology*.

Mating Bears

Eskimo sculpture made in new ivory. Measures 3" to 4½". $29.95. Postage $1.50. *Arctic Trading Post.*

Tin Woodsman

Sculptured and created by Joseph Leone, this conception of a character in the *Wizard of Oz* is made of tin, but has a heart of brass. The piece stands 26" high. $130.00. Postage $3.00. *J. Kenneth Zahn.*

Incan Idol

From Ecuador, hand-carved in cedar-wood. Finished in natural tone, or in brown, or in black. 16" high. $6.00. Postage $3.00. *Akios.*

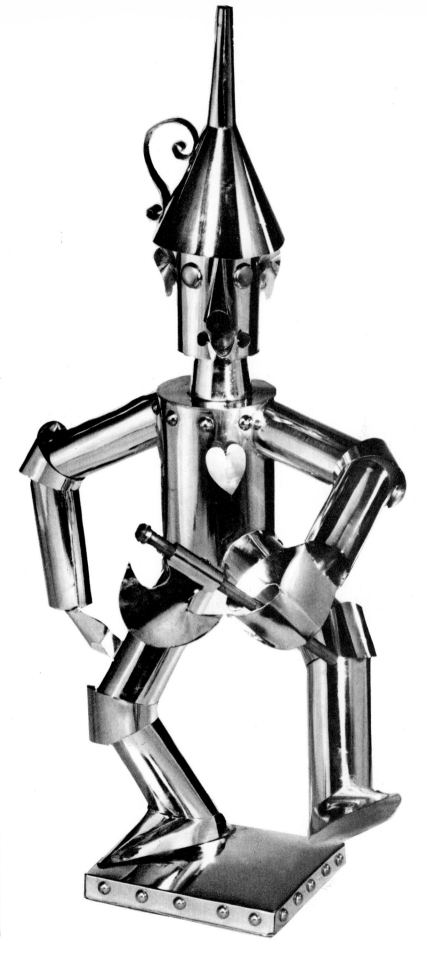

For Smokers

Although it was Sir Walter Raleigh who smoked a bowl of tobacco before the Queen and was promptly rewarded with a dousing by a member of the court who thought Walter was burning, it was the Spanish explorers who discovered the Aztecs smoking crushed tobacco leaves in corn husks some 100 years earlier. Cigarette smoking spread rapidly to Spain, with the beggars of Seville getting credit for the first paper-wrapped variety.

Smoking didn't become popular in Northern Europe until the 1850s, when British soldiers brought Russian cigarettes back from the Crimean War. At the same time, cigarette manufacture and tobacco cultivation spread to the United States, where machinery was developed to replace the tedious hand-rolled technique.

Originally, tobacco derived almost exclusively from Turkey. American cigarette manufacturing dates from the Civil War period. During that era, Greek and Turkish tobacconists in New York City hand-rolled the expensive tobaccos then popular among the carriage trade: Havana, Turkish, Perique, Cavendish, Persian, Cut Navy, Latakia, and St. James. By the 1880s, natural leaf cigarettes, such as Bull Durham, began to dominate the market. The hoi polloi could buy a pack of smokes for a nickel.

Fatima, Sweet Caporal, Vanity Fair, Between the Acts, Melachrino, Murad, Wings, Spud—do these names ring a bell? Well, some of them are still around, but most of them are only nostalgic memories to veteran smokers.

These days, pipes, cigars, and cigarillos are taking an increasing share of the tobacco sales, while the popularity of non-filter cigarettes has declined precipitously in recent years. Yet the Surgeon General's report on the hazards of smoking has hardly meant the last gasp for filtered cigarettes. More filtered cigarettes are now sold each year than the year before. Demon nicotine seems to have secured a niche in the American way of life.

And, by the way, it was Europe—not the United States—that developed the filter cigarette. America only lays claim to the invention of the smoker's cough.

Match Striker
Made with natural materials found in Tennessee, this artifact comes from the mountain district of the eastern part of the state. The match cup is leather trimmed. $10.00 postpaid. *Lynchburg.*

Chinese women, as well as the men, enjoy smoking a pipe. Their pipes are extremely delicate and unusually decorated. Cigarettes, on the other hand, which caught on only in the Chinese metropolises before the advent of Mao, are less common in China today than they were 25 years ago.

* * *

Eskimo boys of three and four years old may be seen smoking pipes! Little girls are not allowed the privilege. A father is very proud when his son picks up the knack, for smoking is considered a sign of manliness.

* * *

If you tried to pay the month's rent or your bus fare with cigarettes, people would laugh at you. But in pre-Revolutionary America, tobacco was acceptable legal tender in several Southern colonies. Virginia even enacted a law that taxes should be payed in tobacco.

Lighter

Billed as the world's most elegant lighter, this precision-crafted, 10 micron gold-electroplate lighter was designed by S. T. DuPont of Paris. Uses butane cylinder for fuel. Has adjustable flame control. 1¾" high, 1¼" wide, ½" deep. $65.00. Postage $1.75. *Abercrombie and Fitch.*

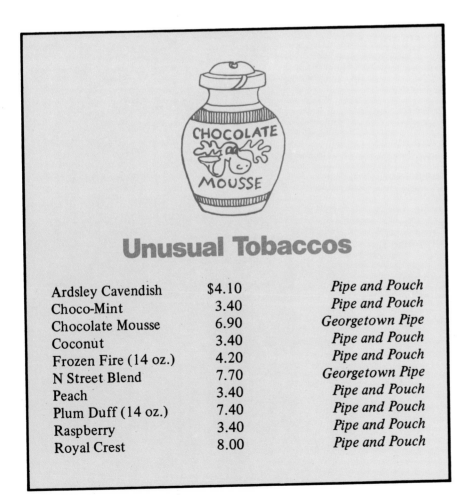

Unusual Tobaccos

Ardsley Cavendish	$4.10	*Pipe and Pouch*
Choco-Mint	3.40	*Pipe and Pouch*
Chocolate Mousse	6.90	*Georgetown Pipe*
Coconut	3.40	*Pipe and Pouch*
Frozen Fire (14 oz.)	4.20	*Pipe and Pouch*
N Street Blend	7.70	*Georgetown Pipe*
Peach	3.40	*Pipe and Pouch*
Plum Duff (14 oz.)	7.40	*Pipe and Pouch*
Raspberry	3.40	*Pipe and Pouch*
Royal Crest	8.00	*Pipe and Pouch*

Pipe-Tomahawk

A replica of an artifact used during the French and Indian War period. It can actually be smoked, and is really a weapon. The wooden stem is 18" long; the tomahawk, made of brass, is 6" long. $15.00 postpaid. *Plume Trading & Sales Co.*

For Smokers

Charles Steinmetz, the electrical wizard, was an inveterate smoker. Although a notice forbidding smoking was posted in the General Electric plant where Steinmetz worked, the great man ignored it until one day an executive asked him rather pointedly if he was not aware of the rule. Steinmetz answered with a cold stare.

The next day, Steinmetz didn't show up for work; and for two days thereafter, no one heard from him. The laboratory of the General Electric plant was practically at a standstill. Without Steinmetz, they just couldn't go ahead.

So the management ordered that a serious search be made throughout the city to locate their genius. After a while, they found him in the lobby of a Buffalo hotel. He was seated in a huge chair, puffing away nonchalantly at a huge cigar. When he was told that the whole company was out looking for him, and was asked why he had, without so much as a goodbye, left his office without notice, he calmly replied, "Well, I just came up here to have a good smoke."

After that, there was never a word mentioned to him about the no smoking rule.

* * *

Pagoda Humidor

Birds and flowers in brilliant enamel interspersed with coral and turquoise adorn the sides of this pekinware humidor. The 7" piece is gold-dipped silver filigree. $175.00. Postage $4.25. *Charlotte Horstmann Ltd.*

No one is quite certain that Rodrigo de Jerez of Spain was the first European to smoke tobacco, but he is more often credited with that distinction than anyone else. As the story has it, he learned to smoke from the natives of the West Indies where he landed with Columbus in 1492. When he returned to Spain, he brought a bit of the plant with him, and greatly astonished the populace by his newly acquired habit. His wife denounced him to the Inquisition as a man who "swallows fire, exhales smoke, and is surely possessed by the devil."

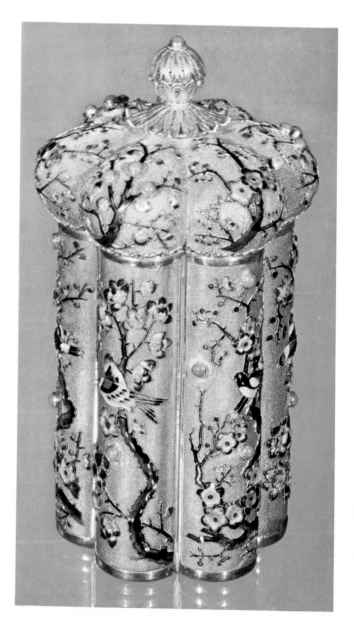

Full Bent Chimney

About 5" high, the lined bowl lies within a smooth surface. $20.25. Postage $2.00. *Pipe Dan.*

Matchless Match

An internal spark system, similar to that of an auto ignition, lights this wand which has no flints, nor wheels, nor gears. Battery-operated. Holds over 250 cc. of standard lighter fuel in its reservoir. Black or white, with gold trim. $12.50. Postage $1.25. *Gallery.*

Brussels Medal Winner

You are supposed to be able to stuff this pipe in your pocket fully lit without even creating a soot mark. This brand new design has a spark-proof grille cover, built-in tamper and cleaner, condensation-free filters, and a washable ceramic bowl. So extraordinary it won a prize at the Brussels fair. $15.00. Postage $1.25. *Joan Cook.*

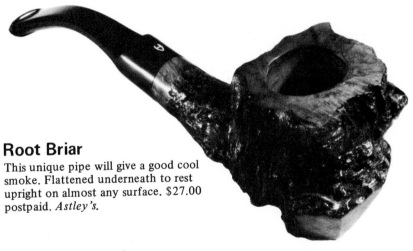

Root Briar

This unique pipe will give a good cool smoke. Flattened underneath to rest upright on almost any surface. $27.00 postpaid. *Astley's.*

Glass Striker

Made of clear hand-blown glass with bubbles, and a "striker" band around the middle. 4" in diameter. Imported. $19.00. Postage $2.25. *Gump's.*

For Smokers

It is recorded that Tennyson and his pipe were almost inseparable. One day, when chatting with several friends, he was taunted about his addiction to tobacco. "Ah!" Tennyson proclaimed, "I can give up tobacco any time I care to!" When further challenged, the poet went over to his pipe rack, took all his pipes and his tobacco, walked over to the window, and threw the whole shebang out down into the yard below.

The next day, Tennyson wasn't his genial self; and still a day later, he was downright morose. He complained, he was grumpy and taciturn, and not at all easy to live with.

On the third day, without a word, he went down to the yard beneath the window, picked up one of his pipes which now lay in two pieces, somehow fitted it together, picked up a few leaves of tobacco, stuffed the pipe, and took a few puffs. He then walked upstairs smiling broadly. Then in a voice of purring contentment, he greeted everyone with the cheeriest of good mornings.

Pipe Smoker's Outfit

This black buffalo case has gold-plated fittings, and contains 31 Dunhill pipes. When the suede inner trays are removed, the case can be used as an overnight bag or as a briefcase. $1,970.00. Shipped express collect. *Harrod's.*

Agate Ashtray

This Brazilian slab cut from an agate nodule has been shaped and then polished into a very sturdy ashtray. Sizes run between 4½" and 6". $20.00. Postage 75¢. *Dover Scientific.*

Electra-Pipe

Odor-free electric smoking provides a different experience, with less tar and nicotine and a cooler smoke. Tobacco is inserted in the holder. You then push the switch and it's on. Chrome base. Tinted globe. $15.50. Postage $1.59. *House of Minnel.*

Keo One o'Clock

Designed in Denmark by the artist, Keo, this pipe is about 6½" long, with a lined bowl. $48.60. Postage $2.00. *Pipe Dan.*

Cobra Pipe

Keo, a Danish artist, designed this pipe, which has a lined bowl to prevent a wood taste in the smoke. About 5" long. Smooth finish, $40.50. Postage $2.00. *Pipe Dan.*

Warden's Clay Pipe

Clay-pipe making is a dying art. These pipes are made in Gouda, Holland. A smooth smoking pipe, this Dutch church warden's pipe has an ultra long stem that cools the smoke. 15½" overall. $4.98. Postage 79¢. *Harriet Carter.*

Golfer's Pipe

The white porcelain bowl resembles a golf ball. Two walls of porcelain separated by a pillow of air comprise its thermo system. Made of Royal Copenhagen. Comes in leather pouch. $34.00. Postage 95¢. *Stern's.*

For Smokers

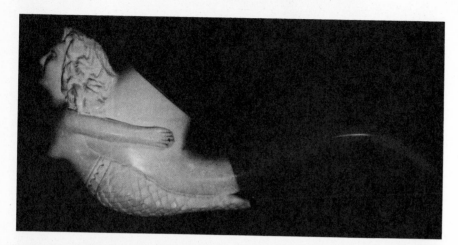

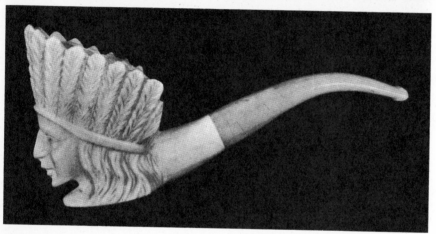

Indian or Mermaid Pipe

Hand carved from a block of meerschaum, these pipes come from Turkey. Meerschaum, an organic substance which is the fossilized remains of sea animals, is found almost exclusively in Asia Minor. One of the most porous substances found in nature, it is very light. Consequently, it absorbs nicotine and filters tobacco. As the meerschaum is smoked, it takes on a rich brown color. The pipe is waxed to give it the velvety finish meerschaum pipes are famous for. Fitted bone mouthpiece. $8.80. Postage $1.00. *Hayim Pinhas.*

Knute Pipe

No two of these handmade sculptured pipes with their natural bark bowl rim are alike. Made of aged Corsican lightweight briar, this pipe yields a mellow smoke. Smooth finish. $30.00 postpaid. *Peterson's.*

Chimney Pipe

The bowl of this lined pipe is 3½" high. About 5" long. Sandblasted surface. $28.35. Postage $2.00. *Pipe Dan.*

Thomas Edison once complained to his friends that his business acquaintances and associates would drop into his office, help themselves to his pure Havana cigars, and just take off. They would just take them by the handful, he said.

"Well," said his friend, "Why don't you lock them up in a humidor?"

"Well, I would find that rather inconvenient. As far as I'm concerned, I wouldn't fancy having them under lock and key. But a friend of mine thought of a clever trick. He knew a cigarmaker, and he had him make me a few boxes of cigars out of cabbage leaves and brown paper. My friend was sure that would fix the freeloaders.

"But that didn't seem to help either; and after my Havanas started disappearing again, I spoke to my secretary, and asked her what happened to those two new boxes of cabbage cheroots."

"Why, I sent those two boxes to your home," she said. When Edison asked his wife about the two new boxes of cigars she said, "Well dear, when you went to California last month, I put them in your trunk."

"Well," confessed Edison, "you wouldn't believe it, but I smoked every one of those damned cigars myself."

* * *

Many First Ladies have smoked a cigarette now and then, but only two have smoked a pipe. The wife of Andrew Jackson, the country's seventh President, was a habitual pipe smoker, but she never got a chance to preside over the White House, briar in hand, for she died shortly after Jackson's election.

Mrs. Zachary Taylor, however, was reported to have often smoked a pipe in her days in the White House, though always in private. Shocking as this may seem today, pipe-smoking was a common enjoyment among American women at the time, especially in the Southwest.

Dolly Madison, wife of the fourth President, took her tobacco in the form of snuff.

* * *

One day, Dr. Creighton, Bishop of London, was riding on a train with a meek curate. The Bishop, who ardently loved his tobacco, took out his cigar case, turned to his companion, and said with a smile, "You don't mind my smoking, do you?"

The curate bowed, and answered humbly, "Not if Your Lordship doesn't mind my being sick."

The tobacco plant was first brought to Europe for cultivation in 1558 by Francisco Fernandes, a physician whom Philip II had sent to the New World to report on its products. Jean Nicot, the French ambassador at Lisbon, sent some tobacco seeds to Catherine de Medici, queen of France, and was immortalized by the application of his name to tobacco's most baleful element, nicotine.

* * *

Thomas Hariot, an English mathematician sent to the colonies by Sir Walter Raleigh, is the first Englishman to have smoked tobacco, but his patron became the most famous smoker of Renaissance England. Raleigh acquired the taste readily, and became a passionate devotee. It is recorded that Raleigh even "tooke a pipe of tobacco a little before he went to the scaffolde."

* * *

For many years, the tobacco habit was bitterly opposed by the English crown and the English church. In his *Counterblast to Tobacco*, King James I described smoking as "a custom loathsome to the eye, hateful to the nose, harmful to the brain, dangerous to the lungs, and in the black stinking fume thereof nearest resembling the horrible Stygian smoke of the pit that is bottomless."

Aladdin's Lamp

The genie in this lamp operates from two D batteries. Just ask it a question, flick the switch, and a spirit-like stream of smoke curls up from the wick. Then in response to your wishes, a small window in the side mysteriously opens and reveals the answer to your question. 12" by 5" by 6". Batteries not included. $10.00. Postage $1.10. *Game Room.*

For Smokers

Chinese Water Pipe
Made of brass. Stands 6" high. $9.50 postpaid. *Art Asia.*

Electronic Cigarette Lighter
Because this lighter electronically generates its own spark, it lights every time, and lasts for years. Works without flint, batteries, or wick. Burns Butane fuel; refills available everywhere. Adjusts for flame level. $16.95. Postage $1.00. *Orvis.*

Korean Pipe
Old bamboo and brass cigar pipe. $9.50 postpaid. *Art Asia.*

Coughing Ash Tray
Looks innocent enough, but coughs and plays "Smoke Gets in Your Eyes" when someone stubs out a butt. Battery-operated (battery not included). $8.00. Postage $1.50. *Haverhill's.*

CHESS

When Bobby Fischer threw a tantrum in Reykjavik, and then arrogantly ceded two games to Spassky before he blew Boris off the board, he performed a commercial alchemy. Thousands of chess books that had been gathering dust in publishers' bins for many years suddenly became prime property, and chess sets—old or new— were transmuted overnight into pure gold.

The boom is still on, and the variety of chess sets is still proliferating. Today, the game— who'd have thunk it?—is the rage of cops, hardhats, and John Wayne.

Roman Chess Set

Each piece has a historical background—the Queen is Livia Drusilla, and the King is Emperor Augustus Caesar. The King stands 4" high; all other pieces are in proportion and hand-antiqued to a fine gold and silver patina. Heavy-weighted and made of styrene, they are packaged in a chest of emerald-green velour with two lift-out leatherette trays. Comes with black and gold 16" chess board, and 16-page instruction book. $35.00. Postage $2.00. *The Gallery.*

CHESS

Beginner's Chess Set

Strictly for the veriest neophyte. The base of each piece identifies the piece, indicates the number of spaces it may move, and shows the directions in which it may move. King is 3 1/4" high; Queen is 2 7/8" high. All other chessmen are in proportion. Pieces are black and oyster white, with weighted felted bases. Black and gold board is 16 1/2" square. Instructions and rules included. $13.00. Postage 50¢. *Brentano's.*

Pre-Mayan Chess Set

An authentic reproduction of an ancient Central American set. Terracotta figures are 3½" to 11" tall. The black and white chess board is 24" square. Comes in a wood box. $150.00. Postage $6.00. *Patio.*

Alice in Wonderland Chess

Lewis Carroll contrived his *Alice in Wonderland* as a chess game. The designers of this chess set sculptured the pieces from John Tenniel's original illustrations. Queen is 4½" high. Board included. $30.90. Postage $1.20. *Game Room.*

Ultra-Modern Chess

This chess set is contemporary plus. Not only do the shapes of the various pieces relate to their movements in the game, but the complete set fits together into a compact 4" by 8" by 1" rectangle. The king and queen are each 3½" high. The other pieces are in proportion. Made of solid aluminum, and finished in black and aluminum. $60.00. Postage $2.50. *Austin Enterprises.*

Nuts and Bolts Chess

Commercial nuts and bolts are used for this chess set. The King stands approximately 2½" high. $25.00. Postage $2.80. *Hammacher Schlemmer.*

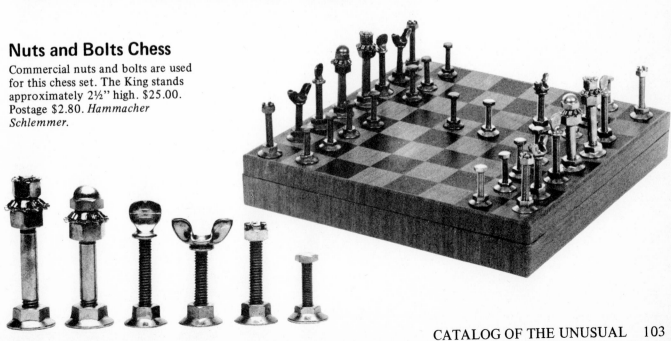

Although many men had attempted to create a telephonic system of communication before Alexander Graham Bell, none invented a practicable device. As early as 1865, Bell, a teacher of the deaf, conceived the idea of transmitting speech by electric waves. Not until 10 years later did he discover the mechanical principle which would implement his theory. Within the next few months, Bell developed his first working apparatus.

On March 10, 1876, he uttered these first electrified—but hardly electrifying—words to his assistant, Thomas Watson, who was in the next room: "Watson, come here; I want you." Later that year, Bell introduced his scientific marvel to the world at the Centennial Exposition in Philadelphia, and the world hasn't stopped jabbering since.

As of 1970, 120.2 million telephones were in use in the United States alone, considerably more than the combined number of phones in Japan, Great Britain, West Germany, Russia, and Canada. Out of 100 households in New York State, 95 had telephones. And Washington, D.C., averaged 102 telephones per hundred households!

The state that has been best able to resist the lure of electronic gab is Mississippi, which has only 75 phones per 100 households—still a fantastic proportion when compared to even the most technologically advanced nations of the world. For example, Japan has less than 40 phones per 100 households, and West Germany has less than 35 per 100.

Fabulous Fones

Cameo Phone

White figures on blue, off-white handset and dial panel, and white cord are the attributes of this attractive Grecian phone. Metal parts are 18K gold-plated brass. $95.00. Postage $2.10. *American Telecommunications.*

All-American Telephone

This handsome instrument is 12" high. Diameter of the base is 7". White cord. 18-carat gold trim. $45.00. Postage $2.10. *American Telecommunications.*

Mediterranean Cradlephone

Fashioned of distressed, dark-grained Polywood. Charcoal handset and dial panel, black scroll decoration, black cord, 18K gold-plated trim. $90.00. Postage $2.10. *American Telecommunications.*

Telephone Booth

In a brown woodtone, this phone holder is made of simulated stainless glass, whose tones are green, amber, and orange. 16" wide, 24" high, and 10" deep. $40.00. Postage $1.00. *Yorkraft.*

Texas Telephone

Ma Bell's itsy little telephones are fine for holding civil conversations, teenage bee-bop talk, and general lady's klatch. But for real man talk and matters of importance, you need a tool of power and persuasion, a Big Deal telephone. Simply place Ma Bell's receiver inside, then use the monster as you would an ordinary telephone. Holes are placed in proper places so you can hear and converse without difficulty. Phone disconnects, just as with an ordinary telephone, when replaced on the cradle. About 16" long, 4" wide. $8.00. Postage $1.50. *A Man's World.*

Telephone Dialer

Automatic telephone dialer programs up to 38 numbers which will be dialed at the touch of a button. Numbers can be easily changed. Plastic apparatus is 11 3/4" long, 10 1/8" wide, and 2 1/2" high. Installs in minutes. $49.95. Postage $2.25. *Abercrombie and Fitch.*

Fabulous Fones

Fold-a-Fone

Except for the ringing components incorporated into the network plug, all the functional elements of this telephone are assembled in one body contained in the two hinged parts. When the telephone is not being used, these parts can be closed, forming what might be the smallest telephone set in the world. $79.95. Postage $2.00. *Hammacher Schlemmer.*

Listening Aid

Attached by means of a suction cup to the side of a phone extension, this electronic gadget enables you to hear both sides of the conversation without holding the receiver. The amplifier is likely to add clarity to your long-distance call. Precision volume control. Long-life battery. Ear plug 2'' wide. $12.98. Postage $1.25. *Bevis.*

Automatic Index

The number you want is selected at a touch of the button. Holds 300 numbers in its plastic case. With batteries. $7.00. Postage $1.50. *Haverhill's.*

Models of Perfection

The 20th-century craze for model trains, cars, and airplanes is merely a continuation of the 19th-century craze for model ships, ships in bottles, and toothpick Towers of Pisa. And before that, man's passion for life in miniature manifested itself in saints' names engraved on a pin and scale models of military equipment.

Model fans might be interested to know that:

The penknife with the greatest number of blades is the Year Knife, made by Joseph Rodgers & Sons Ltd. of Sheffield, England. Built in 1822 with 1,822 blades, the knife has continued to match the year ever since. The knife will finally run out of space for further blades in the year 2,000.

The record run for a model train was set at Nuremberg, West Germany, in 1971, by a Fleischmann "Black Elephant" HO gauge engine. It pulled a 62-axle train 1,053 actual miles. At scale, the run was equivalent to 11,600 miles at 123.9 m.p.h.

The world record for altitude by a model aircraft is 26,929 feet by Maynard L. Hill (U.S.) on September 6, 1970, using a radio-controlled model. The speed record is 213.71 m.p.h. by V. Goukoune and V. Myakinin with a motor piston radio-controlled model at Klementyeva, U.S.S.R. on September 21, 1971.

Western Stagecoach

The pieces of this kit are pre-cut and sanded California redwood and ponderosa pine. Included are trim, wheels, a pamphlet of historical notes, and an instruction sheet. The assembled stagecoach will be 9" long and 6½" high. $4.50. Postage $1.05. *Yield House.*

Models of Perfection

Western Wagon

Model hobbyists and history buffs—convalescents, too—will find assembling this kit entertaining as well as challenging. The wagon is 9" long. Made of California redwood and ponderosa pine, all pieces are pre-cut and sanded. Trim, wheels, a pamphlet of historical notes, and an instruction sheet are included. $3.95. Postage 55¢. *Yield House.*

Hook and Ladder

Handcrafted of cast iron, this beautifully detailed, hand-painted, brilliantly colored model will delight a fire buff. 32" long. $50.00. Postage $3.00. *Haverhill's.*

Mamod Steam Tractor

One quarter of a mile in 15 minutes may not be very fast for a real tractor, but for one that is only 7" high, and 10" long, that's pretty good. The boiler is made of brass and solid copper. The engine is fueled by alcohol. $31.50. Postage $2.00. *A Man's World.*

Radio Control Porsche

Scaled like the real thing, this model racing car measuring 13" long has a 150' range. Hand-held control unit operates steering, forward, reverse, and stop. Four "C" batteries and two 9-volt batteries included. $29.95. Postage $1.65. *F.A.O. Schwarz.*

Rolls Royce
Phantom 11 Coupe

Mounted on mahogany with a mirror base to view the underside of the car, this custom finished model is enclosed in a glass vitrine which is 29" long and 11" high. The model is constructed of over 2,000 parts. Includes suspension steering, brake system, doors which open, spoke wheels, headlamps that work from the dashboard, windows that can be opened. Model is 27" long, 8" high, 9" wide. $495.00. Postage $8.85. *Hammacher Schlemmer.*

Franklin H. Avers of Portage, Wisconsin, made a miniature electric village, which enacts the activities of an average midwestern town from late afternoon to sunrise. This model is mounted on a 5' by 12' stage. As the five-foot curtain opens on the scene, a breeze wafts the scent of flowers out toward the audience and flutters a flag in the park. A motorboat passes a sailboat on the lake, an automobile drives up to a house and honks its horn, and a plane glides in and lands noisily. The sun becomes reddish and finally disappears behind the mountain. Cattle moo, cowbells jingle, the moon appears, stars twinkle. A train pulls into the station, and all is still for a moment to signal the passing of several hours. The day begins to break, a rooster on a fence crows, the flag is raised, a plane roars, the curtain closes, and the five-minute performance is over.

* * *

Elektro, the mechanical man, was made by the Westinghouse Company, and first exhibited in New York City during the World's Fair of 1939-40. The seven-foot, 260-pound robot was set in motion by vibrations of the human voice. He could walk, smoke, count on his fingers up to 10, tell whether an object held before him was red or green, and perform 20 or so other feats. Elektro's electrical system contained 24,900 miles of wire, or enough to encircle the globe.

* * *

The Queen's Dolls' House, presented to Queen Mary of England in 1924, may be the world's most intricate miniature. Constructed on a scale of one inch to one foot, the house is almost nine feet long, five feet wide, and five feet high. It has more than 50 rooms, its own electric generator, a functioning elevator, a plumbing system, and a wine cellar with genuine cobwebs covering its minuscule bottles of real vintage wine. Its library contains hundreds of actual books, most of which were handwritten by such well-known authors as Kipling.

Hunting

All hunting is divided into three parts: trapping and snaring; coursing and falconry; and hunting with implements (firearms, bow and arrow, boomerang, sling). For hunting novices, snaring differs from trapping in that the hunter uses a running noose of wire or cord to entangle his prey. Coursing is the pursuit of game with hounds.

Early methods of trapping involved primarily the pitfall and deadfall. The pitfall was a pit covered with some flimsy material that would not bear weight; the deadfall consisted of a pit plus a weight (a log or stone) which would fall on the trapped animal. But modern trappers rely almost exclusively on spring-snapped, steel-jawed traps.

Falconry is a mode of bird-hunting that was known in ancient China, Persia, and Egypt. It attained its greatest popularity in Europe during the Middle Ages, and went into serious decline after the 17th century. This explains why the sport never caught on in the Americas.

In Great Britain and Western Europe, the sport of hunting often takes the form of the chase. The hunters pursue the game on horseback with the aid of hounds that have a keen sense of smell. In the United States, however, hunting almost always means the field sport of shooting small and large game caught unawares. During the 19th century, big-game hunting in Africa and India became a popular sport among wealthy Westerners.

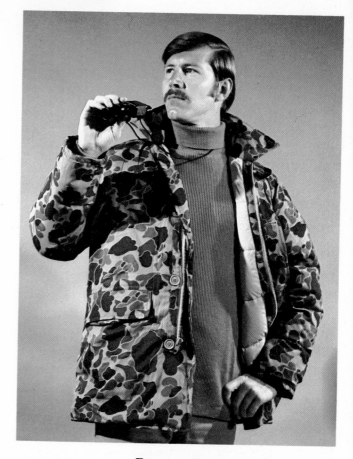

Brown Camouflage Down Coat

Made of waterfowl down with down-insulated sleeves, this 32" jacket weighs less than 3 lbs. Brown camouflage color; big front pockets. Button and zipper front. Sizes to 48. $59.50. Postage $1.00. *Orvis.*

Decoys

This duck decoy is 22" long, 13" high; the swan is 23" long and 17" high. Both made of woodlike latex. $25.00 each. Postage $3.90. *Artistic Latex.*

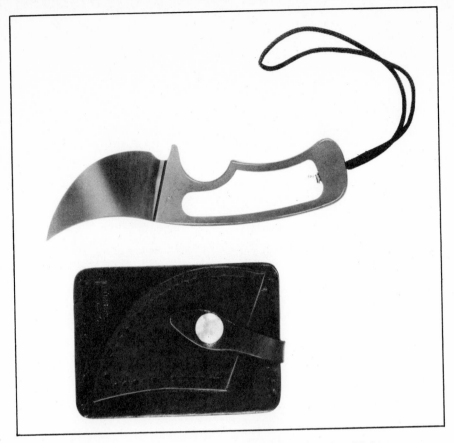

Trailing Point Skinner

The 2 5/8" blade of this lightweight (2½ oz.) hunting knife is made of stainless steel. Hand-made cowhide sheath fits any size belt from 1" to 3". Comes with a woven lanyard to prevent loss during use. $25.00. Postage 75¢. *Collins Bros.*

Camouflage Pants

Designed to provide insulation against the cold for skiers, duckshooters, waders, etc., these pants can be worn over an ordinary pair of trousers for warmth in below-zero temperature. Sizes: 30 to 44. $30.00. Postage $1.00. *Orvis.*

Crooked Hunting Knife

Hand forged of carbon steel, the manufacturer promises that this skinning knife will hold a sharp edge even if it is used to cut wire or split the backbones of big game animals. Blade is 6" long and has a 2" upsweep; overall length, 11". To insure strength, the handle is made of triple-riveted African tiger wood. Sheath and book included. $3.67. 50¢ service charge. Shipped collect. *Herter's.*

Hunting Glasses

The French optical firm that developed these glasses states that in actual trials, a charge of No. 6 shot fired at 20 meters failed to penetrate the Triplex lenses, either the frame or the side shields. Hunters may find the added protection beneficial. With light green sun lenses, $100.00; with yellow lenses which provide increased contrast without dazzling, $125.00. Postage 75¢. *Hunting World.*

Hunting

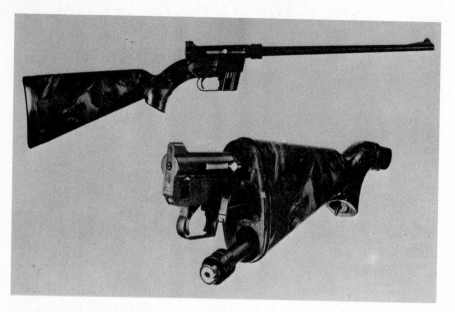

Survival Rifle

This versatile .22 rimfire rifle is designed specifically for survival use. It dismantles to stow in 16½", and is so light it floats. Even when stowed for a long time, rifle is virtually impervious to moisture and corrosion. Semi-automatic action, detachable box-type magazine with eight-round capacity. 16" steel rifling. 2¾ lbs. 34½" long. Includes one magazine. $59.95. Postage $2.10. *Arma Lite.*

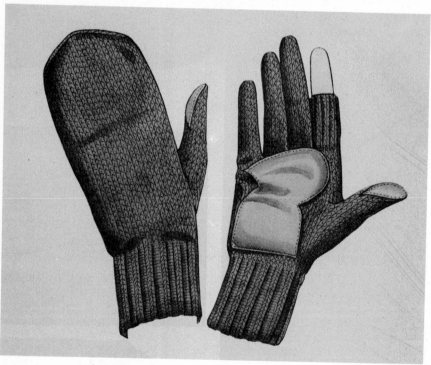

Hunting Gloves

Made in Europe, these forest green, knitted wool gloves stress warmth and mobility. The mitten portion flips back for complete finger freedom. The first joint of the trigger finger is bared. The inner hands and finger tips are made of chamois, trimmed for firm grip. Sizes small through extra large. Made for both righthanded shooters and lefthanded shooters. $14.95. Postage 75¢. *Hunting World.*

Folding Bush Knife

This compact knife is made in Italy. The 7" scimitar folds into a walnut handle. $11.50. Postage $1.15. *Hoffritz.*

For the Executive Desk*

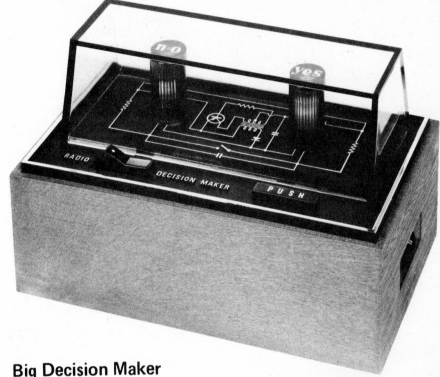

Small Decision Maker

For those rapid unimportant decisions that can go one way or another that harry every businessman. When you just can't make up your mind about some pesky picayune problem, you can settle the matter just by dropping the little blue ball into this lucite contraption. The ball rolls down to either YES or NO, and your dilemma is over. 9½" by 5". $10.95. Postage $1.10. *Game Room.*

Big Decision Maker

This machine is for making important decisions which involve lots of money. Decisions like this should be treated with a good deal of respect. So you push a button and the machine goes through lots of gyrations and does a lot of worrying for you before the answer comes out at the bottom, either either YES or NO. 6" by 3½" by 3". $25.00. Postage $1.20. *Game Room.*

Desk Embosser

You can personalize your stationery by just pressing down on the handle. Envelopes, invitations, announcements, cards, checks, film foil, and a host of other materials are instantly embossed with a raised-letter impression. Special designs can be made on request, for any one-to-four-line message, with a maximum of 24 characters per line. Requires no ink. $10.95 for one to three lines, $1.00 additional for 4th line. 60¢ postage. *Postamatic.*

Portable Desk Fan

Lightweight, compact fan made of plastic adjusts to direct its breeze in different directions. Operates on two D batteries (not included). 3½" in diameter. Stands 8" tall. $3.98. Postage 85¢. *Holiday Gifts.*

Executive Desk: A large wastebasket with drawers.

For the Executive Desk

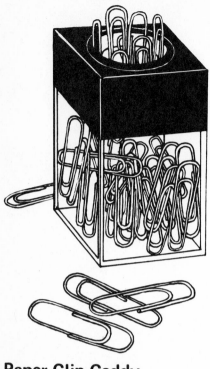

Paper Clip Caddy

Clips are drawn to this attractive paper clip holder like bees to honey. A magnetic inner rim at the top holds the clips, doling them out as needed— one or a few at a time. Pins, nails, bobby pins are also handily held. This 1½"-square, 3"-tall dispenser has a clear plastic bottom and a black top. To refill, you simply remove the top. Comes with a supply of clips. $1.98. Postage 69¢. *Harriet Carter.*

Magnetrix

A limitless variety of interesting forms and shapes are possible with this do-it-yourself magnetic device. With this intellectual erector set, you build with 30 magnetized pieces on a 5½" by 7" hardwood base with 3" metal insert. $8.95. Postage 95¢. *Game Room.*

Investment Advisor

This sage system isn't guaranteed to be foolproof, but it will probably work as well as anything else. You drop a steel ball into the top of the walnut board, and the ball lands in a certain slot which tells you what to do in the market. 9" by 6". $5.00. Postage 85¢. *Game Room.*

Running Wild

More than 200 steel balls scurry helter skelter from top to bottom through eight levels of acrylic plastic. Finally, as if by magic, they arrange themselves in orderly rows on the bottom. Turn it over and the phenomenon repeats. For some unknown reason, this turns out to be fascinating. A handsome kinetic form, 3½" square. $5.00. Postage 75¢. *Game Room.*

Executive Wastebasket

This teakwood-finish basket has a throat opening of 8 5/8", but takes paper many times its size, and will accept up to seven sheets at a time. Operates on 110 volts. 22" high, 14" wide, 11½" deep. Rolls on casters. $279.00. Shipped express collect. *Electric Wastebasket Corp.*

Pilgrim Puzzle

More than a puzzle, this is an opportunity to create your own sculptures. A 7½" walnut wood block has been carefully jig-sawed to provide intriguing pieces. You stack and balance them as you wish, creating an unlimited number of sculptures. Then, if you can bear it, collapse your creation, and produce another. $6.00. Postage 85¢. *Game Room.*

Tapedeck

This battery-operated dispenser ends tangled tape. You get the right length every time. Comes in black or walnut metal case. Takes any type of tape. $12.95. Postage. *Patio.*

Alabaster Ruler

Each of the 12 inches of this imported Italian desk ruler is a different jewel-like color. Doubles as a paperweight. $10.98. Postage $1.25. *Taylor Gifts.*

All Manner of Manna

Salad

To make this condiment, your poet begs
The pounded yellow of two hard-boiled eggs;
Two boiled potatoes, passed through kitchen-sieve,
Smoothness and softness to the salad give;
Let onion atoms lurk within the bowl,
And, half-suspected, animate the whole.
Of mordant mustard add a single spoon,
Distrust the condiment that bites so soon;
But deem it not, thou man of herbs, a fault,
To add a double quantity of salt.
And, lastly, o'er the flavored compound toss
A magic soup-spoon of anchovy sauce.
Oh, green and glorious! Oh, herbaceous treat!
'Twould tempt the dying anchorite to eat;
Back to the world he'd turn his fleeting soul,
And plunge his fingers in the salad bowl!
Serenely full, the epicure would say,
Fate can not harm me, I have dined to-day!

Sydney Smith

If you think Adelle Davis is brewing up a storm over nutrition, you should have been around when Sylvester Graham, the father of the graham cracker, was stirring up the country with his lectures and books in the 1830s-1840s. He antagonized thousands by opposing such standard commodities as tea, coffee, tobacco, liquor, meat, corsets, and featherbeds. He also persuaded thousands to follow his diet, which included bread made of coarse flour, since known as Graham flour. The number of Grahamites became so great that, to accommodate them, scores of Graham boarding houses were established, and restaurants set apart special Graham tables.

* * *

The avocado has three singular features: (1) its protein content is greater than that of any other fruit; (2) its ripeness can be determined only by a laboratory test of its oil content; and (3) its growth is sometimes so prolific that trees have collapsed under the weight of their fruit.

* * *

For great occasions, nomadic Arab tribes usually prepare a feast whose main dish is, at least in size, without equal. This dish consists of eggs which are stuffed in fish, the fish then stuffed in chickens, and the chickens then stuffed in sheep, and the sheep finally stuffed in a whole roasted camel.

* * *

For its merit, I will knight it and make it sir-loin.
Charles II (1630-1685),
on being told that a piece of beef
which particularly pleased him
was called the loin.

* * *

All human history attests
That happiness for man,—the hungry sinner!—
Since Eve ate apples, much depends on dinner.
George Gordon, Lord Byron (1788-1824),
DON JUAN

For economy and ease, you can't beat the food-gathering methods of the Cistercian Monastery in Alcobaca, Portugal. Whenever its cooks want fresh fish, all they do is lower their nets into a branch of the Alcoa River which flows through the heart of their huge kitchen.

Prepared Dishes

Beefsteak & Kidney Pie	15½ oz.	$1.69	*Colonial Garden Kitchens*
Beef Stroganoff	Doz. (7 oz.)	55.00	*Hammacher Schlemmer*
Beef Wellington (Individual)	8 (6½ oz.)	44.00	*Hammacher Schlemmer*
Beef Wellington (Tenderloin)	Doz. (9 oz.)	45.00	*Hammacher Schlemmer*
Boneless Breasts of Chicken			
Stuffed Alfredo Style	Dozen	16.50	*Maryland Gourmet*
Stuffed with apples and almonds	Dozen	15.95	*Maryland Gourmet*
Stuffed Montmartre Style	Dozen	16.50	*Maryland Gourmet*
Stuffed Venezia Style	Dozen	15.95	*Maryland Gourmet*
Boneless Legs of Chicken			
Stuffed with apple and almond	Dozen	10.25	*Maryland Gourmet*
Stuffed a la Paradise	Dozen	10.75	*Maryland Gourmet*
Brunswick Stew	1¼ lbs.	1.29	*Colonial Garden Kitchens*
Canadian Roast	6 lbs.	20.10	*McArthur's Smokehouse*
Cassoulet	15½ oz.	1.69	*Colonial Garden Kitchens*
Clams Casino	2 doz.	23.00	*Hammacher Schlemmer*
Coquilles Saint-Jacques	Dozen	25.00	*Hammacher Schlemmer*
Crab Imperial	Dozen	29.00	*Hammacher Schlemmer*
Crepes a la Reine	Dozen	23.00	*Hammacher Schlemmer*
Crepes Canneloni	Dozen	23.00	*Hammacher Schlemmer*
Crepes de la Mer	Dozen	29.00	*Hammacher Schlemmer*
Curried Beefsteak Pie	15½ oz.	1.69	*Colonial Garden Kitchens*
Fillets of Roe-Deer with Mushrooms	14¾ oz.	2.65	*Bremen House*
Grouse in Wine Sauce	19 oz.	5.50	*Bremen House*
Lobster Cherbourg	Doz. (4 oz.)	29.00	*Hammacher Schlemmer*
Marshalls Guinea Hen in Wine Sauce	3 lbs.	9.50	*Maison Glass*
Partridge in Sherry	15 oz.	5.00	*Maison Glass*
Pigeon in Wine Sauce	15½ oz.	6.00	*Bremen House*
Pheasant in Wine Sauce	3 lbs.	8.95	*Bremen House*
Quenelles Brochet in Shrimp Sauce	15 oz.	2.95	*Maison Glass*
Quiche Lorraine	Doz. 4" pies	26.00	*Hammacher Schlemmer*
Ratatouille	16 oz.	1.25	*Maison Glass*
Roast Wild Boar in Juniper Sauce	14¾ oz.	2.45	*Bremen House*
Seafood Pie	14 oz.	2.98	*Colonial Garden Kitchens*
Seafood Newburg	Doz. (4 oz.)	25.00	*Hammacher Schlemmer*
Seafood Oceania	4½ lbs.	24.00	*Hammacher Schlemmer*
Venison in Wine Sauce	15½ oz.	3.50	*Bremen House*
Vine Leaves Stuffed with Rice	13 oz.	1.10	*H. Roth & Son*

All Manner of Manna

For almost 200 years, a festival called the Fiesta of the Radishes has been held each December 23 in Oaxaca, Mexico. During the festival, immense radishes are sold, and native artists carve them into many shapes—fantastic figures of men and animals. Prizes are awarded for the best and most imaginative shapes.

Vegetables

Cèpes	10 oz.	$4.50	*Maison Glass*
Chanterelle	4 oz.	2.25	*Maison Glass*
Morel	7 oz.	6.25	*Maison Glass*
Salsify	15 oz.	1.85	*Bremen House*

Seafood

Brook Trout (Iceland)	10 oz.	$2.75	*Bremen House*
Cuttlefish (seasoned)	7 oz.	.59	*Nichols Garden Nursery*
Mackerel (in bean paste)	7 2/5 oz.	.69	*Nichols Garden Nursery*
Matjes Herring (from Holland)	2 lbs.	3.00	*Bremen House*
Octopus (sliced, smoked)	3½ oz.	.89	*Nichols Garden Nursery*
Sea-eels (barbecued in sweet sake)	3 2/3 oz.	.79	*Nichols Garden Nursery*
Smoked Salmon (from Scotland)	2 lb. side	22.00	*Ritchie Brothers*
Snails (24, without shells)		2.95	*Maison Glass*
Snails (18, with shells)		3.95	*Maison Glass*

Sauces

Beef Fondue (assorted)	6 jars	$5.95	*Maison Glass*
Béarnaise Sauce	3½ oz.	.59	*H. Roth & Son*
Cumberland	5¼ oz.	1.25	*Maison Glass*
Harissa	4 oz.	.75	*Maison Glass*
Hoisin	16 oz.	.85	*Maison Glass*
Madeira Wine	3½ oz.	.59	*H. Roth & Son*
Oyster	bottle	1.75	*Maison Glass*
Ravigot	3½ oz.	.59	*H. Roth & Son*
Snail	5 1/3 oz.	1.25	*Maison Glass*
Teriyaki Barbecue	12 oz.	1.00	*Maison Glass*
Truffle	3½ oz.	.59	*H. Roth & Son*

Honeys

Acacia	17½ oz.	$1.75	*Bremen House*
Appleblossom	12 oz.	1.50	*Maison Glass*
Belgium	17½ oz.	2.50	*Maison Glass*
Black Forest	16 oz.	3.50	*Maison Glass*
Black Locust	12 oz.	1.95	*Maison Glass*
Buckwheat	16 oz.	1.50	*Maison Glass*
Clover	16 oz.	1.50	*Maison Glass*
Comb	10 oz.	1.75	*Maison Glass*
Dandelion	16 oz.	1.75	*Maison Glass*
Dutch Clover	16 oz.	1.69	*H. Roth & Son*
Dutch Heather	16 oz.	1.69	*H. Roth & Son*
Eucalyptus	16 oz.	1.25	*Maison Glass*
Fireweed	16 oz.	1.75	*Maison Glass*
Fir	17½ oz.	2.25	*Bremen House*
Florida	16 oz.	1.25	*Maison Glass*
French	(6) 5 oz.	7.50	*Maison Glass*
Gatinais	16 oz.	2.25	*Maison Glass*
Heather	5½ oz.	1.00	*Bremen House*
Hymettus	17 oz.	1.95	*Maison Glass*
Irish	12 oz.	1.75	*Maison Glass*
Jungle	12 oz.	3.00	*Caswell-Massey*
Lavender	16 oz.	2.00	*Maison Glass*
Lime Blossom	16 oz.	1.59	*Bremen House*
Linden	17½ oz.	1.65	*Bremen House*
Ling	16 oz.	2.50	*Maison Glass*
Lotus Blossom	16 oz.	1.29	*Bremen House*
Mountain Flora	12 oz.	1.75	*Maison Glass*
Manley's English	16 oz.	3.00	*Caswell-Massey*
Manuka	16 oz.	1.29	*Bremen House*
Natural Wild	13 oz.	1.25	*Maison Glass*
Orange Blossom	16 oz.	1.25	*Maison Glass*
Pinewood	16 oz.	1.65	*Maison Glass*
Ramat Gan	16 oz.	1.75	*Maison Glass*
Rosemary	16 oz.	2.00	*Maison Glass*
Safflower	16 oz.	1.25	*Maison Glass*
Tamara	12 oz.	2.95	*Maison Glass*
Trappist	(6) 3 oz.	3.50	*Maison Glass*
Wild Flower	12 oz.	1.95	*Maison Glass*
Wild Rose	16 oz.	2.50	*Maison Glass*

All Manner of Manna

Uncommon Cereals

Couscous	1 lb.	$ .98	*Colonial Garden Kitchens*
Lumberman's Mush	5 lbs.	1.65	*Vermont Country Store*
Oat Groats	5 lbs.	1.65	*Vermont Country Store*
Rye (cracked)	5 lbs.	1.65	*Vermont Country Store*

Desserts

Fruits in Cointreau	20 oz.	$6.50	*Maison Glass*
Fruits in Jamaica Rum	17 oz.	6.49	*Colonial Garden Kitchens*
Oranges in Cointreau	20 oz.	6.50	*Maison Glass*
Spiced Seckel Pears	16 oz.	1.29	*Colonial Garden Kitchens*

Baking Ingredients

Marzipan (Danish)	8 oz.	$.69	*H. Roth & Son*
Prune Lekvar	Per lb.	.98	*H. Roth & Son*
Strudel Dough (Hungarian)	Pkg.	.69	*H. Roth & Son*

Unusual Syrups and Flavors

Black Currant	12 oz.	$1.75	*Maison Glass*
Cassis-Dijon	24 oz.	3.50	*Maison Glass*
Cheese	1 pt.	4.00	*Fioretti*
Citron	25 oz.	3.00	*Maison Glass*
Date	28 oz.	2.00	*Maison Glass*
Falernum	12 oz.	1.50	*Maison Glass*
Fleurs Des Alpes	16 oz.	5.50	*Fioretti*
Golden	16 oz.	1.00	*Maison Glass*
Lemon Barley Water	25 oz.	1.50	*Maison Glass*
Mandarin	16 oz.	5.50	*Fioretti*
Mango	1 pt.	4.00	*Fioretti*
Orange Flower Water	4 oz.	1.00	*Maison Glass*
Orgeat	24 oz.	3.50	*Maison Glass*
Pecan	1 pt.	4.00	*Fioretti*
Rose Water	4 oz.	1.00	*Maison Glass*

Oils

Almond, bitter	½ oz.	$1.70	*Caswell-Massey*
Amber	½ oz.	3.15	*Caswell-Massey*
Anise	½ oz.	1.45	*Caswell-Massey*
Balsam Pine	½ oz.	1.75	*Shuttle Hill Herb Shop*
Basil	½ oz.	6.00	*Caswell-Massey*
Bayberry	½ oz.	1.75	*Shuttle Hill Herb Shop*
Bay Leaf	½ oz.	3.95	*Caswell-Massey*
Bergamot	½ oz.	3.50	*Shuttle Hill Herb Shop*
Camelia	½ oz.	5.35	*Caswell-Massey*
Caraway	½ oz.	2.85	*Caswell-Massey*
Carnation	½ oz.	4.35	*Caswell-Massey*
Cedar	½ oz.	1.85	*Shuttle Hill Herb Shop*
Celery Seed	½ oz.	9.75	*Caswell-Massey*
Citronella	1 oz.	1.35	*Nichols Garden Nursery*
Clove	1 oz.	2.25	*Nichols Garden Nursery*
Coriander	½ oz.	3.85	*Caswell-Massey*
Cyclamen	½ oz.	4.20	*Caswell-Massey*
Dill	½ oz.	1.90	*Caswell-Massey*
Eucalyptus	1 oz.	1.95	*Nichols Garden Nursery*
Fennel Seed	½ oz.	1.60	*Caswell-Massey*
Fougère	½ oz.	5.00	*Caswell-Massey*
Frangipanni	½ oz.	9.35	*Caswell-Massey*
Frankincense	½ oz.	7.00	*Caswell-Massey*
Freesia	½ oz.	4.95	*Caswell-Massey*
Gardenia	½ oz.	5.45	*Caswell-Massey*
Heliotrope	½ oz.	4.00	*Caswell-Massey*
Honeysuckle	½ oz.	12.70	*Caswell-Massey*
Hyacinth	½ oz.	7.40	*Caswell-Massey*
Iris	½ oz.	5.90	*Caswell-Massey*
Jasmine	1 oz.	1.50	*Nichols Garden Nursery*
Lemon	½ oz.	2.90	*Caswell-Massey*
Lilac	1 oz.	1.95	*Nichols Garden Nursery*
Lily of the Valley	½ oz.	4.50	*Caswell-Massey*
Lime	1 oz.	1.95	*Caswell-Massey*
Lotus	½ oz.	12.00	*Caswell-Massey*
Magnolia	½ oz.	5.35	*Caswell-Massey*
Mignonette	½ oz.	4.85	*Caswell-Massey*
Mimosa	½ oz.	5.10	*Caswell-Massey*
Myrrh	1 oz.	2.50	*Nichols Garden Nursery*
New Mown Hay	½ oz.	1.85	*Shuttle Hill Herb Shop*
Narcissus	½ oz.	16.65	*Caswell-Massey*
Nutmeg	½ oz.	3.10	*Caswell-Massey*
Oak Moss	½ oz.	4.15	*Caswell-Massey*
Oleander	½ oz.	3.90	*Caswell-Massey*
Orange	1 oz.	2.15	*Nichols Garden Nursery*

All Manner of Manna

Oils

Orange Blossom	½ oz.	5.80	*Caswell-Massey*
Parsley	½ oz.	9.50	*Caswell-Massey*
Patchouli	½ oz.	3.50	*Shuttle Hill Herb Shop*
Pennyroyal	½ oz.	1.75	*Shuttle Hill Herb Shop*
Peppermint	½ oz.	2.70	*Caswell-Massey*
Pine Balsam	½ oz.	2.80	*Caswell-Massey*
Potpourri	½ oz.	5.00	*Caswell-Massey*
Rose	1 oz.	2.50	*Nichols Garden Nursery*
Rose geranium	1 oz.	2.65	*Nichols Garden Nursery*
Rosemary	½ oz.	1.35	*Caswell-Massey*
Russian Leather	½ oz.	11.85	*Caswell-Massey*
Sage	½ oz.	2.90	*Caswell-Massey*
Sandalwood	½ oz.	2.50	*Shuttle Hill Herb Shop*
Spearmint	½ oz.	2.30	*Caswell-Massey*
Sweet Pea	½ oz.	4.50	*Caswell-Massey*
Sweet Grass	½ oz.	2.75	*Shuttle Hill Herb Shop*
Tangerine	½ oz.	2.45	*Caswell-Massey*
Thyme	½ oz.	2.80	*Caswell-Massey*
Tuberose	½ oz.	6.00	*Caswell-Massey*
Verbena	½ oz.	8.20	*Caswell-Massey*
Vetiver Bourbon	½ oz.	5.40	*Caswell-Massey*
Violet	1 oz.	2.95	*Nichols Garden Nursery*
White Rose	½ oz.	6.70	*Caswell-Massey*
Wintergreen	1 oz.	1.95	*Nichols Garden Nursery*
Wisteria	½ oz.	6.05	*Caswell-Massey*
Ylang-Ylang	½ oz.	3.35	*Caswell-Massey*

Next to apple pie, nothing is considered more American than the doughnut. During the two World Wars, special doughnut-making machines went from one battle area to another to provide soldiers with this favorite American treat.

So it may come as quite a surprise to learn that the doughnut is not American. It was brought over from the Netherlands more than 300 years ago by the Dutch colonists, and then became a popular accompaniment to coffee and milk.

Sonnet to a Clam

Inglorious friend! most confident I am
   Thy life is one of very little ease;
   Albeit men mock thee with their similes
And prate of being "happy as a clam!"
What though thy shell protects thy fragile head
   From the sharp bailiffs of the briny sea?
   Thy valves are, sure, no safety-valves to thee,
While rakes are free to desecrate thy bed,
And bear thee off—as foemen take their spoil—
   Far from thy friends and family to roam;
   Forced, like a Hessian, from thy native home,
To meet destruction in a foreign broil!
   Though thou art tender yet thy humble bard
   Declares, O clam! thy case is shocking hard!
                 John G. Saxe

In general, mankind, since the improvement of cookery, eat twice as much as nature requires.
        Benjamin Franklin (1706-1790)

He that takes medicine and neglects to diet wastes the skill of his doctors.

        Chinese Proverb

A man once asked Diogenes what was the proper time for supper, and he made answer, "If you are a rich man, whenever you please; and if you are a poor man, whenever you can."
        Diogenes Laertius (2nd or 3rd C. A.D.),
                    DIOGENES

He may live without books,—what is knowledge but grieving?
He may live without hope,—what is hope but deceiving?
He may live without love,—what is passion but pining?
But where is the man that can live without dining?
        Owen Meredith (1831-1891), LUCILE

Tell me what you eat, and I will tell you what you are.
        Anthelme Brillat-Savarin (1755-1826),
             PHYSIOLOGIE DU GOUT

Among the great whom Heaven has made to shine,
How few have learned the art of arts,—to dine.
        Oliver Wendell Holmes (1809-1894),
             THE BANKER'S SECRET

If you wish to grow thinner, diminish your dinner,
And take to light claret instead of pale ale;
Look down with an utter contempt upon butter,
And never touch bread till it's toasted—or stale.
        Henry Sambrooke Leigh (1837-1883),
             CAROLS OF COCKAYNE

All Manner of Manna

Condiments

Apricot Relish Chutney	7 oz.	$ .75	*Maison Glass*
Green Peppercorns (in Wine Vinegar)	3½ oz.	1.50	*H. Roth & Sons*
Moutarde á Poivre Vert	9 oz.	1.50	*Maison Glass*
Moutarde Bocquet	5½ oz.	2.50	*Maison Glass*
Mustard Dessaux	5 oz.	1.00	*Maison Glass*
Mustard Dusseldorf	3½ oz.	.60	*Maison Glass*
Mustard (with Green Pepper)	9 oz.	1.59	*H. Roth & Son*
Onion Relish Chutney	7 oz.	.75	*Maison Glass*

Invited to dinner by a friend, Will Rogers replied, "No, thanks, I've already et."

"You should say 'Have eaten,' " his friend admonished.

"Well," drawled Rogers, "I know a lot of fellers who say 'have eaten' who ain't et!"

The first dining establishment to print a menu offering a variety of foods and liquors was Boulanger's Restaurant, which opened in Paris in 1765. Previously, coffee houses and taverns served "Ordinaries," regular meals at a common table at a fixed time and price. Parisians so enjoyed eating when and what they liked that, 50 years later, the city had more than 125 restaurants—one of which served 197 differently prepared meat dishes!

At a certain dinner party, Daniel Webster found himself the prey of a hostess who endlessly and mercilessly worried her guests. They were not eating enough, possibly they did not like this or that, and wouldn't they have more, and so forth.

"You're hardly eating a thing, Mr. Webster," she protested for the umpteenth time.

"Madam," said Webster solemnly, "permit me to assure you that I sometimes eat more than at other times, but never less."

Unusual Appetizers

Butterfish in Oil	3 2/3 oz.	$ .95	*Nichols Garden Nursery*
Fish Cakes (Tempura Fried)	7 1/4 oz.	.79	*Nichols Garden Nursery*
Pheasant Paté	2 oz.	1.00	*Maison Glass*
Rainbow Trout Paté	3¾ oz.	1.00	*Maison Glass*
Sanma Kabayaki	3½ oz.	.49	*Nichols Garden Nursery*
Shrimp (Smoked)	3 2/3 oz.	.95	*Nichols Garden Nursery*
Taki Taki	4 oz.	.69	*Nichols Garden Nursery*
Terrine Bordelaise (au Vin de Sauterne)	4½ oz.	.89	*H. Roth & Son*
Truffles (Brushed)	7/8 oz.	6.50	*H. Roth & Son*

All Manner of Manna

Jams and Jellies

Chestnut	$.89	*H. Roth & Son*
Ginger-Rhubarb	.80	*Shuttle Hill Herb Shop*
Loganberry	.80	*Shuttle Hill Herb Shop*
Marjoram Herb	.80	*Shuttle Hill Herb Shop*
Mountain Brook Mint	.80	*Shuttle Hill Herb Shop*
Papaya	.95	*Colonial Garden Kitchens*
Peach Butter	.89	*Colonial Garden Kitchens*
Plum Butter	.75	*H. Roth & Son*
Rhubarb	.98	*Colonial Garden Kitchens*
Rose	1.30	*Manganaro's*
Rose Hips	.95	*Colonial Garden Kitchens*
Scuppadine	1.25	*Colonial Garden Kitchens*
Thyme Herb	.80	*Shuttle Hill Herb Shop*
Wild Elderberry	.80	*Shuttle Hill Herb Shop*

I always eat peas with honey,
I've done it all my life,
They do taste kind of funny,
But it keeps them on the knife.

Grace
Good bread,
  Good meat;
Good God!
  Let's eat!

Cakes and Biscuits

Amaretti	10 oz.	$1.65	*Manganaro's*
Pappadums	5 oz.	1.95	*Colonial Garden Kitchens*
Petits-Babas-au-Kirsch	10 oz.	3.75	*H. Roth & Son*
Trappistine Penuche	1 lb.	2.19	*Colonial Garden Kitchens*

Giant Sausage

This one can feed the entire San Marino army. It's 30 feet long. Honest! Weighs 4½ lbs. $14.95 postpaid. *Swiss Colony.*

After a good dinner, one can forgive anybody, even one's own relations.

Oscar Wilde (1854-1900),
A WOMAN OF NO IMPORTANCE

According to the Spanish proverb, four persons are wanted to make a good salad: a spendthrift for oil, a miser for vinegar, a counsellor for salt, and a madman to stir all up.

Abraham Hayward (1801-1884),
THE ART OF DINING

When I demanded of my friend what viands he preferred,
He quoth: "A large cold bottle, and a small hot bird!"

Eugene Field (1850-1895),
THE BOTTLE AND THE BIRD

One must ask children and birds how cherries and strawberries taste.

Johann Wolfgang von Goethe (1749-1832),
CONVERSATIONS WITH ECKERMANN

You must reflect carefully beforehand with whom you are to eat and drink, rather than what you are to eat and drink. For a dinner of meats without the company of a friend is like the life of a lion or a wolf.

Epicurus (342-270 B.C.), FRAGMENTS

There is no love sincerer than the love of food.
George Bernard Shaw (1856-1950),
MAN AND SUPERMAN

An apple-pie without some cheese
Is like a kiss without a squeeze.

English Popular Rhyme

Whether woodcock or partridge, what does it signify, if the taste is the same? But the partridge is dearer, and therefore thought preferable.

Martial (c. 66 A.D.), EPIGRAMS

Whatsoever was the father of a disease, an ill diet was the mother.

Proverb

Strictly for Golf Nuts

"It looketh like a silly game," quoth King James IV of Scotland in 1491, signing a law that prohibited the playing of golf. "I'll not have our braw boys beating up the pasture with a stick when they could be out a-practicing with the trusty bow-and-arrow!"

"Why do ye not try it yourself, sire?" queried a crafty courier.

"Aye," said the King. "I'll do that. But only to show ye that it be a silly game."

"If Your Majesty would borrow my sticks. . ." volunteered another.

And that's why the law of 1491 was repealed. But you can be sure that the Scots would have continued to play their game, law or no law. Golf is the national game of Scotland, and no land has ever had a fiercer devotion to a sport.

Since the mid-15th century, golf has enjoyed great popularity in Scotland, but the origins of the game probably go back much further in time. The word "golf" is commonly supposed to be an adaptation of the Dutch word *kolf* ("club"), but this is highly uncertain, for there is no record of the Dutch having played a game analogous to the Scots' golf.

The most famous of all golf courses and clubs is the Royal and Ancient of St. Andrews. Founded in 1774, its basic rules were soon accepted throughout the world. After 1888, the game gained in popularity in the United States, the year when the St. Andrews Golf Club of Westchester County, New York, was founded.

Although most women (and many men) cannot for the life of them fathom the pleasure to be obtained from chasing a little white ball over 6,000 yards of grass, shrubs, and sand, there is one point on which almost everyone is agreed: Of all games devised by mortal man, golf is far and away the most difficult to learn and the most exasperating to play. It's a case of out of the rough and into the sand.

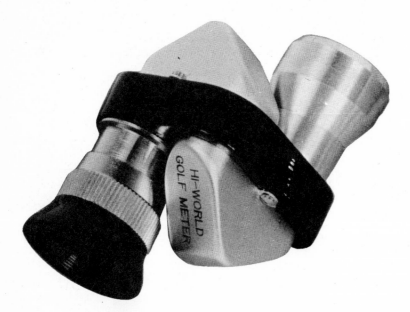

Golf Meter

This precision range finder enables the golfer to see at a glance the exact distance his ball lies from the flag. No calculation is necessary: the distance is indicated on the viewing lens itself. Magnification of 6X power. Telescope is so small you can hold it in your hand. $19.95. Postage $1.15. *Sleepy Hollow.*

Electronic Golf Balls

The most useful gift in the world for the duffer who slices his ball off the fairway into the woods, and spends hours searching for the lost spheroid. A tiny transmitter is embedded in the *Bleeper* electronic golf ball. If the ball is out of sight, the guy who hit it takes out his *Bleeper*. The louder the bleep, the closer he is to the lost golf ball. Two golf balls and Bleeper receiver $30.00. Postage. $1.25. *Stern's*.

Golf Exerciser

Fifteen minutes of exercise each day keeps you in golfing shape all year long, and provides the equivalent of 18 holes of golf for your forearm and your grip. These instruments provide means for flexing and rotating exercises, and pronate, supinate, and isometric exercises for biceps and shoulder muscles. Regulation golf grip on a stainless steel shaft. 18½" long. $15.00. Postage $1.25. *Gallery*.

Divot Fork

You can lift and level on-the-green divots in a matter of seconds with this little fork which can also be used to clean your shoe cleats and remove unwanted turf from a golf ball. Five tiny nubs on the top of the handle can be used to scrape clean the grooves of your irons. 2½" long. Stainless steel. Three initials of your choice are engraved free of charge. Symbols—Caduceus or Scales—engraved for $1.00 additional. Businessmen's logos or names engraved free when 20 or more are ordered. $5.00 each. Postpaid. *Elgin*.

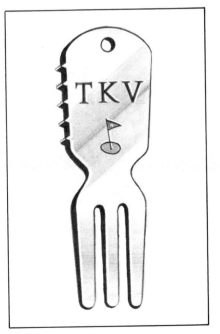

Strictly for Golf Nuts

Can you believe that a woman player—and not a novice either—took 166 strokes on a single hole? Well, it happened. In 1912, in the qualifying round of the Shawnee Invitational for Ladies in Pennsylvania, a poor female who shall remain nameless teed off at the 130-yard 16th hole. Her drive flew directly into the Binniekill River. With the ball floating insolently in the water, she set out in a rowboat to continue play, with her husband at the oars. After flailing away for what must have seemed an eternity, she finally drove the ball to dry land. Unfortunately, the thing landed in a dense wood and again she hacked away for what seemed forever to extricate it from the woods, into the rough, into the sand, into the rough. Before this nightmarish hole was played out, the poor woman had taken 166 strokes, all meticulously recorded by her loving husband.

* * *

The longest recorded drive of all time is 445 yards, achieved by E.C. Bliss in 1913. Playing on the Old Course at Herne Bay, Kent, England, Bliss—a 12-handicap player—put all of his 182 pounds behind his swing and sent the ball flying over a quarter of a mile. There was a 57-foot drop over the course of the drive. On that particular day, Bliss was blessed with luck, for a registered surveyor was on the scene to accurately measure his shot forthwith.

* * *

Norman L. Manley stepped to the seventh tee at the Del Valle Country Club course at Saugus, California. The date was September 2, 1964. He hit a prodigious drive, and the ball bounced unerringly to the green and into the cup. He had scored an ace, one of the longest ones on record. But the best was yet to come. On the very next hole, the 290-yard eighth, Manley, bubbling with excitement and confidence, hit another mammoth drive. As if directed by radar, that ball landed smack in the hole! Manley had hit two holes-in-one, back to back, scoring six strokes under par for the pair.

* * *

Justice McKenna of the United States Supreme Court was a dedicated golfer, but a rather unsuccessful performer. Hoping that his game might be improved if he took instruction, he engaged a professional for a course of lessons.

One day, while practicing on a course just outside the Capitol, he placed his ball on the tee, swung mightily, and missed. The same thing happened on three successive strokes: each time his club hit several inches behind the ball. The golf pro watched in silence.

The Justice was chafing. Finally, in white heat, he glared at his ball, which hadn't moved a fraction of an inch, and muttered, "Tut! Tut!"

The instructor gravely walked towards the jurist, and said, "Sir, you'll never learn to play golf with *them* words."

* * *

The longest hole in the world is the 17th hole at the Black Mountain Golf Club in North Carolina. It measures 745 yards, and is a par 6.

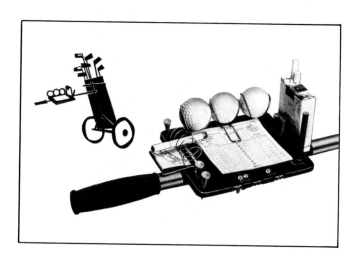

Golf Valet

Scorecard, three golf balls, tees, pencils, and cigarettes are stored within easy reach on the handle of your cart. Counter keeps track of which hole is next, plus your total number of strokes. $4.50. Postage 79¢. *House of Minnel.*

The day was August 19, 1962. Longview, Texas was agog. Homero Blancas, a 24-year-old graduate of the University of Houston, had just completed the first round of the Premier Invitational Tournament in 55 strokes! His card of 27 for the front nine and 28 for the back was the lowest round of golf ever played on a course measuring more than 5,000 yards.

* * *

Five golf partners teed off at the Ithaca Country Club one fine summer day in 1938, and achieved one of the most remarkable scores in the entire history of golf. Playing a short par-three hole, the five golfers posted respective scores of 1, 2, 3, 4, and 5.

* * *

White shot a par 72 after taking 13 strokes on one hole.

Dave White's round at the Winchester Country Club started fine, but he blew up on the fifth hole and took a horrifying 13! Then the Massachusetts pro settled down with a vengeance. He shot 10 straight birdies to salvage a par round of 72.

* * *

Lew Worsham leaned over his putter on the 18th green of the Jacksonville Country Club. He needed to sink the ball in 2 to win the 1948 Jacksonville Open Championship, a $10,000 feature. He moved his putter carefully behind the ball. Suddenly, he straightened, dropped his club, and went to the side of the green.

"I touched the ball," he told the tournament official. "Call a penalty stroke."

Worsham then returned to take the 2 putts that would have won, the 2 putts that now gave him only a tie.

The next day, Lew lost the playoff to Clayton Haefner on the 21st green.

But even in defeat Worsham was marked as a great champion—a champion in sportsmanship. Not even his victory in the 1947 National Open earned him the respect he won by calling against himself a penalty nobody else had seen.

Golf Counter

Worn on the wrist like a watch, the golf counter keeps track of strokes. Comes in red and green dial. $12.95. Postage $1.50. *Haverhill's.*

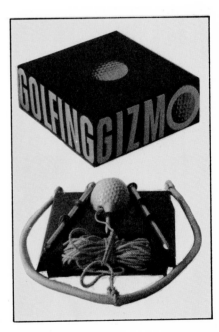

Golfing Gizmo

Only 40' of space is required to practice your golf drives at full power. A real golf ball is attached to a line for return to the tee. When hit correctly, the ball returns near the tee, indicating a straight drive. If sliced, the ball returns left of the tee. If hooked, the ball returns right of the tee. A topped ball will not return, but must be retrieved. Safe for use in limited space. $3.95. Postage 79¢. *House of Minnel.*

Strictly for Golf Nuts

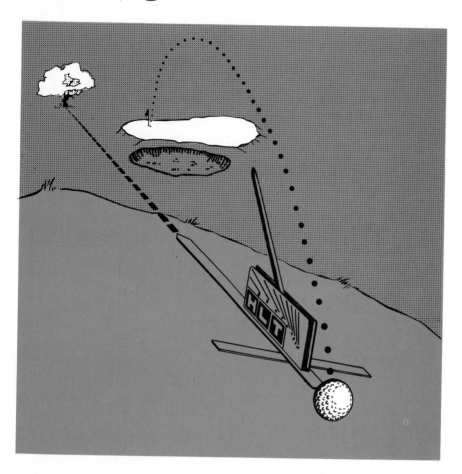

Galloping Golf

Tee off anytime with these five dice.
Each roll of the dice plays one hole.
Great for passing the time while
waiting to tee off. Comes in a miniature
golf bag, complete with instructions.
$5.50 postpaid. *Gokey.*

The "Holocator"

This gadget is supposed to groove your
swing so you will be able to make
decent iron shots off a side hill lie.
Folds to a flat 2½" by 12" and clips to
your bag. Comes in vinyl case with
illustrated instructions. $9.95. Postage.
$1.00. *Deluxe Saddlery.*

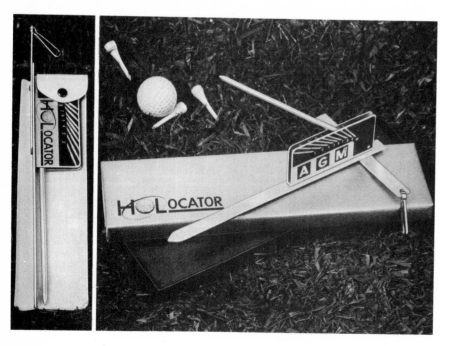

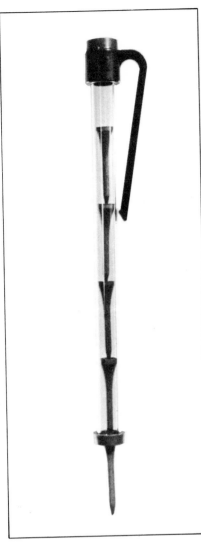

Golf Tee Dispenser

A sturdy, see-through tube clips securely to your golf bag and dispenses tees. $3.50. Postage 70¢. *Sleepy Hollow Gifts.*

Golfer's Mugs

What's funnier than one of these hilarious golf mugs? Six of them, of course. Created by the famous golf humorist, George Houghton. English bone china. Set of 6. $25.00. Postage $3.15. *Plummer-McCutcheon Ltd.*

Golf Ball Alarm

A white golf ball set on a yellow tee, which again is set into a green base. The ball opens in half to reveal a green removable alarm clock. The dial is green, the Arabic numbers white. The hands are shaped like golf clubs. 5 1/4" by 3 7/8". $12.95. Postage $2.10. *Invento.*

Tee-Off Practice

A convenient golf practice aid which requires only room for a swing. It anchors solidly in the ground, and the spin of the ball indicates whether you've hooked, sliced, or hit straight. $6.95. Postage $1.00. *Deluxe Saddlery.*

Strictly for Golf Nuts

Lighthorse Harry Cooper was at the top of his golfing fame when he took a job as pro at the Oahu Country Club in Hawaii. On his arrival at those sunny shores, he was made aware that the committee members weren't completely satisfied with his press clippings. They wanted to see an exhibition.

Harry obliged. Using a driver, he drove ball after ball straight down the fairway. Then he changed to an iron and called each shot for distance and direction for a full half-hour.

The Hawaiians still remained unconvinced, and Harry thought it was time to haul out the clincher. For his trick shot, he borrowed a watch from one of his audience. He rested his ball on the watch, drew back his club, and swung carefully.

The ball sailed off down the fairway—a perfect shot—and Harry bent down to retrieve the watch. Oh-oh! The crystal was smashed to pieces. For a brief instant Harry looked down at the fractured timepiece. Then he calmly returned the watch to its owner. "The trick of this shot," he said genially, "is to crack the crystal without damaging the watch itself!"

* * *

If you gave Bobby Jones a golfing riddle, he gave you an answer. Long putts are the greatest problem in golf, and Jones showed everybody how to handle them.

In 1928, for 10 consecutive rounds, Jones averaged 30 putts a round.

Confronted with the longest putt in the game—a 120-foot affair on a green at St. Andrews, Scotland—Bobby unsheathed his putter, *Calamity Jane*, and knocked the little white ball into the little green cup for a world's record.

* * *

C. Arthur Thompson of Victoria, British Columbia, Canada, had played golf for many a year. It kept him so agile that he even was able to tour the links when he was past 100 years of age. On October 3, 1966, at the age of 97, he managed to shoot a round lower than his age. Thompson scored a 96 on the 6,215-yard Uplands course.

Out at the Inverness Golf Club in Toledo, they still call the seventh hole "Ted Ray's Hole." It is so named in honor of the great Britisher who won the U.S. Open there in 1920.

The hole itself is a 320-yard dogleg which can be straightened out to 290 yards—*if* you carry the forest between the tee and the cup.

Four times in the U.S. Open, Ted Ray cleared those woods: twice, he got directly on the green; once, he landed in a trap beside the green; and once, he came to rest on the fairway at the edge of the green.

The British pro scored four birdie 3's at this tough hole—and he won the championship by a single stroke!

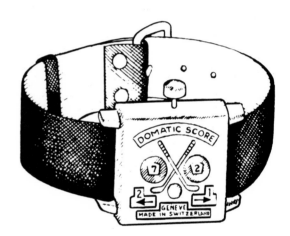

Wrist Golf Scorer

This Swiss precision instrument keeps track of your golf strokes up to 99. The mechanism, encased in gold-tone steel, is tarnish-proof. The leatherette strap fits all sizes. $8.50. Postage $.65. *Hoffritz.*

Preposterous Pets

"Honey, take the orangutan out for a walk."

While these words are not yet heard every day in homes across America, there is a growing number of adventurous souls who are not content with just having a dog or a cat for a pet. Lizards, snakes, raccoons, otters, foxes, chimps—all sorts of thoroughly undomesticated creatures are finding their way into American homes. Today, there is hardly an animal that is not available for purchase; and only a few locales have restrictive ordinances against the ownership of such unusual pets.

I know an old gent in lower Manhattan who keeps his pet tarantulas under glass; and I know a lady who's just crazy about her baby boa constrictor. And there used to be a fellow whose pet was a black widow spider, but . . .

Animals coming from all climes will be shipped to you via express collect. Just about every one of these firms guarantees the live delivery of what you have ordered. The animal will be crated and insured. Carriers used by these shippers will follow the feeding instructions on the crate; and barring an accident, your new pet should arrive in good health, to your delight and—what might be when you lay your eyes on the arrival—your consternation! Caveat emptor!

Available Reptiles

Alligator (baby)	$3.95	*Grove Pet Ranch*
Anaconda (South American)	39.75	*Grove Pet Ranch*
Blacksnake	5.00	*Trails End Zoo*
Chickensnake	8.50	*Trails End Zoo*
Chameleon (6)	3.50	*Trails End Zoo*
Chuckawala	6.50	*Trails End Zoo*
Copperhead	5.00	*Trails End Zoo*
Cornsnake	10.00	*Trails End Zoo*
Cottonmouth Moccasin	10.00	*Trails End Zoo*
Gecko (banded)	4.50	*Trails End Zoo*
Gecko (Indian Tokay)	8.75	*Grove Pet Ranch*
Hog-nosed snake	7.00	*Trails End Zoo*
Iguana (desert)	6.00	*Trails End Zoo*
Iguana (green)	3.95	*Grove Pet Ranch*
Iguana (Rhinoceros)	75.00	*Trails End Zoo*
Indigo	39.50	*Grove Pet Ranch*
Jacara	35.00	*Trails End Zoo*
Kingsnake	10.00	*Trails End Zoo*
Lizard (Leopard)	5.50	*Trails End Zoo*
Python	17.95	*Grove Pet Ranch*
Rattlesnake (large)	25.00	*Trails End Zoo*
Skink (red-head)	3.98	*Trails End Zoo*
Tegu	15.00	*Grove Pet Ranch*

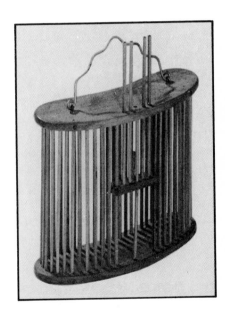

Cricket Cage
Bamboo slats. Made in Hong Kong. $2.00. Postage $1.50. *Charlotte Horstmann Ltd.*

Preposterous Pets

Available Mammals

Achuni	$30.00	*Trails End Zoo*
Agouti	25.00	*Trails End Zoo*
Anteater	100.00	*Trails End Zoo*
Armadillo	14.50	*Trails End Zoo*
Badger (pup)	129.50	*Grove Pet Ranch*
Bear (black)	250.00	*Trails End Zoo*
Bobcat (kitten)	225.00	*Grove Pet Ranch*
Capuchin Monkey	93.95	*Grove Pet Ranch*
Capybara	50.00	*Trails End Zoo*
Cheetah	2,395.00	*Grove Pet Ranch*
Chimpanzee (baby, tame)	795.00	*Grove Pet Ranch*
Chipmunk	17.50/pair	*Trails End Zoo*
Coatimundi	42.50	*Trails End Zoo*
Coyote	47.50	*Trails End Zoo*
Ferret	17.50	*Trails End Zoo*
Fox (grey)	25.00	*Trails End Zoo*
Fox (red)	25.00	*Trails End Zoo*
Gibbon (white-handed)	275.00	*Grove Pet Ranch*
Grizzly bear	350.00	*Trails End Zoo*
Kinkajou	77.50	*Grove Pet Ranch*
Marmoset	35.00	*Grove Pet Ranch*
Monkey (Ringtail)	47.50	*Trails End Zoo*
Monkey (Spider)	29.95	*Grove Pet Ranch*
Monkey (Owl)	19.95	*Grove Pet Ranch*
Monkey (Squirrel)	13.95	*Grove Pet Ranch*
Ocelot	335.00	*Grove Pet Ranch*
Opossum	12.50	*Trails End Zoo*
Otter	225.00	*Grove Pet Ranch*
Paca	50.00	*Trails End Zoo*
Porcupine	27.50	*Trails End Zoo*
Porpoise	875.00	*Trails End Zoo*
Puma	495.00	*Grove Pet Ranch*
Raccoon (tame)	40.00	*Trails End Zoo*
Serval (kitten)	375.00	*Grove Pet Ranch*
Skunk (baby)	35.00	*Trails End Zoo*
Skunk (spotted)	25.00	*Trails End Zoo*
Squirrel (Flying)	20.00/pair	*Trails End Zoo*
Squirrel (grey)	15.00	*Trails End Zoo*
Squirrel (red)	27.95/pair	*Trails End Zoo*
Sloth (two-toed)	37.50	*Trails End Zoo*
Tayra	50.00	*Trails End Zoo*

The rabbit has a charming face:
Its private life is a disgrace.
I really dare not name to you
The awful things that rabbits do;
Things that your paper never prints—
You only mention them in hints.
They have such lost, degraded souls
No wonder they inhabit holes;
When such depravity is found
It only can live underground.

The bee is such a busy soul
It has no time for birth control,
And that is why in times like these
There are so many sons of bees.

Life Span of Animals

Animal	Years
Pig	10
Rabbit	13
Coyote	14
Chicken	14
Timber Wolf	15
Reindeer	15
Pronghorn	15
Kangaroo	16
Cheetah	16
Bullfrog	16
Goat	17
Beaver	19
Sheep	20
Rattlesnake	20
Moose	20
Cow	20
Cougar	20
Domestic Dog	22
Domestic Cat	23
Leopard	23
Zebra	25
Tiger	25
Camel	25
Black Bear	25
Sea Lion	28
Giraffe	28
Lion	30
Dolphin	30
Grizzly Bear	31
Gibbon	31
Gorilla	33
Toad	36
Chimpanzee	37
Polar Bear	41
Baboon	45
Jackass	46
Domestic Horse	50
Pelican	51
Eagle	55
Owl	68
Freshwater Oyster	80
Elephant	84
Eastern Box Turtle	138
Giant Tortoise	190

The list above reflects the maximum life span of animals while in captivity.

Sardinian Donkey

A pure-bred Sardinian donkey makes an ideal pet for young people of any age. The smallest breed of the species, it grows to be 32" to 36" high at the shoulder and can be ridden by a small child. The donkey can also be trained to pull a small cart. Feeds on hay and grain. Specify light tan or light grey color. Male: $275.00; female: $375.00. Air freight collect. *Box Hill Farm.*

Preposterous Pets

A Southern psychologist installed two chimpanzees in adjoining cages, and tried to determine how quickly they could distinguish between two different-colored coins. One cage contained a slot machine that dispensed water only after the insertion of a white coin; the other cage contained a machine that dispensed food and worked only with a black coin. On the first day, each chimp was given a bagful of mixed coins, and soon learned which coins worked his machine.

A few days later, the chimp with the water dispenser was deprived of water for 24 hours, and the one with the food dispenser was deprived of food for 24 hours. Then the thirsty monkey was given food coins, and the hungry one water coins. Instead of being baffled by the ploy, the chimps reached through the bars of their cages and exchanged coins with each other.

*   *   *

When in mortal danger, many animals feign death. But none do this as convincingly as the American opposum and the dingo, a wild dog of Australia. The dingo will allow its captor to beat it unmercifully until the chance to escape presents itself. The entrapped opossum will assume its famous "possum" pose, which is to lie limp with its tongue hanging out of its mouth and its eyes open and rolled back.

Speed is so essential to the survival of the gazelle that nature has endowed it with the ability to run almost from the moment it is born. While most animals are weak and wobbly in the first few days after birth, a two-day-old gazelle can outrun a full-grown horse.

*   *   *

Gazelles, prairie dogs, wild asses, and many other animals never drink water. They have a special chemical process which transforms a part of their solid food into water.

*   *   *

I think I could turn and live with animals, they
*   are so placid and self-contained;*
I stand and look at them long and long,
They do not sweat and whine about their
*   condition;*
They do not lie awake in the dark and weep for
*   their sins;*
They do not make me sick discussing their duty
*   to God;*
Not one is dissatisfied—not one is demented with
*   the mania of owning things;*
Not one kneels to another, nor to his kind that
*   lived thousands of years ago;*
Not one is respectable or industrious over the
*   whole earth.*

                                Walt Whitman

The wildcat is the most vicious fighter in the animal kingdom. Asleep, it resembles a gentle housecat—in a fight, it is a furry ball of rage. This spitfire's speed gives it an advantage over most other animals. In one swift leap, it can rip open its enemy's throat with its razor-like teeth.

* * *

The world's largest rodent is the capybara, also called the carpincho or water hog. A native of tropical South America, it can attain a length of 3½ to 4½ feet and a weight of 150 pounds.

* * *

The keenest sense of smell exhibited in all nature is that of the male silkworm moth. It can detect the sex signals of a female which is 6.8 miles away!

* * *

The longest and heaviest of all snakes is the anaconda of South America. Specimens have been reliably reported to be as heavy as 950 pounds, and as long as 37½ feet.

* * *

The Gaboon viper has the longest fangs of any snake. The specimen kept in the Philadelphia Zoo in 1963 was a little careless and bit itself to death

* * *

A woman visitor to a zoo was having a hard time extracting an intelligent reply from the zoo keeper. Finally she ventured one more query.

"Is that hippopotamus a male?" she asked. "Or a female?"

"That, madam," replied the keeper, "is a question which should interest only another hippopotamus."

* * *

The blue whale is the largest and most powerful animal ever to have graced the planet. The largest accurately measured specimen was captured off Scotland in 1926; it measured 109 feet 4¼ inches in length. A whale caught off Argentina five years later is said to have weighed 195 tons.

The longest of all worms is the *Lineus longissimus,* or "living fishing line worm." In 1964, a specimen washed ashore at St. Andrews, Scotland, after a storm. It measured more than 180 feet in length.

* * *

Before eating anything, a raccoon will first wash the food in the nearest available water. Some raccoons will go hungry rather than eat unwashed food; others will go through the motions of washing when there is no water around.

* * *

The tusks of some male African elephants eventually become so heavy that their owners must frequently rest them in the forks of trees. The longest African elephant tusk on record was some 11 feet long.

* * *

The world's fastest animal is the cheetah. It has been timed at 70 miles per hour, but many believe that it can do even better over a short haul. Sometimes called the hunting leopard, the cheetah has long been used in India to track down the black buck, the Indian antelope, and other fast game.

* * *

The animal that takes the longest time to make its debut is the elephant. Its gestation period is 645 days or more than 21 months.

* * *

The most long-lived animal is the giant tortoise of the Galapagos Islands. Specimens have been estimated to be as old as 190 years.

* * *

Talk about your fat cats! The heaviest domestic cat was a feline named Gigi who weighed 42 pounds.

* * *

Although the whale weighs over a hundred tons and the mouse tips the scales at only a few ounces, they develop from eggs of approximately the same size.

When It Rains

The rain it raineth every day,
    Upon the just and unjust fella,
But more upon the just, because
    The unjust hath the just's umbrella.

Rain keeps the earth dry. It is the rain process that takes the moisture out of the air and gathers it into concentrated rain clouds. Were it not for this, moisture would condense on every solid surface; and all humanity, bathed in tepid, humid perspiration, would slide over the damp and slippery earth, like life prisoners in a steam bath!

*   *   *

Sometimes, in Europe, the rain is red. The so-called "blood rains" of Europe used to plunge the people of that continent into a frenzy. The scientific cause of the phenomenon was not known, and the pinkish rain was thought to be diluted blood.

There are still "blood rains" at odd intervals in Italy, southern France, and southeastern Europe. It seems that storms lift reddish desert dust from the Sahara, and blow billions of these particles across the Mediterranean into the cloudbanks above Europe. Then they are washed down as red rain.

*   *   *

New York City, with an average annual rainfall of 43 inches, is pretty bad. Foggy London has only 25, and sunny Los Angeles gets by with 15. Bergen, Norway, seems wet indeed with 73 inches. But Bergen is dry as a desert compared with Cherrapungi, India, which has an annual downpour of 432 inches, or 36 feet!

*   *   *

The greatest single rainfall fell in the Philippines. In 1911, from July 14 to July 17, the floodgates of heaven opened wide over Baguio, and down gushed a record 88 inches of rain—or more than *seven feet of water!*

Milk Can Umbrella Stand

This antique-looking milk can is an early American design. Hand-rubbed and waxed. Its detailed workmanship includes 30 contrasting layers of knotty pine. Accented with immense brass handles. Personalized with a 4½" solid brass name plate. 23" high; 11" diameter. $85.00 postpaid. *The Pennsylvania Dutchman.*

Collapsible Raincoat

This single-breasted, nylon raincoat comes in its own little pouch which opens into a waterproof beret. Self belting. Fits into your pocket. Navy. 38 to 46 in regular and long. $20.00. Postage $1.75. *Abercrombie and Fitch.*

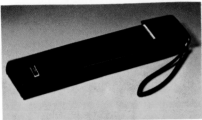

Stowaway Umbrella

This flat-folding umbrella, which telescopes at a touch of the button, fits neatly into an attache case. Black nylon. 12" long, 2¼" wide, 1" deep. $20.00. Postage $1.75. *Abercrombie and Fitch.*

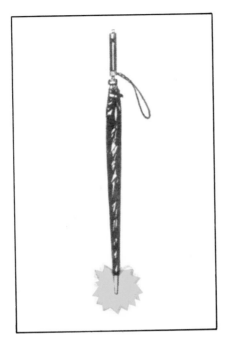

Pop-Out Umbrella

This 100% windproof umbrella pops in and out from inside its walking stick in an instant. The walking stick is almost 3' tall from the top of its golden tip. The umbrella has a steel mechanism which opens to 42". Man's umbrella comes in black; woman's, in beige. $14.95. Postage $1.25. *Taylor Gifts.*

Light-Up Umbrella

A gleaming white, see-through illuminated tip lets you see and be seen in the dark from any direction. A push button, powered by two AA batteries, manages the whole thing. Made of nylon. 36" wide. Complete with batteries and slip-in case. $9.95. Postage $1.15. *Bevis.*

When It Rains

The intense heat of lightning is sometimes responsible for odd accidents. One lady's earring was melted by lightning, and another bolt soldered all the links in a one-yard chain. The U.S. National Safety Council's Report for 1943 told of a soldier being welded into his sleeping bag when the zipper was struck by lightning. The startled soldier had to be cut loose.

* * *

In 1918, at Bahia Felix, Chile, rain fell on all but 18 days of the year. And on those 18 it drizzled!

What could be drier than a desert? Answer: The town of Arica, on the border between Chile and Peru.

With a population of 14,000 inhabitants, Arica receives a mere .02 inches of rain per year. This is all the more remarkable because Arica is situated on the Pacific Ocean. To give you an idea of how dry this town is, the rainfall of Arizona—the driest of the 50 American states—is almost 400 times as heavy.

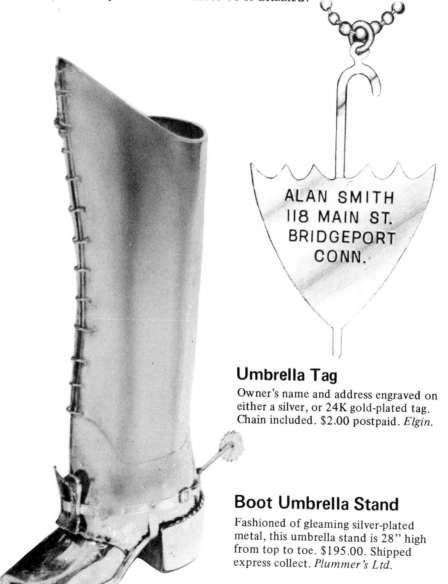

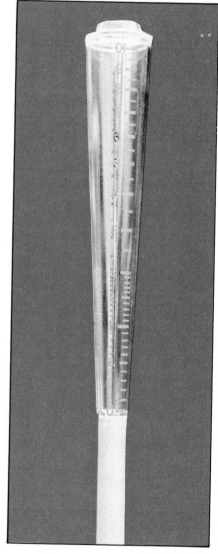

Umbrella Tag

Owner's name and address engraved on either a silver, or 24K gold-plated tag. Chain included. $2.00 postpaid. *Elgin.*

Boot Umbrella Stand

Fashioned of gleaming silver-plated metal, this umbrella stand is 28" high from top to toe. $195.00. Shipped express collect. *Plummer's Ltd.*

Rain Gauge

Up to 10" of rain can be measured with this 23" high conical-shaped rain gauge. Made of a clear plastic with red numerals. $4.50. Postage $1.00. *Adirondack.*

Rain Gauge

Made of Plexine plastic, this precision instrument has a permanently marked, easy-to-read graduated scale. 13" long, with a top opening of 2½" by 2¼". Accurately measures 1/100th to 6" of rainfall. $3.95 postpaid. *Gokey.*

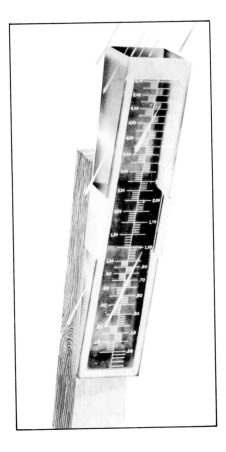

Disposable Rubbers

Lightweight, see-through plastic throwaway boots are high enough for a snow storm, yet store away like a sheet of paper. Tuck in pocket or purse. One size fits everyone. Roll of 36, $3.00. Postage 75¢. *Joan Cook.*

It sometimes rains frogs. Scientists explain the phenomenon of raining frogs in this way: Spawn are sucked up from rivers and lakes into the atmosphere by whirlwinds. The lightweight embryos are carried through the air for great distances. The spawn hatch en route. When the wind is spent, the animals drop to the earth!

* * *

Rain never falls on parts of the Sahara Desert. Though clouds pass over these areas, and raindrops actually fall, the water itself never reaches the ground. The sizzling heat of the desert air evaporates the moisture as it falls, changing it back to invisible vapor.

* * *

Rainbows may be seen at night. Lunar rainbows were observed and recorded in ancient times and are not uncommon. When the sun shines through a sheet of falling rain, it is very apt to form a rainbow. The same effect is caused, now and then, by moonlight. Even strong electric lights shining through rain and mist have caused this phenomenon.

What does it mean when the weatherman says that one inch of rain fell in your area yesterday? For instance—say one inch of rain fell on one acre of ground. Since an acre equals 43,560 square feet, a rainfall of one inch over this area would produce 6,272,640 cubic inches of water, or 3,630 cubic feet of water. A cubic foot of water weighs about 62.4 pounds, the exact weight varying with the water's density. Therefore, one inch of rain over one acre of surface would equal 226,512 pounds, or better than 113 tons of liquid.

* * *

Contrary to folk wisdom, lightning does strike twice in the same place, and may even strike as many as ten times in a single spot! Successive photographs of lightning flashes have been taken by engineers of the General Electric Company during electrical storms in the Berkshire Mountains of Massachusetts.

One can get an appreciable shock from an ordinary electric socket in a house wired at a voltage of 115. A single flash of lightning has been estimated to carry a charge of 100 million volts.

THE HOME BAR

Mead may have been the nectar of the Olympian gods, but here on earth, man sought something a bit stronger.

Already somewhat light-headed from the altitude, the Tibetans went a step further by inventing a crude distillery. A similar contraption was contrived in ancient Peru. The Tahitians developed a still which drew off the vapors into a long pipe. The distillate was then cooled by water to condense the alcohol. Basically similar methods are in use today in Scotland, in Ireland, and in France.

The use of liquor is so widespread that almost every country in the world utilizes some native product to make an alcoholic beverage. Asian liquors, distilled from rice, from millet, or from palm sap originated around 400 B.C., and took the names of *sautchoo, arrack, arika,* and *skhou.* Around the year 300, Ireland brewed up some *usquebaugh* from oat and barley beer. Around the year 900, Italy began distilling grapes to produce brandy. Around 1500, the Scots got the hang of making whiskey from malted barley. In 1750, France distilled cognac from grapes.

In almost any home there is a corner or room, cozy or elaborate, where refreshments are served. Call it bar, call it den, call it what you will, be it room or nook, or just a simple table—it's probably the most convivial spot in that castle you call home.

If all be true that I do think,
There are five reasons we should drink;
Good wine—a friend—or being dry—
Or lest we should be by and by—
Or any other reason why.

Goose Pitcher

Well-named, isn't it? From the Aegean island of Lesbos comes this hand-painted and glazed 13½" high pitcher. $13.50. Postage $1.50. *Greek Island Ltd.*

Insulated Tumblers

Perfect for double old-fashioneds. Keep the drinks cold and the ice unmelted for hours in these non-shatterable glasses. Specify any of the following designs: 19th Hole, Life Preserver, Tennis Racquet, Fishing Flies. Set of four $15.00. Postage $2.00. *Lewis & Conger.*

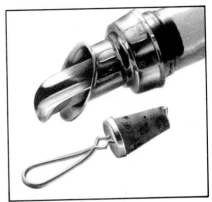

Dripless Wine Pourer

Eliminates stained tablecloths. Double lip ensures non-spilling. When pouring, that extra unwanted drop falls off first lip into channel, and goes back into bottle. Silver-plated. $7.50. Postage $2.00. *Plummer's Ltd.*

Sterling Silver Jacks

There is probably a lady in your life who would like to be a girl again. This nostalgic pastime will bring back fond memories. Besides, jacks were always a lot of fun, and still can be—even if played on your fine mahogany table in your home bar. Boxed set consists of 10 jacks and a rubber ball. $20.00. Postage 45¢. *Windfall.*

Aquarius 2000

This is an astrology computer which gives you daily and monthly forecasts, as well as complete personality reports. Information about marriage, children, sex, jobs, and the future have been programmed into the computer. The manufacturer claims that 200 years of knowledge in this occult science is contained in this set-up. All you need to know is a birthdate—any date between January 1, 1906 and December 31, 1975. By rotating the discs, you recreate the heavens as they existed on the day of birth. Zodiacal cards—270 of them—interpret the meaning of the celestial pattern. $29.95. Postage $2.00. *Gallery.*

THE HOME BAR

An irreverent wag has pointed out that two drinks are mentioned in the Bible—Wine: *which gladdeneth the heart of man*, and Water: *which quencheth the thirst of the jackasses*.

* * *

It was Louis Pasteur's research in the 1850s into the actions of yeasts and molds that resulted in the development of controlled fermentation that makes for a consistently good product.

Freshly distilled spirits are stored in wooden casks for a minimum of two years to age and mature, during which time the bite of the tannin is lost. In the United States, spirits are aged at 103 proof (51½% alcohol); in Scotland, the alcoholic content is 124 proof (62% alcohol). Cognac is aged to 140 proof pure, which means 70% alcohol.

The casks in which the spirits are stored are made of American white oak; but French cognac is aged in Limousin oak and black oak. The casks are then stored in draft-free surroundings.

* * *

There was the Montreal drunk who kept muttering, "It can't be done! It can't be done! It can't be done!" as he stood looking up at a big electric sign that read, "Drink Canada Dry."

Turn-Tac-Toe

If the game itself isn't too much of a bore, those people who find it a bore to keep redrawing tic-tac-toe boxes on paper, might enjoy this outfit. Rings drawn on the 8" square board meets lines, forming four tic-tac-toe boxes at the north, east, south, and west sides of the board. Players choose red or blue pins. As they complete one game, they turn the board and go onto the next. $5.95. Postage 85¢. *Game Room.*

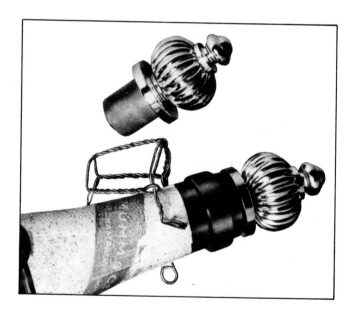

Adjustable Corks

How exasperating when you pull a cork out of a bottle and you can't get the cork back in! These adjustable stoppers have bright silver-plated crowns. They'll fit any bottle. A pair for $12.95. Postage $2.00. *Plummer's Ltd.*

Champagne

A beverage that makes you see double and feel single.

Irish Coffee Rack

This pinewood rack holds four mugs, which come along with the sign. $25.50. Postage $1.00. *Yorkraft.*

Leaning Tower Glasses

Actually, they rest as solidly as the old Pisa landmark itself—they are just made to stand tipsy. Which can be very disconcerting to teetotaling guests, and completely devastating for those who aren't. 6½" high. 13 oz. capacity. Brown and white design. Dishwasher safe. Set of four, $6.95. Postage $1.00. *Joan Cook.*

People Feeder

This food dispenser keeps hands out of the bowl by dispensing a pre-measured serving of munchables and diet-destroyers. Sturdy 6" plastic globe is suspended on a chrome pedestal; tilts about 120° both ways, and automatically returns upright. Easily refilled. Can be capped to keep contents fresh. Stands anywhere or mounts on wall. $12.50. Postage $1.25. *Gallery.*

Viking Drinking Horn

This silver horn, so graceful in its Viking styling, can be filled with water, wine, or beer and used as a pitcher. Or keep the removable flower spreader under its lid, and the vessel becomes a distinctive vase. It is 9" long and 9½" high. $50.00. Postage 75¢. *Norwegian Silver.*

German Roulette

A new twist for an old game. Consists of a polished hardwood playing surface, six wooden balls, and a top. The balls are put into the center, and the top is spun. The balls will be knocked by the top into the scoring holes. The board is 9½" across. $4.95. Postage $1.35. *Clymer's.*

THE HOME BAR

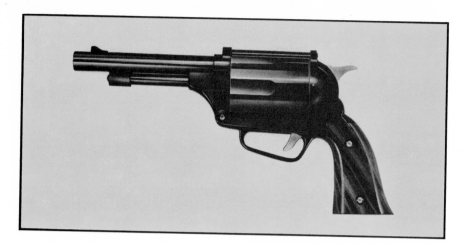

Booze Shooter

"Give me a shot of scotch!" And the request is filled literally by means of this 13" long replica of a Wild-West six-gun shooter which shoots booze—not bullets. Cock the hammer and pull the trigger. The firewater you loaded the gun with will squirt out. For added excitement, you can load caps in the revolving chamber so when you shoot the booze, your guest will get a bang out of it. Made of high-impact plastic and metal. Loads easily. $9.95. Postage $1.10. *Game Room.*

Champagne Bottle Sizes

Split	6½ oz.
Pint	13 oz.
Quart	26 oz.
*Magnum	52 oz.
Jeroboam	104 oz.
Rheoboam	156 oz.
Methuselah	208 oz.
Salmanazar	312 oz.
Balthazar	416 oz.
**Nebuchadnezzar	520 oz.

*A magnum is equal to 4 pints..
**A Nebuchadnezzar is a little over 4 gallons.

Gurgling Decanter

This green-glazed pottery pitcher holds 28 oz. and is a lot of fun. As it pours out a drink, it emits a gurgling sound. Imported from Italy. $10.50. Postage $1.25. *J. D. Brown.*

Brisk methinks I am, and fine
When I drink my cap'ring wine;

Then to love I do incline,
When I drink my wanton wine;

And I wish all maidens mine,
When I drink my sprightly wine;

Well I sup and well I dine,
When I drink my frolic wine;

But I languish, lower, and pine,
When I want my fragrant wine.

Robert Herrick.

Bar Sign

One side says "Bar Open"; the other, "Off Duty." Size: 15" by 7¼". Price $12.00. Postage $1.00. *Yorkraft.*

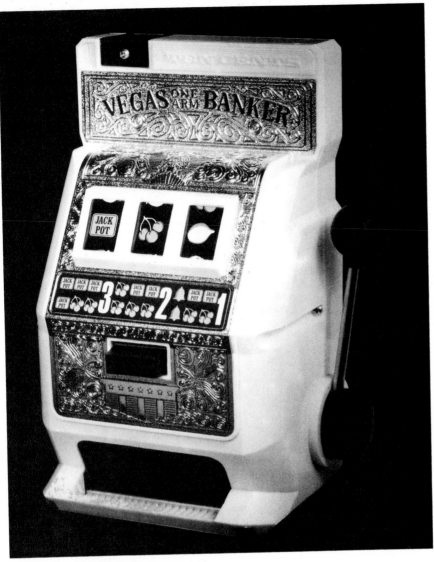

Jackpot Banker

Running your own slot machine is a great way to help pay the rent. The six winning combinations in this machine pay off handsomely. How many losing combinations there are, deponent sayeth not. Encased in colorful antique-looking plastic 9" high, and 5" wide. Accepts only dimes, which can be easily removed—that's why it's legal. $15.00. Postage $1.25. *Game Room.*

Brandy Warmer

Pour your choice cognac or brandy in this snifter, ignite the alcohol burner, and your glass will emit a wonderful bouquet. The swan holder is made of oxidized silver-plated metal. $20.00. Postage $2.00. *Plummer's Ltd.*

Wine Vault

This storage house comes in many sizes. The smallest will hold 132 bottles; the largest, a walk-in affair, will hold 1,824. The idea is to provide a natural cellar environment with the temperature ranging between 53 and 57, plus proper humidity and darkness. All bottles are held in a horizontal position so that the wet corks keep out the air. Every unit plugs into 110-volt outlet, which is vibration proof. Locking panels permit easy assembly and disassembly for relocation. The smallest unit is 6', 8 3/8" high, 4' wide, and 2' deep. Cost $795.00 (unstocked). The largest is the same height, but is 12' wide and 6', 3½" deep. $2,995.00. Shipped by express. There are a number of sizes in between. *Hammacher Schlemmer.*

THE HOME BAR

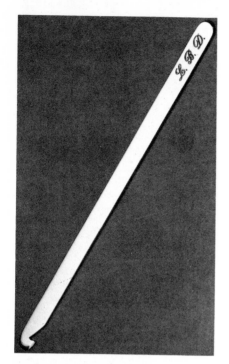

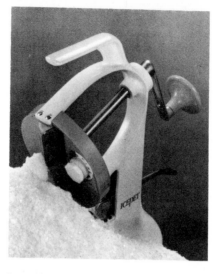

Wine Rack
Wrought iron wine rack, imported from Spain, holds eight bottles on red or black leather straps. 18" by 6" by 14" high. $8.50. Postage $4.00. *Herley Imports.*

Ice Shaver
Shaves ice for seafood cocktails, drinks, and desserts. No-slip suction base is 8" in diameter. $8.95. Postage 99¢. *House of Minnel.*

Silver Citrus Peeler
Peels oranges, lemons, grapefruits, avocados, with ease—and class. Hooked end goes under skin, rind slips off, leaving fruit whole. Sterling silver. Any three initials engraved. 5" long. $7.00. Postage 80¢. *Downs.*

Ice Bucket
Fine china "Vienna Woods" ice bucket is 7½" high, 7" in diameter. $19.95. Postage $2.10. *Seymour Mann.*

The horse and mule live thirty years
And nothing know of wines and beers.
The goat and sheep at twenty die
And never taste of Scotch or Rye.
The cow drinks water by the ton
And at eighteen is mostly done.
The dog at fifteen cashes in
Without the aid of rum and gin.
The cat in milk and water soaks
And then in twelve short years it croaks.
The modest, sober, bone-dry hen
Lays eggs for nogs, then dies at ten.
All animals are strictly dry:
They sinless live and swiftly die;
But sinful, ginful rum-soaked men
Survive for three score years and ten,
And some of them, a very few,
Stay pickled till they're ninety-two.

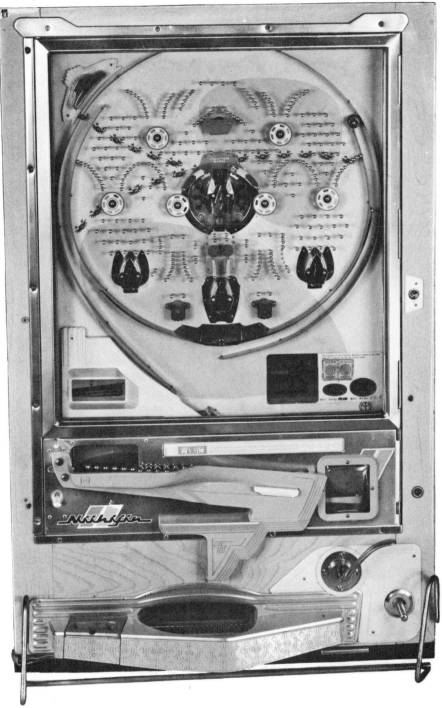

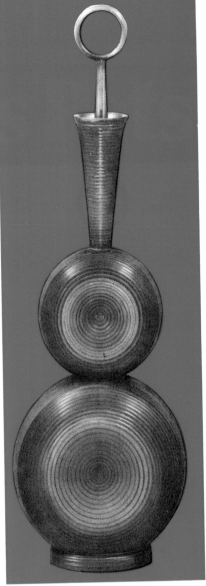

Norwegian Decanter

An aperitif offered from this delicately designed decanter should stimulate the right mood. The silver is oxidized to create a distinctive pattern of light and dark. Stands 14" high; holds 27 oz. $55.00. Postage 75¢. *Norwegian Silver.*

Pachinko

One of the most popular games in Japan, this pinball game is perfect for a bar or game room. Tiny steel balls fight their way through a maze of obstacles, and lights flash celebrating a winner. 300 balls. Instructions. $75.00. Postage $1.95. *Stern's.*

Roped Tankards

Branded with 1" high letters burned into the handcrafted maple, these tankards make highly personalized gifts. The roped handles have been treated for durability and are decorated with copper bindings. Holds 16 oz. 6" high. $7.95. Postage $1.10. *Artisan Galleries.*

THE HOME BAR

Dicing Box

So Lady Luck shouldn't forget who she's supposed to be with, this black leather dice cup comes embossed with his initials, name, or alias. Comes with five plastic dice. $7.50. Postage $1.50. *Charlotte Horstmann Ltd.*

Wheel of Fortune

The plastic, battery-operated wheel spins at a push of the button to win you a fortune, tell your fortune, or make your decisions. A 17" by 9" cardboard Las Vegas betting board is included. The 6" wheel is on a plastic stand, 9" high. Instructions manual included. $11.95. Postage $1.10. *Game Room.*

5¢ Beer

Completely fanciful and nostalgic. Would that those days were here again! Wooden sign is 8" by 12". $7.50. Postage $1.00. *Yorkraft.*

Odds at Dice

A Roll Totaling	Odds Against
2	35 to 1
3	17 to 1
4	11 to 1
5	8 to 1
6	31 to 5
7	5 to 1
8	31 to 5
9	8 to 1
10	11 to 1
11	17 to 1
12	35 to 1

Whiskey is obtained through the distillation of the fermented mash of grain. It is then aged in wood. Whiskey is produced principally in the United States, Canada, Scotland, and Ireland. Scotch whiskey gets its distinctive smoky flavor due to the use of peat in drying the barley malt and also through the quality of Scotch water.

* * *

Vodka is an unaged spirit obtained from potatoes or grain. It is then filtered through vegetable charcoal. In the United States, this process produces a liquid that must be "without distinctive character, aroma, or taste," but which packs quite a noticeable wallop at over 190 proof.

* * *

Rum, obtained from fermented sugarcane or fermented molasses, is produced primarily in the Caribbean. Different varieties derive from Puerto Rico, Cuba, Jamaica, and Mexico.

* * *

Brandy is obtained from wine or the fermented mash of fruit. It is made from grapes, or cherries, or apples, or plums, or apricots, or peaches, or blackberries.

* * *

Tequila, indigenous to Mexico, is obtained from the heart-sap of the mescal cactus.

* * *

Okolehao, an exotic Hawaiian contribution, is made out of molasses, Koji rice, and the juice of the Kalo plant.

* * *

Ng ka py is how you order a shot in Peking. It's made from millet, with various aromatics added.

* * *

Flavored spirits, including gin, aquavit, absinthe, and zubrovka are produced by redistilling alcohol with a flavoring agent. Juniper is used to flavor gin; caraway seeds, to flavor aquavit.

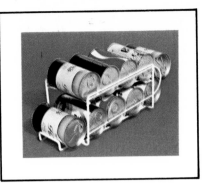

Can Dispenser

Saves space in the refrigerator. Rack loads from the top. Cans rotate one at a time to the bottom, as you use them. Easy to refill right in the refrigerator. Made of heavy steel wire with white plastic finish. Rust proof. 15" long; 5½" high; 5½" wide. Holds ten 12 oz. cans. $2.69. Postage 59¢. *House of Minnel.*

Ice Shaver

Shaves large quantities of ice in seconds. Accepts cubes, hunks of ice of any shape. Made of chrome and plastic. Glass container for the shaved ice. $85.00. Postage $4.00. *Hammacher Schlemmer.*

Take the glass away:—
I know I hadn't oughter:—
I'll take a pledge—I will—
I never will drink water.

The Pampered Kitchen

Guatemalan Pot Holders

These hen and rooster pot holders are made of heavy, durable cotton, hand loomed in Guatemala. A choice of black and white or white and yellow exotic Indian patterns is available. $3.95 a pair. Postage 75¢. *Elizabeth McCaffrey's.*

Self-Stirring Saucepan

Did you ever try to make chocolate mousse or some other dish which says "Stir constantly"? After five minutes or so, your hand feels as if it has gone through the Punic Wars. Now comes this new-fangled pot which eliminates all work and fatigue. There's a stirring mechanism in the cover which is operated by two D-cell batteries. The pot itself is made of red enamel cast iron which is lined with teflon. Three-quart capacity. Weighs 4 lbs. $29.95. Postage $2.00. *Hammacher Schlemmer.*

Cookie Mold

You might well achieve an intriguing result with this Dutch cookie mold which bears the pattern of a 15th century vessel. Made of 1" thick beechwood, the mold might also serve as a wall decoration. No duty. $15.00 postpaid. *Holland Handicrafts.*

Bean Slicer

From France comes this device which French-shoe-strings your stringbeans. Made of white plastic with a steel crank and wooden handle. $15.98. Postage $1.50. *Paprikas Weiss.*

Plate Warmer

Heats 10 12" dinner plates by electricity. Made of gold or white cotton. Cover is white washable fabric. $20.00. Postage $2.00. *Invento.*

Casserole Paw

Assume you have a big roaster or an enormous casserole to take out of the oven. How to do it without burning your hands? Here are two mitts connected by a wide quilted band which surround the surface of the pan. 34" long. Washable cotton. $2.98. Postage 59¢. *House of Minnel.*

The Pampered Kitchen

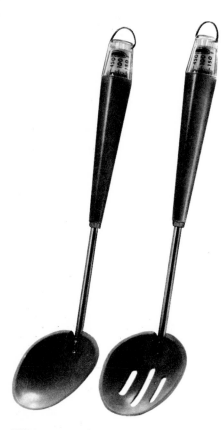

Thermo Spoon

A quite accurate thermometer built into the handle of a cooking spoon records the complete range of cooking and serving temperatures from 80°F. to 450°F. Designed for all top-of-the-range cooking, the spoon bowl slides off the spoon stem so that the 5½" long handle can be used as a thermometer. Available with solid bowl or slotted bowl. $4.50. Postage 28¢. *Gaydell Inc.*

Jam Crock

This heavy English piece of stoneware is just the thing in which to pack your own home-prepared preserves—especially if you want to nicely personalize a gift. The crock ovenproof and has a sturdy metal collar and handle. The oatmeal color, black lettering, and shape of the crock is American, 1903. $4.95 postpaid. *Aunt Jane's Cupboard.*

Bread-Making Machine

Dough sufficient for four loaves of bread is mixed and kneaded by turning the crank. The 10-quart aluminum, 11" diameter kettle fits into a vinyl-covered metal frame, which sticks firmly to any counter by four suction cups. Comes with an extra lid. $24.95. Postage $2.30. *Vermont Country Store.*

Infra-red Food Warmer

This stainless steel electrical gadget will keep your food warm for hours without drying it out. Can also be used to warm up your serving plates or to thaw out frozen food. $35.00. Postage $3.00. *Hammacher Schlemmer.*

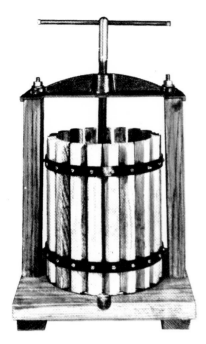

Fruit Press

A handy instrument which presses juice for making wine and cider. Just place fruit in the tub, and screw down the iron bar at top, and the juice will run out of the groove in base. 21" tall with a 9"-diameter by 11" tub. Constructed of red oak. All cast iron parts are finished with acid-resisting enamel. $45.00. Postage $6.10. *Vermont Country Store.*

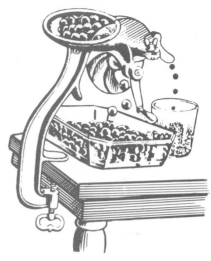

Cherry Stoner

Looks like a Rube Goldberg contraption, but operates with efficiency. The hopper is filled with cherries and the crank is turned. The stones roll out of one end, and the pitted fruit pops out from the center. The cherries are never bruised. Made of heavily-tinned rust-proof metal. $14.95. Postage $1.50. *Paprikas Weiss.*

Your Own Salad Jar

If you have a particular pride in the kind of salad dressing you can turn out, you can dispense your creation to your friends from this bottle which reads: MY OWN SALAD DRESSING. White porcelain with a cork top, multicolor label on fired ceramic. 7½" tall. $1.98. Postage 49¢. *Country Gourmet.*

Vegetable Basket

These gaily painted Chinese baskets are toted around in Hong Kong on shoulder poles. They make excellent storage units for onions, potatoes, radishes, etc. $6.00. Postage $1.75. *Charlotte Horstmann Ltd.*

The Pampered Kitchen

Spatzle Machine
For making those delicious Viennese miniature dough dumplings. $8.98. Postage $1.50. *Paprikas Weiss.*

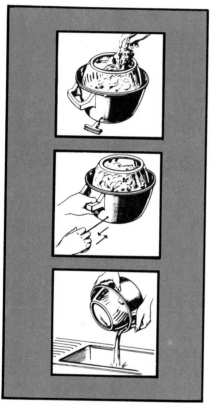

Cookie Mold
Black cast iron cookie mold is a reproduction of Old Sturbridge Village molds. 6" by 5 1/2" by 3/8". $1.50. Postage $1.20. *B. Altman.*

Fruit Crusher
This electrically driven machine crushes apples, pears, and plums, and is excellent if you want to make cider, perry, or jam. Made of red oak. Price $110.00. Postage $1.50. *Paprikas Weiss.*

Spin-Dryer
Should give you better salads every time. Drip dries lettuce and other vegetables. You simply place greens in the rotating basket. While you alternately pull and release the cord, the basket will spin. It takes just a half a minute for the lettuce to dry. Then pour out the accumulated water from the bottom of the container. When the drying operation is finished, your lettuce is ready to be chilled and then served. Made of polystyrene. $10.00. Postage $3.00. *Rainbow Wood Products.*

Multiple Chopper
Known in France as a hache-tout or something that cuts everything, this five-blade chopper is razor sharp and well equipped for all dicing and mincing. $3.75. Postage $1.10. *Bazar Francais.*

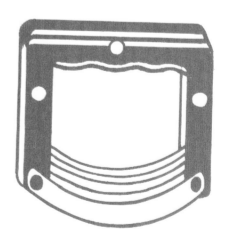

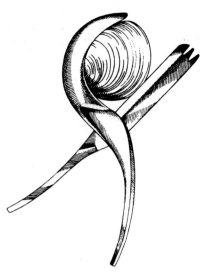

Honey Dispenser

A leakproof, finger-tip-controlled valve dispenses honey, ketchup, syrups. Made in Germany of glass. $10.00. Postage $1.25. *J.D. Browne.*

Clam Opener

From Italy comes this fast-action implement, made of chromed-brass with a stainless steel blade. The forked end on the blade side can be used to disengage the clam from the shell. Strangely enough, the same forked end can also be used for eating the disengaged clam since the two halves of the implement detach. $6.50. Postage 90¢. *Hoffritz.*

Thermo Probe

A quick way to test the internal doneness of any food. A thermometer at the end of a sturdy fork is safe in a dishwasher. No glass to break, no mercury to spill. $5.98. Postage 75¢. *Gallery.*

Pasta Maker

This chrome-plated steel pasta maker turns out spaghetti, vermicelli, ravioli, macaroni, and oodles of noodles in six thicknesses. 4" long, 6" high. $32.50. Postage $3.65. *Invento.*

Giant Toaster

This toaster has a 10" slot and will toast a piece of bread suitable for a hero sandwich. Heating element is 1500 watts, 120 volts. 6¾" high; 15" long; 5" wide. 5½' cord. $20.69 postpaid. *The Hoover Company.*

The Pampered Kitchen

Cornbread Skillet

If you have a yen for cornbread cooked the old-fashioned way, this 9" cast iron skillet will yield individual wedges. $3.98. Postage 75¢. *The Gallery.*

Snail Dough Maker

This gadget which comes from Germany, is made of wood, and measures 7" by 3¾". It is designed to make the dough which, in Hungarian cuisine, is wrapped around the snail. $1.98. Postage $1.50. *H. Roth & Son.*

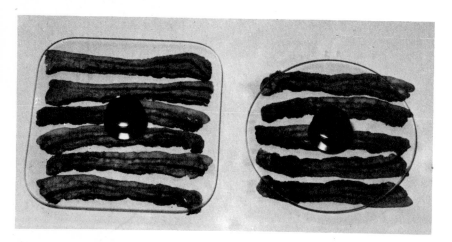

Bacon Press

A seemingly simple device which eliminates many of the complications of bacon-frying. Prevents spattering and shrinkage and cooks the bacon fully without turning it over. Made of ¼" tempered glass, with bakelite handle. 9" diameter. Specify round or square. $4.00. Postage 25¢. *Gokey.*

Homemade Broom

A family in Tennessee has been making these one-of-a-kind brooms for three generations. They grow the straw and cut the laurel handles in the mountains. 35" high. $3.50. Shipped express collect. *Storehouse.*

Food-Steaming Trivet

This steamer folds to fit any size pan. Instructions included. In stainless steel, $8.00. In aluminum, $4.50. Postage $1.25. *J.D. Browne.*

Burger Maker

How many burgers do you want to get out of every pound of chopmeat? No need to guess. Use this automatic patty maker and it will cut burgers to yield the exact results you are seeking. $1.98. Postage 75¢. *Bevis.*

Squash Cutter

This 15" long, 5" wide squash cutter is equipped with a stainless steel blade and wood frame. It cuts the vegetable into very thin strips. From Germany. $6.95. Postage $1.50. *H. Roth & Son.*

Snail Dish

This aluminum dish, 8" in diameter, holds 12 snails. It can be used for cooking and for serving. $1.50. Postage $1.50. *H. Roth & Son.*

Julienne Potato Cutter

Potatoes are not all this gadget cuts. Its stainless steel blades also work on cabbage, carrots, celery, beets, onions, and apples. 14¼" by 4¾". From France. $6.95. Postage $1.50. *H. Roth & Son.*

The Pampered Kitchen

Cream Machine

Make your own fresh cream. Use milk and butter, or margarine and skim milk. Recipes are included for clotted cream, cake fillings, mayonnaise. $10.95. Postage $2.10. *Invento.*

Cake Mold

This 12" high Breton mold makes a six-story cake for any occasion. Made of tin. From France. $19.95. Postage $1.50. *H. Roth & Sons.*

Wastecan Trolley

How embarrassing when guests trip over your wastecan, or when the odors therefrom are less than pleasant. This trolley which attaches to a right- or left-hand cabinet door can end the trauma by hiding away that ugly container. The can will now conveniently glide out as the door is opened, and disappear as the door is closed. Sized at 12" by 16", this board contraption can hold any can. Comes in honeytone pine. $4.50. Postage $1.75. *Yield House.*

Electric Brisker

This is not a breadbox, it's a brisker. It keeps crackers, cookies, cereals, nuts, pretzels, and potato chips crisp, crunchy and fresh. Electrically dehumidified. 10" by 18" by 9". Chromeplate. Black plastic. $25.00. Postage $3.15. *Lewis & Conger.*

Yogurtera

Brew your own yogurt. Create your own unusual flavor combinations with this electric 2-quart set. Complete with instructions. $15.00. Postage $2.10. *Invento.*

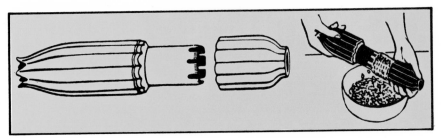

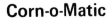

Corn-o-Matic

A plastic gadget which strips kernels automatically. $1.25. Postage 50¢. *Bazar Francais.*

Chocolate Mill

Have you admired those gorgeous cakes in a bake shop on which the whipped cream is decorated with scads of thin chocolate strips? Well, you can achieve those decorations with this mill, which looks and works like a pepper grinder. It shaves and flakes curls of chocolate. $6.95 postpaid. *Bissinger's.*

Flour Mill

Mill your own flour and save the precious nutrients. This machine will grind a pound of grain in a minute. Makes whole wheat flour, corn flour, oatmeal, rice flour, chestnut flour, lentil flour, peanut flour, cottonseed, or barley flours. Cast iron construction. Tinned to prevent rust. Adjustable to desired grind. $15.95. Postage $2.72. *Colonial Garden Kitchens.*

Couscous Cooker

A pot in which to cook the traditional dish of North Africa. Tiny moistened pellets of semolina are steamed over boiling couscous sauce. 8 quarts. $18.00. Postage $4.00. *Bazar Francais.*

Pineapple Corer

With one simple downward stroke, this device cuts and cores the pineapple meat from a fresh pineapple. $2.95. Postage 86¢. *Colonial Garden Kitchens.*

Apple Parer

In just five seconds, this machine will peel, core, and slice an apple. $5.95. Postage 75¢. *Casco Bav.*

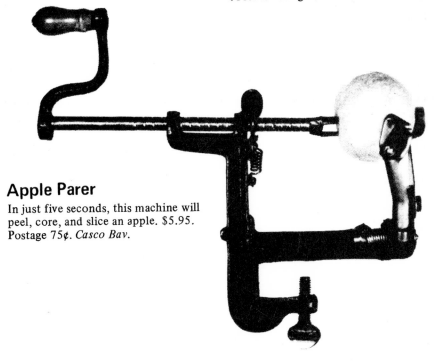

The Pampered Kitchen

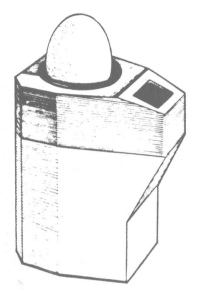

Eggs Ray

Now you can tell if your eggs are really fresh. Put egg—big end down—in the opening. A light shows how big the bubble is. The smaller the bubble, the fresher the egg. Complete with instructions and batteries. $8.95. Postage 95¢. *Hammacher Schlemmer.*

Fat and Cheese Strainer

This contraption is excellent for straining jellies, soups, or fats after deep frying. Also fine for making cottage cheese. Rust-resistant metal frame. Adjustable legs fit any kettle up to 12" in diameter. Folds for storage. Filter bag included. $1.98. Postage 86¢. *Colonial Garden Kitchens.*

Asparagus Steamer

Asparagus may be cooked to perfection in this upright copper steamer with brass handles. This 10" high pot is lined with tin. The inner arrangement permits easy removal of the asparagus. $45.00 postpaid. *Bazar De La Cuisine, Inc.*

Pickle Tongs

Made of wood. 11½" long. $2.50. Postage $1.50. *H. Roth & Son.*

Electric Bun Warmer

Will keep your bread, rolls, buns, and English muffins nice and warm. 7" by 16". $13.95. Postage $2.00. *Rainbow Wood.*

Tapwater Filter

This attachment ensures a constant supply of pure water, but does not interfere with the use of the faucet. Contaminants are removed by a disposable charcoal filter which has a life of about six months. 4 lbs. $24.95. Postage $2.00. *Hammacher Schlemmer.*

Pound and Gram Scale

Imported from Germany, this plastic kitchen scale measures up to one pound or 500 grams. 3" by 7". $9.50. Postage $1.50. *H. Roth & Son.*

Kernel Kutter

Do you ever get a yen for corn fritters? Or perhaps you like corn relish? If you want to get your kernels right off the ear with one stroke, this solid stainless steel gadget with saw-toothed cutting edges will do the job. No adjustments, no moving parts. The flexible cutting circlet will expand to fit any size ear. $1.95. Postage 70¢. *Postamatic.*

Indoor Herb Garden

Parsley, chives, dill, sweet basil, sage, thyme, and sweet marjoram grow in your kitchen. The kit includes seven red clay pots, a nickel-plated wall rack, nutrient potting mix, a pair of scissors, seed assortment and instructions. 14" wide, 16" high. $9.50. Postage $1.00. *Lewis & Conger.*

Get Going!

Even before the invention of the wheel, man realized that there were better means of locomotion than his own feet. A bird could cover in one hour the distance a man could make in a day. A fish could swim tirelessly for days on end, while an average man would poop out in an hour or two. Even the other land mammals could do a lot better on four feet than a human could do on two.

Once man reconciled himself to his physical limitations, he began to put his superior intellect to work to find ways to get about as well as Nature's more fortunately endowed creatures. Although the wheel was certainly the prime of man's inventions, it is pretty tame compared to some of the more unusual—and generally unsuccessful—inventions of later years. To give you a small idea of the trials man has endured in his striving for mobility, here are a few of the odder modes of locomotion contrived by homo sapiens:

One of the strangest land vehicles ever devised was the marsh buggy, an enormous four-wheeled contraption designed by the Gulf Oil Company to traverse the treacherous Louisiana bayous in search of mineral deposits. Looking like a giant's roller skate, the marsh buggy had wheels 10 feet tall mounted on an ordinary automobile frame.

Trying to get the best of both worlds, the Caudron company of France devised an airplane-automobile with foldable wings. It was an entirely conventional airplane except for a small outboard motor mounted on a rear third wheel. In March, 1935, a writer for the *Scientific American* declared that he "saw no reason why some day such a combination should not be practicable for general use." But the "aviocar," as it was called, took a few trials spins down the boulevards of Paris, and that was the end of that.

Scientists at the U.S. Air Force Missile Development Center at Holloman, New Mexico constructed a train that traveled so fast that no human could ride in it. The rocket-powered sled attained a speed of 3,090 mph on a 6.62-mile-long rail track.

A much more leisurely mode of getting about

Horseless Carriage

Here's an exact replica of the 1901 Olds, finished in fireman red. Has a put-up, take-down top of vinyl with a tubular steel frame. The chassis is made of welded steel, and the whole outfit turns in eight feet of space. It runs on a 3-horsepower air-cooled gasoline motor, and a 12-volt battery. $1,895.00. Shipped express collect. *Hammacher Schlemmer.*

is a pair of stilts. Though a stilt-walker isn't very speedy, he does get a unique perspective on the world around—and under—him. Hop pickers commonly go about their business on 15-foot stilts, but Albert Yelding ("Harry Sloan") of Great Britain mastered the art of walking on stilts that measured 22 feet from his ankles to the ground.

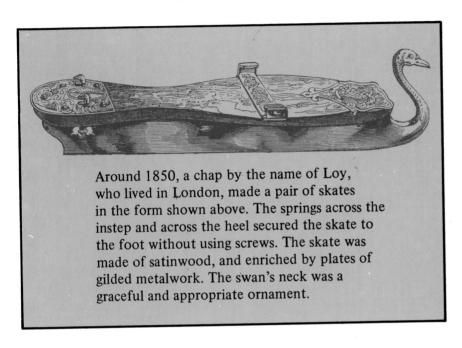

Around 1850, a chap by the name of Loy, who lived in London, made a pair of skates in the form shown above. The springs across the instep and across the heel secured the skate to the foot without using screws. The skate was made of satinwood, and enriched by plates of gilded metalwork. The swan's neck was a graceful and appropriate ornament.

Unicycle

Stop, start, turn, and reverse at will on this rugged unicycle, which is 18" in diameter. Enamel finish. Riveted spokes. Adjustable seat. Semi-pneumatic tires. $19.95. Shipped express collect. *F.A.O. Schwarz.*

Mobile with Surrey Top

This fun car has a four-cycle engine, a foot-throttle brake, an automatic clutch, a full circle steering wheel, and Goodyear tires. It can run to a speed of approximately 15 miles per hour. Uses regular gasoline. Seats one adult or two children. $239.50. Shipped express collect. *Hammacher Schlemmer.*

Get Going!

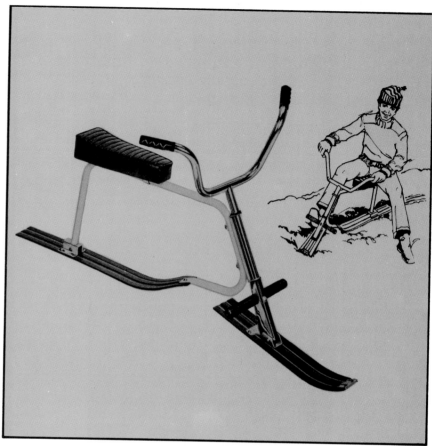

Snow Bike

Tough, extra wide skis added to a sports-styled frame provide the fun of bike riding with the exhilarating adventure of skiing. The skis, measuring 3½" wide, are aluminum; the front ski has a 60° arc to minimize bumps. The frame is made of brightly colored tubular steel, with a chrome-plated steering assembly. Upholstered mini-bike seat. 28" high, 60" long. $39.95. Postage $2.00. *House of Minnel.*

Viceroy Carriage

The wheels are 20", the shafts 5' long. Chrome axle points; laminated hardwood body; patent leather dash board. Painted and striped to order. $1,225.00 postpaid. *Pearson's.*

Pony Wagon

Can be used with either one or two ponies. Seat is foam padded. Measures 7' long by 34" wide. Step board on the side of the wagon. $224.95. Shipped express collect. *Pearson's.*

Jumping Shoes

Strong springs generate a lot of bounce, while rubber knobs protect the floors and avoid slips. Shoes are adjustable to fit every size. $5.95. Postage $2.00. *F.A.O. Schwarz.*

Horse Cart

Made of a tubular steel frame with 1"-thick waterproof cypress wood-work. The tread width is 44", and the seat is 50" wide. The cart is 34" high. The 24" wheels are chrome and have ball bearings. The shaft length is 7'. Price $124.50. Additional for surrey top with fringe, $30.00. Additional for sleigh runners, $17.95. Shipped express collect. *Pearson's.*

Nome Snowmobile

Powered with a 39 h.p. twin cylinder engine, this vehicle is capable of travel-ing at over 60 m.p.h. The power tread is poly track with internal-drive slide rail. 18-inch wide track. Two sealed-beam headlights, two tail-lights, two safety side lights. Weighs 360 lbs. Off-white and red. $1000.00. Shipped collect. *Herter's.*

Get Going!

Three-Wheel Bicycle

There are eight gearing combinations on this adult vehicle. The foamrubber seat is 10" wide. The basket is 23" by 19" by 9". Available in red, dark blue, light blue, gold, green, or white. $159.95. Shipped express collect. *Adultrike.*

Non-Sinkable Sailboat

Made of polystyrene, this boat weighs only 41 lbs fully rigged, and can be transported in a stationwagon or on the top of a car. It has a 3' beam. The aluminum mast is 8' high. The nylon blue and white sail is 55' wide. $240.00 postpaid. *Patio.*

Dune Buggy

Brush, mud, snow, sand, surf, streams, and ponds are no obstacle to this eight-horsepower vehicle. Fiberglass body is finished in metallic gold-flake. Seats two adults or one adult and two children. Steering sticks can be moved to the middle. Weighs 425 lbs., yet is easy enough to lift at either end with one hand. 54" wide, 87" long. Automatic electric starter. $1,195.00. Shipped express collect. *Hammacher Schlemmer.*

Model T Ford

This miniature is capable of chugging along at 10 mph powered by a four-horse-power lawn mower engine. Fueled with gasoline. 5' long steel body. $650.00. Shipped express collect. *Hammacher Schlemmer.*

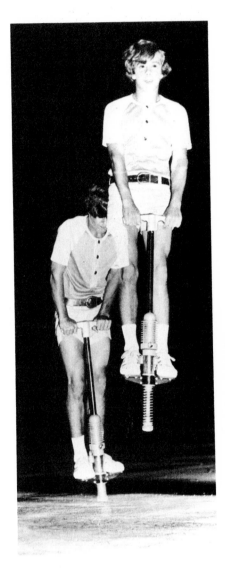

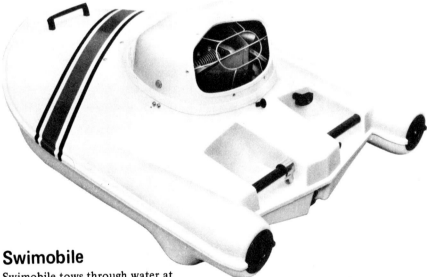

Swimobile

Swimobile tows through water at speeds up to 15 mph, and goes 30 miles on a tank of gas. The air-cooled engine will not pollute the water. Supports 3 adults; tows five persons on an air matress. Tough hull construction of laminated acrylic fiberglass withstands jolts and scrapes on rock and sand. Will fit in a car trunk. Safe and simple enough for a child to run. Cannot sink. $329.50. Shipped express collect. *Hammacher Schlemmer.*

Hop Rod

A gas-powered pogo stick. Put in a gasoline mix—the same kind you use in a lawn mower. Add batteries. Stand on the foot pedals, and you're off. Your weight activates the machine. As long as you keep your balance, you'll keep hopping. Just jump off to stop. $69.95. Postage $4.15. *Hammacher Schlemmer.*

For Men

With the notable exception of man, in the animal kingdom the most colorful feathers and furs have generally been bestowed on the male of the species. Whereas female attire has changed whimsically, men's garb has tended to be more functional. The Cro-magnon male was fashionably attired for all occasions, as long as he first killed a bear.

The demand for the dye of royal purple, derived from particular shellfish and used to color the togas of friends, Romans, and countrymen, was so great that it stimulated the exploration that helped Rome build its great empire. But other than color, the only difference in men's togas was the length; there were long togas for winter, short togas for summer. While the toga was de rigueur for a patrician, the masses had to be satisfied with a belted tunic of rough material.

Stylistically, men's pants remained essentially the same for hundreds of years until a revolutionary development catapulted this essential item into the fashion whirl: pockets. Now pants could go anywhere, and hold their own.

After that high point, the men's fashion parade sort of bogged down; and for four hundred years, it was hard to distinguish one era from another. While women went from the floor-length dress to the pinch-waisted bustle, with many variations in between, male styles remained depressingly the same. Trouser legs got a little wide, shirts grew collars, long hair and moustaches came in and out of fashion, but wedding and funeral suits stayed the same.

Then from a little area in the most staid and conservative country in the world, the fashion explosion hit. London's Carnaby Street tailors went wild with colors and styles. Outrageous hues, matching, clashing, flashing! Bright-colored shoes with high heels and bizarre decorations. And in just a few short years, all the old rules for men's dress flew out the window.

Today, unisex is the prevailing fashion trend, with men's styles, at last, vying with those of women. However, there are dangers inherent in styles that are so similar. The next coifed, wide-trousered, high-heeled, long-haired beauty you whistle at may be your son.

Indian Hat

Indians wore this black "Tommy Grimes"-style hat as far back as the 1890s. Features a high crown and 4" brim, with a hatband and sweatband. Made of wool felt. Sizes 6 5/8 to 7 5/8. $6.95. Postage 70¢. *Grey Owl.*

An Italian nobleman, the Marchese Del Grillo, was invited by a well-known London hostess to a reception. The Marchese begged to be excused. He explained he had a previous engagement, and that he would be bound to be late. "Never mind," said the lady, "just come as soon as you can."

So upon the termination of his first appointment, the Marchese drove straight to her house. The hostess met him at the front door, and looked him up and down. She was visibly disappointed and frowned. "Oh my goodness!" she exclaimed, "My dear Marchese, you are not in evening clothes. Impossible!"

The Marchese never moved a muscle. He simply said he'd return promptly, properly attired, and left her home. In an hour, he came back in full evening dress, covered with orders and decorations.

He was announced, approached his hostess, politely bowed, and bent to kiss her hand. She offered him a cup of consomme, while a butler brought him a cocktail. The Marchese accepted both. He then took the soup which was in one hand and the cocktail which was in the other and poured them both over his splendid raiment, saying, "It is you, dear clothes who are invited, not I. Therefore, I am treating you, not myself." Then he bowed once again, and immediately left the room.

* * *

Determined to lose weight, a rather stout gentleman who was on vacation in New Hampshire, hustled to the general store to buy himself a pair of overalls, so he could labor in the fields. He picked out a pair that was big enough for energetic exercise.

Then a thought struck him. He turned to the clerk and said, "Wait a minute. These overalls are big enough for me now, but I expect to lose a lot of weight. Maybe I'd better get a smaller pair."

The clerk looked at him and said, "Mister, if you can shrink as fast as these overalls will, you'll be in pretty good shape, and they'll fit you all the way."

North Bay Jacket

World-renowned Hudson Bay stripes bedeck this wool jacket with Orlon pile lining. Built-in hand-warming muff. Flap patch pockets. 32" deep. Sizes 36 to 46. $50.00. Postage $1.00. *Deerskin Trading Post.*

For Men

Costly thy habit as thy purse can buy,
But not express'd in fancy; rich, not gaudy;
For the apparel oft proclaims the man.
> William Shakespeare (1564-1616), HAMLET

Trust not the heart of that man for whom old
clothes are not venerable.
> Thomas Carlyle (1795-1881), SARTOR RESARTUS

Eat to please thyself, but dress to please others.
> Benjamin Franklin (1706-1790),
> POOR RICHARD'S ALMANACK

Strip the bishop of his apron, or the beadle of his
hat and lace; what are they? Men. Mere men.
Dignity; and even holiness, too, sometimes are
more questions of coat and waistcoat than some
people imagine.

> Charles Dickens (1812-1870)

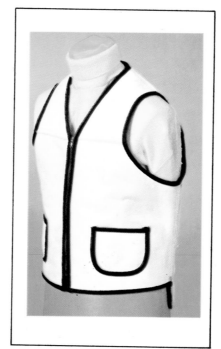

Lock Belt

A stretch-weave cotton belt, with an antique-looking icebox latch made of zinc. Sizes: 24 to 36. $3.98. Postage 80¢. *Lillian Vernon.*

Traditional Scottish Garb

Following the 1745 uprising in Scotland, wearing of the tartan was forbidden until 1782. Over the years, the tartan has become a symbol of Scottish freedom to clansmen all over the world. The full traditional outfit is offered here: Montrose doublet in fine black barathea with Celtic buttons, lace jabot, and cuffs; full kilt (available in most tartans) made to measure for waist, hips, and length; evening belt; Piper's horsehair sporran; hand-knitted clan hose (specify shoe size). $212.10. Postage $8.35. *Tartan Gift Shop.*

Outdoorsman's Vest

Shaggy lamb on the outside and fluffy shearing on the inside make this piece of clothing warm and comfortable. Zip front; two pockets; piped in black. Sizes: small through extra-large. $15.00. Postage $1.00. *Deerskin Trading Post.*

Latigo Top Hat

Cattlehide leather, tanned with alum and gambier, has been fashioned into a smart top hat. Sizes: Small, medium, and large. $32.00. Postage $1.00. *Western Brands.*

Sherlock Holmes Cape

This garment, technically known as a Harris/Loden Cape, is available in either green Harris tweed or green Loden cloth. A gift that will feed the fantasy of some dear male who has dreamed of being the great sleuth. The coat length is about 39", with a finger-length over-cape which leaves the arms free. Comes in one size that fits a chest size from 38" to 44". Six to eight weeks for delivery. Subject to duty. $94.00. Postage $4.50. *J.C. Cording.*

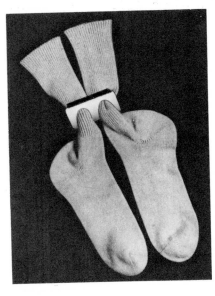

Sock Tucker

Keeps socks permanently paired through the entire washing and drying process. Guaranteed to withstand the high temperatures of clothes dryers. Made of practically indestructible plastic. Comes in red, green, yellow and blue. 32 (8 of each color) for $4.50 postpaid. *C. A. Gordon.*

Electric Pants Presser

Jacket, tie, and trousers are held and pressed with gentle heat. Slip-proof tie-rod. Built of dark wood. Has an automatic 30-minute timer and signal light. 17" wide; 14" deep; 40" high. Made in England. $150.00. Postage $6.05. *Hammacher Schlemmer.*

Raw-Wool Jacket

Natural raw sheep wool is what this Tibetan jacket with two pockets is made of. The five buttons are made of wood or bamboo knots. Sizes: small or medium. With sleeves: $34.00; sleeveless: $28.00. Postage $3.00. *Tibetan Arts and Crafts.*

For Men

Moneypak

Eight zippered compartments separate the coins and the currency of four countries in this leather wallet. Passport and papers are stored as well. A belt attachment permits concealment under a coat. Finished in black, brown, or red calf. Two sizes: standard, 5-7/8" by 8⅓/4"; wallet, 4-¾" by 8-1/8". $35.00. Postage $1.00. *Hunting World.*

Until the time of the French Revolution, most everyone wore knee breeches rather than trousers. But in 1789, supporters of the Revolution separated themselves from the royalists by adopting trousers. Accordingly, they were known as the *sans-culottes* ("without breeches").

In token of their sympathy with the French rebels, many ordinary Americans sported trousers between 1790 and 1800. But it was not until a decade or so later that trousers substituted for breeches on formal occasions. The first President who habitually dressed in long trousers was James Madison.

* * *

Tradition has it that the greatest fop in all history was one Prince Wenzel von Kaunitz-Rietburg, an 18th century Austrian statesman. It is reported that over a period of 57 years the prince changed his clothes no less than 30 times a day. His obsession occupied him no less than four hours a day. Since the prince was a multimillionaire, he could well afford to spend a half a million dollars each year on his clothes and decorations. Resplendent in the world of fashion, von Kaunitz was also a statesman of renown. For more than 30 years, he took a leading part in his country's political affairs.

Tibetan Fur Cap

Made of otter, marmot, etc., in various combinations. Decorated with gold trim and red flowers. Inner circumference, 20". $16.00. Postage $2.00. *Tibetan Arts and Crafts.*

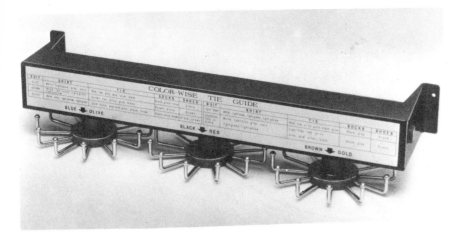

Electric Tie Rack

This cordless contraption holds over 36 ties and organizes them by color. A pushbutton selector rotates the ties. Walnut color. 14½" long, 4½" deep, 2¾" high. Batteries included. $9.00. Postage $1.90. *Lewis & Conger.*

Flotation Vest

If you spill into the water wearing this light, action-free, reversible vest, you float face up. Can be worn as outer wear, or under hunting coat. Sizes: 36 to 48. $19.95. Postage $1.00. *Orvis.*

Marrakesh Robe

A Moroccan-inspired kaftan styled for informal entertaining. Made of washable nylon tricot. Comes in black, beige, or royal purple. One size fits all. $19.95. Postage $1.50. *Lew Magram.*

Safari Jacket

This sweater jacket derives from Ireland, where it is woven in pure wool in a traditional Irish pattern. Small and medium, $29.15; large and extra-large, $30.25. Postage $5.50. *Creation Boutique.*

Ponytrack Hat

Made of finest quality fur felt, hand-creased to a horseshoe shape. 3½" brim. Raw edge. Beige or black. Sizes 6 7/8 to 7 5/8. $16.50. Postage $1.00. *Western Brands.*

Pranks and Wiles

ASK THE MAGIC MIRROR
"Mirror, mirror on the wall
am I the best looking
one of all...?"

PRESS BUTTON FOR REPLY!

Magic Mirror

Just ask the age-old question, "Who's the fairest of them all?" and the magic mirror will tell it like it is, in a voice that sounds like it was packed in dry ice. Sixteen wisecrack answers are programmed at random so you never know what the reply will be. Mirror is set in a gilded frame. Operates on one C battery (not included). $9.95. Postage $1.10. *Game Room.*

The Practical Joker

Oh, what a fund of joy jocund lies hid in harmless hoaxes!
    What keen enjoyment springs
    From cheap and simple things!
What deep delight from sources trite inventive humour coaxes,
    That pain and trouble brew
    For every one but you!

Gun powder placed inside its waist improves a mild Havana,
    Its unexpected flash
    Burns eyebrows and moustache.
When people dine no kind of wine beats ipecacuanha,
    But common sense suggests
    You keep it for your guests—

Then naught annoys the organ boys like throwing red hot coppers.
    And much amusement bides
    In common butter slides;
And stringy snares across the stairs cause unexpected croppers.

    Coal scuttles, recollect,
    Produce the same effect.

        A man possessed
         Of common sense
       Need not invest
         At great expense—

        It does not call
         For pocket deep,
       These jokes are all
         Extremely cheap.

If you commence with eighteenpence—it's all you'll have to pay;
You may command a pleasant and a most instructive day.

A good spring gun breeds endless fun, and makes men jump like rockets—
    And turnip heads on posts
    Make very decent ghosts.
Then hornets sting like anything, when placed in waistcoat pockets—
    Burnt cork and walnut juice
    Are not without their use.

No fun compares with easy chairs whose seats are stuffed with needles—
    Live shrimps their patience tax
    When put down people's backs.
Surprising, too, what one can do with a pint of fat black beetles—
    And treacle on a chair
    Will make a Quaker swear!

    Then sharp tin tacks
      And pocket squirts—
    And cobbler's wax
      For ladies' skirts—

    And slimy slugs
      On bedroom floors—
    And water jugs
      On open doors—

Prepared with these cheap properties, amusing tricks to play
Upon a friend a man may spend a most delightful day.
W. S. Gilbert

Talking Toilet

When a guest sits on your john, a laughing voice says, "Hey! We're working down here!" There's an assortment of other rude comments and sounds. This small battery-operated unit, hidden from view when in use, speaks out whenever there's pressure on the seat. $5.00. Postage 45¢. *Game Room.*

Hand Decanter

"I'll have a finger of scotch," your guest declares. This gadget handles the request literally. You unscrew the digit and pour an exact fingerful from this handpainted, wood-grain 13" hand which rests on its own bar stand. $7.95. Postage 95¢. *Game Room.*

Pranks and Wiles

The Man on the Flying Trapeze

A reproduction of the antique toy, this little man flies on the principle of sand displacement. Performs for two minutes. Man is made of hardwood; box is decorated with fabric. 4" by 8" $10.00. Postage $2.00. *Hammacher Schlemmer.*

Party Truth Meter

This transistorized version of the renowned polygraph (lie detector) is made of plastic. 5" by 2" by 1½" high. Battery and instruction book included. $11.95. Postage $2.00. *Invento.*

Coin Rustler

Every time you put a coin in the slot of this machine, a green hand darts out, grabs the coin, and deposits the loot inside. This box, 2¾" wide by 4" long, operates on two C batteries (not included). $4.00. Postage 75¢. *Game Room.*

The Nothing Box

It blinks and that's all. It can't be turned off. It will keep on winking its eight eyes in no recognizable pattern for no apparent reason for nearly a year. Then it's dead. It can't be fixed. Made of metal, with red light bulbs for eyes. 6" wide, 4" high, 4" deep. $25.00. Postage $2.80. *Hammacher Schlemmer.*

In the summer of 1824, two retired New Yorkers, named Lozier and DeVoe, perpetrated a wild hoax on their numerous friends. They convinced a crowd that they had obtained the mayor's approval to saw off Manhattan from the mainland, and *turn the island around!*

The purpose of this grand plan was to keep Manhattan's southern end from sinking into the harbor under the weight of the many new buildings. DeVoe and Lozier started immediately to sign up laborers, and to award contracts for food, equipment, and even for a huge anchor to prevent the island from being swept out to sea. After eight weeks of preparation, all those associated with the project were instructed to meet the following Monday morning so they could proceed to the north end of Manhattan where the work was to begin. As instructed, hundreds of workmen plus scores of contractors arrived at the spot. They waited for hours before they learned that Lozier and DeVoe had, for reasons of health, gone on an extended journey.

* * *

At noon, on a spring day in Paris in 1910, a truck broke down in the center of the Place de l'Opera. The driver got out, went underneath his vehicle, and emerged a half hour later, evidently having made the repair. After apologizing to the police for the traffic snarl he had caused, the man drove away. That night he collected several thousand English pounds from friends whom he had bet that he could lie on his back for 30 minutes at the busiest hour in the busiest traffic center in Paris. The man's name was Horace De Vere Cole, England's greatest practical joker of the day.

* * *

For the 1886 and 1888 editions of Appleton's Cyclopedia of American Biography, the policy of the editors was to accept all material received by mail. Their trusting nature made them the unwitting prey of some practical joker who sent them at least 84 biographies of fictitious persons. These phony bios were all published, and went unnoticed until 1919, when 14 of the frauds were discovered by a librarian. This led to a search that brought to light 70 more by 1936.

* * *

When Lord Halifax was a young man, he traveled one day from London to Bath, seated in the railway between two sober-faced spinsters. During the long journey, not one of the three said a word. Just before reaching Bath, the train entered a tunnel. Young Halifax put the back of his hand to his lips and made loud kissing noises.

As the train emerged into the daylight, the young man looked from one spinster to the other, rose, tipped his hat, and said, "To which of you two charming ladies am I indebted for that most delightful interlude?" Then he stepped out of the train, leaving the two ladies glaring suspiciously at each other.

Gotcha

Pull the ball out, and the ball somehow finds its way back into the box. When it does, the door snaps shut like a trap door. $6.00. Postage 90¢. *Sleepy Hollow Gifts.*

For Tots

What is the little one thinking about?
Very wonderful things, no doubt;
Unwritten history!
Unfathomed mystery!
Yet he laughs and cries, and eats and drinks,
And chuckles and crows, and nods and winks,
As if his head were as full of kinks
And curious riddles as any sphinx!
Josiah Gilbert Holland (1819-1881),
BITTER-SWEET, FIRST MOVEMENT

Who would not tremble and rather choose to die,
than to be a baby again, if he were given such a
choice.
St. Augustine (354-430),
THE CITY OF GOD

Sweet babe, in thy face
Soft desires I can trace,
Secret joys and secret smiles,
Little pretty infant wiles.
William Blake (1757-1827),
CRADLE SONGS

An infant crying in the night;
An infant crying for the light:
And with no language but a cry.
Alfred Lord Tennyson (1809-1892),
IN MEMORIAM

A babe in a house is a well-spring of pleasure.
Martin Farquhar Tupper (1810-1889),
OF EDUCATION

Automatic Baby Swing

This swing has two legs instead of four, which makes it easier to put your baby in the seat. This construction also takes up less room. A strong one-piece leg brace, 7/8" plated tubing, and non-skid tips make for good balance. A completely enclosed motor swings the baby for 17 to 20 minutes on a single wind-up. Locks in place. Folds easily. $19.95. Postage $2.00. *Jackson.*

Musical Spoon

Made of silver plate. Handle shows a bunny. Music can be turned on and off. Comes in blue, yellow, or pink. $8.50. Postage $2.00. *Plummer's Ltd.*

Musical Toilette Trainer

A wind-up music box merrily plays "How Dry I Am." Contoured seat is stainproof. Comes with hinged lid, potty, deflector, and safety belt. Available in white, avocado, or hot pineapple. $10.00 postpaid. *Century.*

Bentwood Cradle

A throwback to the days of our American forefathers. It rocks, then can be locked for the sleeping child. The graceful arm is for a canopy or a mobile. Soft walnut finish. 46" long, 24½" wide, and 22" from floor to cradle bottom. $138.50. Shipped express collect. *Storehouse.*

BABY:

1. An alimentary canal with a loud voice at one end and no responsibility at the other.
2. The most extensive employer of female labor.
3. The morning caller, the noonday crawler, the midnight brawler.

GLASSWARE

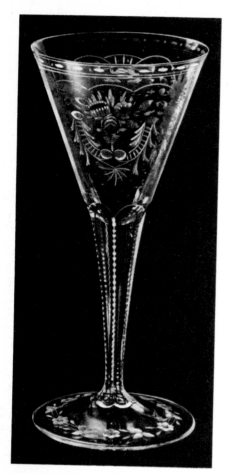

Maharani Glass

The Maharajah of Alirajpur was first to use this richly engraved lead crystal glass. Such notables as King Mohammed V of Morocco, President Sukarno of Indonesia, and Crown Prince Asfa Wossen of Ethiopia, have since used this pattern. Goblet measures 8½" high. Twenty-five different sizes of glassware are available in the pattern. Set of six goblets: $135.00, which includes customs duty, postage, and handling. *Superlux Ltd.*

Deer Park Prism

Hand engraved in clear crystal. 7" high. $151.48 postpaid. *Svenskt Glas.*

Engraved Vase

Hand-engraved in clear crystal. 8¾"
high, $68.38; 4½" high, $23.07
postpaid. *Svenskt Glas.*

Vase

Handmade crystal vase from Sweden.
5" high. $36.00. Will bill for postage.
Svenskt Glas.

Dalecarlia Wine Glass

The engraving is of Karl XIV of
Sweden (1818-1844) on a royal
progress through the province of
Dalecarlia. 6¼" high. $61.33 postpaid.
Svenskt Glas.

Glass is a liquid, though it feels hard enough to be
called a solid. If left standing long enough in one
position, the particles that make up glass will flow
downward. Old windows are thicker on the bottom
than on the top!

GLASSWARE

Polar Bears

The bear in the front of this scene is
engraved from underneath the ice
block; the one in the background is
engraved on the back of the glass. This
creates the three-dimensional impression. Hand-cut green glass. 10" high,
11" wide. $660.15 postpaid. *Svenskt
Glas.*

Wellington Glass

This hand-cut crystal, distinctively
British pattern, would enhance any
table. Ice bucket is $49.40. Old-
fashioned tumblers are $10.00 each.
Claret glass, $11.00. Decanter, $68.00.
Shipped collect. *Harrods.*

Glass was made in prehistoric times, and glass-making was already a well-established industry in Egypt by the 16th cent. B.C. The Romans refined the art of glassmaking to a level unequaled until modern times. They made small windowpanes, hollow ware, and colorful millefiori (thousand flowers) vessels.

After the Crusades, Venice was the leader in making fine glassware for almost four centuries. The city officials tried to monopolize the industry by strictly controlling the glassworkers at Murano. Artisans were severely penalized for betraying the secrets of their art.

France became dominant in the 18th century with the invention of a process for casting glass. French plate glass was used to line the magnificent Galerie des Glaces at Versailles.

The first glass manufactory on this side of the Atlantic was built in 1608.

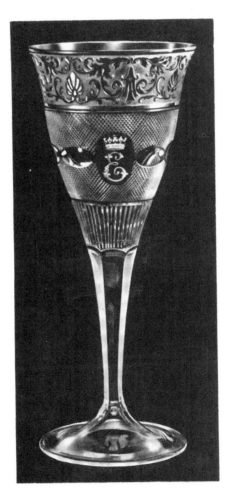

"Splendid" Glass

Designed for Queen Elizabeth II of Great Britain, this hand-cut lead crystal pattern has been used by President Paasikivi of Finland, King Mohammed V of Morocco, King Alphonso XIII of Spain, King Fuad of Egypt, King Faisal of Saudi Arabia, the President of the Czechoslovak Republic, as well as by an assortment of maharajahs, premiers, and marshals. The goblet is 8 5/8" high. Upper rim is gilded. Assortment of different glasses available in the pattern. Set of six goblets: $126.00, which includes customs duty, postage, and handling. With Queen Elizabeth's emblem, approximately 10% more. *Superlux Ltd.*

Romeo and Juliet

The romance of Romeo and Juliet's balcony scene is depicted in this hand-carved crystal, 8" high. $49.25 postpaid. *Svenskt Glas.*

Tableware

Though we commonly think of prehistoric man grappling with his dinner with his bare hands, evidence has come to light that primitive man used a rudimentary spoon of shell, horn, or flint.

The first civilization to dine with stylized spoons of wood, slate, or ivory were the Egyptians. The Greeks and Romans preferred spoons of bronze which generally had spike handles. Craftsmen of medieval Europe topped their spoons with knobs, and later with effigies of the Madonna, saints, or apostles. The spoon as we know it today, with its spatulate handle, dates only from the 18th century.

The earliest forks were probably forked sticks. These evolved into the wooden forks of Egypt, and eventually into the silver and bronze forks of Renaissance Italy. The English resisted using this "foreign" implement until the 17th century.

Table knives were a rather late innovation. Until about 1600, individuals brought to the table their own knives, which between meals, served as daggers.

The place of origin of chinaware is rather obvious. This translucent pottery with its soft glaze differs from the later European porcelain of Italy (c. 1600) and Meissen (c. 1700) in the method of firing. After the first firing of European porcelain, the body and glaze are fired together at a very high temperature.

Hammersley Bell
This fine bone china bell by Wedgwood commemorates John Donne. $18.00. Shipped collect. *Gered.*

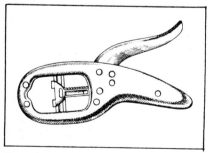

Crackerjack
A chrome-plated instrument which cracks nuts, lobster claws, and ice. Imported from England. $6.25. Postage 65¢. *Hoffritz.*

Cordless Peppermill
This walnut finished, 9" high peppermill grinds pepper automatically. Uses batteries. $12.95. Postage $2.00. *Hammacher Schlemmer.*

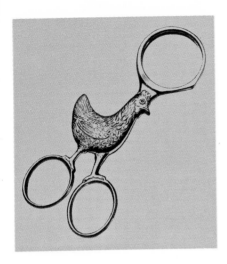

Egg Scissors
One snip slices off the top of a soft-cooked egg, without crushing the shell. Gold-plated; 5" long. $9.00. Postage $2.00. *Invento.*

Pepper Mill
A twist of the silvery tail brings a sprinkle of freshly ground pepper from this fish's mouth. 6" long. $25.00. Postage $1.10. *Plummers Ltd.*

Wine-Bottle Coaster
Trimmed with braid, this silver-plated table accessory is entirely suitable for formal wine service. The cork-stopper is a dripless pourer. $18.50. Postage $2.00. *Plummer's Ltd.*

Sterling Silver Toothpick
The idea here is that one man's sterling silver toothpick shouldn't get mixed up with another man's sterling silver toothpick. Therefore the initial. This 2" dental aid comes in an alligator case. Specify one initial. $6.00. Postage 80¢. *Downs.*

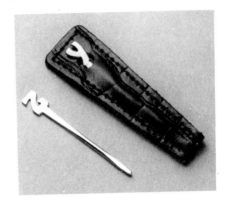

Danish Spice Mills
Designed in Denmark for Georg Jensen, this pepper mill and salt mill, each 7¼" tall, will handle the daily grind. See-through acrylic. $10.00 each. Postage 90¢. *Kenton Collection.*

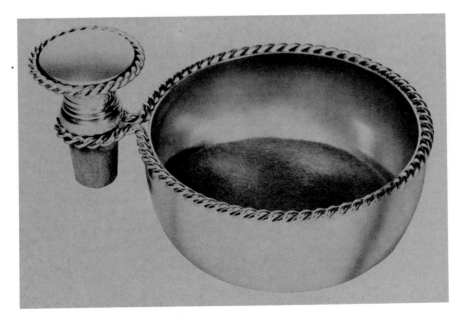

French Wine Region Plates
Map of the main French wine regions decorates each of six porcelain plates imported from France. Set of six, $22.10. Shipped collect. *Harrods.*

Tableware

Today we would not laud the manners of a person who picked up a piece of steak with his hands and then licked the gravy off each digit. But until the 17th century, the English believed that Providence had provided them with fingers for the purpose of eating, and thus no utensil was necessary.

When in 1608, Thomas Coryat, an Englishman who had visited Italy, introduced the Italian custom of eating with a dinner fork, everyone thought the idea was an insult to human dignity. But little by little, of course, this affront became standard practice.

Mustard Dish
This sterling silver condiment container is glass-lined with a spoon height of 3¼". Spoon included. $21.50. Postage $5.00. *Carlo Mario Camusso.*

Balloon Mugs
This richly styled set of eight-ounce beakers might give anyone a lift. $12.00. Postage $1.20. *Kenton Collection.*

Moustache Spoon

A bit of nostalgia for a gentleman of today, this is an exact reproduction of a 19th century moustache spoon. It has the practical function, however, of protecting moustaches from food and soups. Comes in a red flannel bag. In silver plate, $5.95. In 24-K gold Vermeil, $12.50. Postage $2.00. *Plummer's Ltd.*

Cherub Centerpiece

The centerpiece is composed of four white bisque pieces, each a cherub 17" long. Each piece holds a candle cup. Arranged in a circle, the four pieces make a 4-candle centerpiece 11" in diameter. They can also be arranged in a long serpentine effect, or used as individual candleholders on a bridge table. Set of 4, $7.95. Postage $1.10. *Artisan Galleries.*

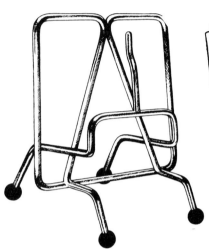

Newspaper Stand

What some of us have dreamed about is to be able to sit at breakfast and read the daily newspaper unimpeded. With this smart gadget, you can sip your coffee and cut your ham—in other words, use both hands and still read the news. Chrome-plated ball feet. 11" high. Imported from England. $10.00. Postage 90¢. *Hoffritz.*

Swinging Susie

This tray seemingly defies gravity. Will hold anything on it, including drinks, without spilling, sliding, or tipping, even though you swing it back and forth. Diameter 15". Made of plastic. $7.95. Postage 99¢. *House of Minnel.*

Silver-Plated Chopsticks

For lovers of Chinese food, this set of 8" silver-plated chopsticks may even enhance the flavor. Pair, $8.50. Postage $1.50. *Lewis and Conger.*

Fossils for You

A fossil can be either the actual remains of a plant or an animal, or the imprint of a plant or animal, preserved from prehistoric times by nature. Quick burial in material that excludes bacteria and oxygen prevents decay and permits whole preservation. Preservation for aeons creates fossils. The scientific study of fossils is called paleontology.

Insects that lived millions of years ago are often found in amber. This hard substance was originally a sticky resin which enveloped the insect. Through the years, the fragile tissues of the insect dried, until all that remained was the mold, sometimes so precise scientists can conduct microscopic studies of its structure.

Fossilization is often the result of petrification. Mineral material from underground streams may be deposited in the interstices of bones, shells, or plants, and render the subject more stonelike, thus protecting it from the ravages of time. Over the millennia, the original live material may be replaced entirely by minerals, so that the original structure and appearance are maintained, as in petrified wood. Petrified logs from the Triassic period may be seen in the Petrified Forest in the Painted Desert of Arizona.

Multiple Trilobite Slab

If you want something really old around the house that won't smell, you could do worse than pick up this 500 million-year-old fossil. This shale slab from Utah reveals the fossilized forms of two or more *Elrathia Trilobites* of the Middle Cambrian age. Each slab is 3" to 4" in length. $25.00. Postage 75¢. *Dover Scientific.*

Trilobite, Grapholite, Nautilus pie;
Seas were calcareous, oceans were dry.
Eocene, miocene, pliocene Tuff,
Lias and Trias and that is enough.

The Society Upon the Stanislaus

I reside at Table Mountain, and my name is Truthful James:
I am not up to small deceit, or any sinful games;
And I'll tell in simple language what I know about the row
That broke up our society upon the Stanislow.

But first I would remark, that it is not a proper plan
For any scientific man to whale his fellow-man,
And, if a member don't agree with his peculiar whim,
To lay for that same member for to "put a head" on him.

Now, nothing could be finer or more beautiful to see
Than the first six months' proceedings of that same society,
Till Brown of Calaveras brought a lot of fossil bones
That he found within a tunnel near the tenement of Jones.

Then Brown he read a paper, and he reconstructed there,
From those same bones, an animal that was extremely rare;
And Jones then asked the Chair for a suspension of the rules,
Till he could prove that those same bones was one of his lost mules.

Then Brown he smiled a bitter smile and said he was at fault,
It seemed he had been trespassing on Jones's family vault:
He was a most sarcastic man, this quiet Mr. Brown,
And on several occasions he had cleaned out the town.

Now, I hold it is not decent for a scientific gent
To say another is an ass—at least, to all intent;
Nor should the individual who happens to be meant
Reply by heaving rocks at him to any great extent.

Then Abner Dean of Angel's raised a point of order, when
A chunk of old red sandstone took him in the abdomen,
And he smiled a kind of sickly smile, and curled up on the floor,
And the subsequent proceedings interested him no more.

For, in less time than I write it, every member did engage
In a warfare with the remnants of a palaeozoic age;
And the way they heaved those fossils in their anger was a sin,
Till the skull of an old mammoth caved the head of Thompson in.

And this is all I have to say of these improper games
For I live at Table Mountain, and my name is Truthful James;
And I've told, in simple language, what I know about the row
That broke up our society upon the Stanislow.

Bret Harte

Fossil Crab

This Australian fossil crab (*Galene aispinosa*) is over 60 million years old. Size 1½" to 2". $15.00. Postage 75¢. *Dover Scientific.*

Fossil Camel Tooth

These Ice Age fossil camel teeth were dug up in—of all places—Nebraska, and offer unassailable evidence that camels once roamed the United States. A souvenir from the Ice Age. 1" to 1½". $7.50. Postage 75¢. *Dover Scientific.*

Boots & Shoes

Man did very nicely without shoes for thousands of years, and in many sections of the world still does so today. Yet, once accustomed to a shoe, a foot will not easily tread bare on asphalt or concrete.

The earliest form of shoe was the sandal, worn in ancient Egypt, Greece, and Rome. Next came the boot, generally worn for hunting and traveling, until the Romans took to wearing boots for ordinary outdoor activity.

Though the sabot had been in use much earlier, by the 11th century wooden clogs became the standard footwear of the European peasant. In the 1400s, people began to mount their shoes on separate wooden blocks to protect their footwear from mud and water. Soon, both the platform and the shoe were combined,

to become the forerunner of the heeled shoe.

It was not long before Europe's fashion designers went to work. Among the more bizarre footwear developed were shoes with points so long that they had to be fastened at the knee; platform shoes with soles a foot high; shoes which were extraordinarily wide at the toes; and boots faced with fur.

Yet shoes are more outrageously styled today than they have been in centuries. Witness silver lamé shoes with Cuban heels for men; platform shoes with six-inch heels for women, and women's boots in every color of the rainbow. We've even been told of a pair of women's heels which are made of clear, hollowed-out plastic, and are filled with water and live goldfish—to create a walking aquarium.

Rolling Shoe Rack

This compact rack holds any size and style shoe along with cleaning and polishing gear. Made of pine. Your choice of honeytone or antique finish. 22" wide; 16" deep; 26½" high. $35.95. Postage $5.75. *Yield House.*

In medieval France, society was strictly divided into separate classes. Philip Augustus, the king of France, enacted a law that points on one's shoes should be between six and twelve inches, depending upon one's station—the longer the point, the higher the rank.

* * *

When a Manchurian child is ready to learn how to walk, his parents often embroider a cat's head, whiskers and all, on the toes of his shoes. The parents hope that this will make their child as sure-footed as the cat.

Electric Boot Dryers

Damp boots dry in one hour or less, wet boots dry overnight, without damaging the leather. Also stops mildew and rot in humid climate. Plugs into any 110-120 volt AC or DC outlet; draws 8 watts. $10.00 postpaid. *Gokey.*

Driving Shoes

The soles and heels of these shoes were designed to reduce muscular tension and provide more positive pedal control. Moccasin construction in supple leather gives a foot-hugging fit. Madras kidskin, black or white. Both men's and women's sizes. $19.00. Postage $1.50. *Hunting World.*

Sailing Shoes

Molded of fine latex, these shoes fit to the skin, with or without socks. Soles have a molded network of suction cups and cross bars to provide safer, more secure footing under difficult weather conditions. White. Both men's and women's sizes. $15.00. Postage $1.50. *Hunting World.*

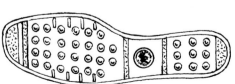

Boots & Shoes

Boot Rack

Five pairs of boots and galoshes are held in shape, upside down, for fastest drying. Stained wood dowels have protective caps. This rack takes two pairs of boots up to 17½" high, and three pairs up to 14½". Entire shebang takes up 18" by 9". Comes in easily assembled parts. $3.98. Postage 80¢. *Lillian Vernon.*

Electric Boot Dryer

This contraption, made in Norway, is designed to allow warm air to circulate over, under, and through a shoe. The heat will not damage the leather. The process stops mildew, and also controls odors which are apt to generate in a hot and humid climate. Operates on either a 110 or 220-volt AC or DC. Made of light-weight, rust-proof aluminum. 8 1/3" x 2 3/4". Weight 1 1/4 lbs. $10.00. Postage $1.00. *Windfall.*

Lounging Boot

Fluffy goose down provides the warmth. Insoles are made of thick thermal foam, protected by a fitted sole of glove leather. Upper is ankle-hugging nylon. Specify regular shoe size. For men, taupe, $14.95 postpaid. For women, powder blue, $14.95 postpaid. *Eddie Bauer.*

SPICES

What is a spice? According to Christopher Morley, *spice* might be the plural of "spouse." According to Webster a spice is an aromatic vegetable such as pepper, cinnamon, nutmeg, mace, allspice, ginger, cloves, or such, used to season food and to flavor sauces and pickles.

An herb, on the other hand, is defined as "a seed plant which does not develop a woody tissue as that of a shrub or tree, but is more or less soft or succulent." An herb may be used for medicinal purposes; or because of its scent or flavor, for culinary purposes.

There is but a thin line of distinction between an herb and a spice.

In ancient times, spices were used for incense, for embalming preservatives, as ointments, as perfumes, as antidotes against poisons, as cosmetics, and for medicinal use.

In the Book of Esther, it is stated that when the candidates for the Persian queenship were assembled by King Ahasuerus, they were brought to the royal harem and there treated for "six months with balm and six months with spices."

The first record of the use of spices dates from the age of the pyramids in Egypt— approximately 4,600 years ago. Onions and garlic were fed to the 100,000 laborers who toiled in the construction work under Cheops. These vegetables were administered as medicinal herbs to preserve the health of the laborers.

When herbs became essential in the embalming process, cassia and cinnamon were imported into Egypt from China and Southeast Asia. The interior of the deceased was rinsed with cumin, anise, marjoram, cassia, and cinnamon.

Ancient cuneiform records of medicinal literature have been found in Mesopotamia, dating from the 3rd millennium B. C. These Sumerian clay tablets mention various odoriferous plants. A scroll of cuneiform writing from the great library in Nineveh established by King Ashurbanipal of Assyria (668-633 B.C.) records a long list of aromatic plants, among them thyme, sesame, cardamon, ptarmicha, saffron, poppy, garlic, cumin, coriander, silphium, dill, and myrrh. The Assyrians utilized sesame at a very early date as a vegetable oil.

Spices and herbs were also used at a very early date in China. According to legend, one Shen Nung, the founder of Chinese medicine, is said to have discovered the curative virtues of herbs. Around 2,700 B.C., he is alleged to have written the Pen Ts'ao Ching or The Classic Herbal, the earliest treatise on medicine. It mentions more than 100 medicinal plants. Chinese folk tradition holds that Shen Nung used to plant grasses and then test their properties on himself, sometimes taking as many as 12 of these somewhat poisonous plants a day during his experimentation.

From India, nutmegs and cloves, native to the Moluccas—the Spice Islands—were introduced into China. A tradition has come down to us that in the 3rd century B. C., the courtiers of the royal court were required to carry cloves in their mouths in order to sweeten their breath when addressing the emperor.

Columbus made his journey to America seeking a short way to India in order to import spices. The spices were extremely important to Europe at a time when refrigeration was not known.

Nowadays, international trade in spices amounts to something over $170 million a year. Pepper alone normally accounts for over one-fourth of the world's total trade in spices.

Saffron, from Spain, enjoys the distinction of being far and away the world's costliest spice. Its average import price in the U.S., between 1967 and 1968, exceeded $100.00 per pound, while Portuguese rosemary and Canadian mustard seed have been the least expensive of all spices and herbs. Between 1967 and 1968, the price for these last two has averaged somewhere between 7¢ and 8¢ per pound.

The United States is by far the world's largest importer of spices and herbs. In 1968, this country imported over 150 million pounds of spices, with a value in excess of $60 million.

SPICES

Unusual Spices

Agar	1 oz.	$1.35	*H. Roth & Son*
Alfalfa	4 oz.	1.20	*H. Roth & Son*
Ambrette Seed	4 oz.	4.70	*Caswell-Massey*
Angelica Root	4 oz.	1.50	*Nichols Garden Nursery*
Anthemis	4 oz.	5.10	*Caswell-Massey*
Balm of Gilead Buds	4 oz.	4.20	*Caswell-Massey*
Bayberry Powder	4 oz.	1.50	*Nichols Garden Nursery*
Benzoin Gum Pieces	4 oz.	3.25	*Caswell-Massey*
Bishopswort	1 oz.	.60	*H. Roth & Son*
Black Walnut Hulls	4 oz.	1.30	*H. Roth & Son*
Black Walnut Leaves	4 oz.	1.30	*H. Roth & Son*
Blue Mallow Flower	4 oz.	2.00	*H. Roth & Son*
Blue Stone	4 oz.	2.40	*H. Roth & Son*
Boldo Leaf	4 oz.	1.70	*H. Roth & Son*
Boemboe Bali	¾ oz.	.60	*Maison Glass*
Boemboe Opar	¾ oz.	.60	*Maison Glass*
Boemboe Sesate	¾ oz.	.60	*Maison Glass*
Burdock Root	4 oz.	4.50	*Caswell-Massey*
Calendula	4 oz.	3.35	*Caswell-Massey*
Cassia Buds	4 oz.	7.75	*Caswell-Massey*
Cherry Stalks	4 oz.	4.00	*Caswell-Massey*
Chickweed	4 oz.	4.25	*Caswell-Massey*
Cyani	4 oz.	5.90	*Caswell-Massey*
Deertongue	4 oz.	4.60	*Caswell-Massey*
Elder Flowers	4 oz.	4.95	*Caswell-Massey*
Elderberry Blossom	4 oz.	1.20	*H. Roth & Son*
Elecampane Root	4 oz.	1.50	*Nichols Garden Nursery*
Elm Bark	1 oz.	.40	*H. Roth & Son*
Eucalyptus Leaf	4 oz.	1.20	*H. Roth & Son*
Fenugreek (ground)	4 oz.	.80	*H. Roth & Son*
Flax Seed (ground)	4 oz.	.80	*H. Roth & Son*
Figwort	Pkg.	1.00	*Nichols Garden Nursery*
Flea Seed (whole)	4 oz.	1.20	*H. Roth & Son*
Frankincense	4 oz.	3.85	*Caswell-Massey*
Gumbo File	4 oz.	1.20	*H. Roth & Son*
Hawthorne Berries	4 oz.	1.20	*H. Roth & Son*
Heather	4 oz.	3.20	*Caswell-Massey*
Hops	4 oz.	3.50	*Caswell-Massey*

Unusual Spices

Hyssop Herb	Pkg.	1.00	*Nichols Garden Nursery*
Irish Moss (Carageen)	4 oz.	1.40	*H. Roth & Son*
King Solomon Root	4 oz.	1.65	*Nichols Garden Nursery*
Knotgrass	4 oz.	1.20	*H. Roth & Son*
Krazy Mixed Salt	8 oz.	1.00	*Maison Glass*
Lavender	4 oz.	3.70	*Caswell-Massey*
Lemon Balm	4 oz.	3.85	*Caswell-Massey*
Licorice Root	1 oz.	.45	*H. Roth & Son*
Lime Flower	4 oz.	5.00	*Caswell-Massey*
Maidenhair Fern	4 oz.	4.50	*Caswell-Massey*
Malve	1 oz.	.50	*H. Roth & Son*
Mullein Leaves	Pkg.	1.00	*Nichols Garden Nursery*
Nettles	4 oz.	3.50	*Caswell-Massey*
Origanum	4 oz.	3.50	*Caswell-Massey*
Orris Root Powder	4 oz.	1.50	*Nichols Garden Nursery*
Patchouli Leaves	1 oz.	1.35	*H. Roth & Son*
Plantain	4 oz.	3.75	*Caswell-Massey*
Peppercorn (green)	3½ oz.	1.50	*Maison Glass*
Pesto Alla Genovese	6 oz.	.55	*Manganaro's*
Ragwort	4 oz.	4.95	*Caswell-Massey*
Raspberries (dried)	1 oz.	1.55	*H. Roth & Son*
Red Saunders	4 oz.	3.35	*Caswell-Massey*
Rose Buds	4 oz.	1.40	*H. Roth & Son*
Rose Hips	Pkg.	1.00	*Nichols Garden Nursery*
Rue	4 oz.	4.85	*Caswell-Massey*
Salt, Hickory-smoked	5 oz.	.70	*Maison Glass*
Sambal Nasi Goring	1¾ oz.	.75	*Maison Glass*
Sambal Oelek	1¾ oz.	.60	*Maison Glass*
Sambal Petis	1¾ oz.	.75	*Maison Glass*
St. John's Wort	4 oz.	1.50	*Nichols Garden Nursery*
Saltpeter	4 oz.	1.20	*H. Roth & Son*
Sassafras	1 oz.	.50	*H. Roth & Son*
Star Anise	1 oz.	.45	*H. Roth & Son*
Southernwood	4 oz.	4.95	*Caswell-Massey*
Sumac	4 oz.	1.20	*H. Roth & Son*
Szechuan Pepper	1 oz.	1.98	*H. Roth & Son*
Tamarind	4 oz.	1.70	*H. Roth & Son*
Tansy Herb	4 oz.	1.75	*Nichols Garden Nursery*
Tonka Beans	each	.20	*H. Roth & Son*
Valerian Root	4 oz.	2.50	*H. Roth & Son*
Woodruff	4 oz.	2.15	*H. Roth & Son*
Yarrow	4 oz.	1.20	*H. Roth & Son*

Birds

The bird on the wing is a symbol of man's aspiration to be more than man, to soar above the natural world. The combination of grace and power epitomized by a bird in flight is both nature's pride and man's joy.

The bird's evolutionary progenitor was the reptile, and several birds—such as the ostrich, the penguin, and the kiwi—remain bound to earth. As the bird moved up the evolutionary scale, it developed many fantastic traits. For example, a bird can focus its eyes more quickly than any other living creature. Its sight is astonishingly keen; so is its sense of hearing; its smell, however, is poor.

Before a baby bird is hatched, it has a temporary tooth that enables it to break out of the egg. Full grown, a bird may have a beak strong enough to crack seeds, or long enough to snap up little creatures from the bottom of a stream.

Yet a bird's most extraordinary physical attribute is, of course, its power of flight. Its

wings, breast muscles, streamlined body, and tail feathers work in concert to produce a vision unparalleled in the natural world.

Danish Bird Feeder

This Danish unglazed stoneware bird feeder is 9¾" high and 7" in diameter. $14.68. Postage $6.20. *Den Permanente.*

Live Birds Available For Purchase

Crane (demoiselle)	$165.00	*Trails End Zoo*
Curassow (razor-billed)	87.50	*Trails End Zoo*
Eagle (crested serpent)	125.75	*Grove Pet Ranch*
Eagle (harpy, male)	995.00	*Grove Pet Ranch*
Eagle (harpy, female)	1250.00	*Grove Pet Ranch*
Eagle (tawny)	187.50	*Grove Pet Ranch*
Falcon (luggar, male)	99.50	*Grove Pet Ranch*
Falcon (luggar, female)	129.50	*Grove Pet Ranch*
Falcon (shaheen)	275.00	*Grove Pet Ranch*
Flamingo	185.00	*Trails End Zoo*
Goose (Sebastopol)	17.50	*Trails End Zoo*
Goshawk (shikra)	67.50	*Grove Pet Ranch*
Hawk (Cooper's)	99.50	*Grove Pet Ranch*
Hawk (Savannah, baby)	55.00	*Grove Pet Ranch*
Hawk-eagle (Bonelli)	225.00	*Grove Pet Ranch*
Hawk-eagle (Orante)	475.00	*Grove Pet Ranch*
Kestrel (Indian)	59.50	*Grove Pet Ranch*
Macaw (blue and gold)	150.00	*Trails End Zoo*
Macaw (scarlet)	150.00	*Trails End Zoo*
Ostrich	750.00	*Trails End Zoo*
Owl (brown fish)	69.50	*Grove Pet Ranch*
Owl (great horned)	29.50	*Grove Pet Ranch*
Parrot (Amazon)	45.00	*Trails End Zoo*
Parrot (bee bee)	27.50	*Trails End Zoo*
Parrot (double yellow-head)	70.00	*Trails End Zoo*
Parrot (half-moon)	30.00	*Grove Pet Ranch*
Parrot (red-head)	50.00	*Trails End Zoo*
Pelican	75.00	*Trails End Zoo*
Penguin	125.00	*Trails End Zoo*
Stork (black)	110.00	*Trails End Zoo*
Stork (jabiru)	100.00	*Trails End Zoo*
Stork (white-neck)	110.00	*Trails End Zoo*
Stork (European)	125.00	*Trails End Zoo*
Swan, black	165.00	*Trails End Zoo*
Swan, white	87.50	*Trails End Zoo*
Toucan	45.00	*Trails End Zoo*
Vulture (King)	87.50	*Trails End Zoo*

Yankee Bird Feeder

Each feeding hole has a perch and a baffle inside to keep the feed from spilling. Metal-edged feeding holes will defy the bite of the toughest-toothed squirrel. Hang it near your house and watch the steady flow of birds as they come to dine. 15" long. 2½" in diameter. Made of clear plastic tubing. Not affected by snow or rain. $11.95. Postage $1.29. *House of Minnel.*

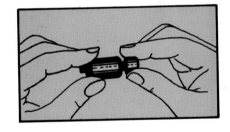

Audubon Bird Call

Imitates birds at a turn of the knob. $1.95 postpaid. *Vermont Country Store.*

Birds

The pioneer people of Salt Lake City, Utah, had watched the summer sun of 1884 bring forth a good crop. They needed the food to get through the coming winter. But out of nowhere an all-consuming mass of crickets swept across the fields. The pioneers fought them in every way they knew, but the crickets kept on eating.

Suddenly, a flock of seagulls arrived to feast on the crickets, gorging themselves until all the marauders were consumed. Fortunately, enough of the crop was left to sustain the people through the winter.

The people of Salt Lake erected a monument to their unexpected saviors and passed a law prohibiting anyone from killing a seagull.

* * *

An unusual bird indeed is the hoatzin, a rare South American species with no close relatives. A crested bird smaller than a pheasant, the hoatzin dines on leaves. But the strangest thing about this bird is that the young have claws on their *wings* in addition to those on their feet. These claws help the baby hoatzins climb about in the trees.

* * *

The social weaver bird of Africa really deserves its name. As many as 90 couples may join to build a huge community nest. A favorite location is a big acacia tree. After the nest is built, each pair of weavers goes to work fashioning its own individual chamber inside the large structure—a bird version of the modern apartment house.

* * *

The fastest bird alive is the swift which comes rightly by its name. This speedster can wing along at better than 200 miles per hour!

Hummingbird Feeder

A nectar of one part sugar and four parts water will attract hummingbirds from miles around to this feeder. For best results, add red vegetable coloring. $6.95 postpaid. *Gokey.*

Tunisian Bird Cage

In the village where these originated, Tunisian craftsmen today faithfully reproduce these 16th-century styled bird cages. Made of hand-woven wire and wood. Colored with non-toxic white enamel. 10' in circumference, 5' high. Base is 27" square. Holds 20 to 30 birds. $350.00. Shipped freight collect. *Treasures of the Universe.*

The Egyptian plover has worked out a mutually satisfactory arrangement with the crocodile: the bird gets food and the crocodile gets service. The plover rides on the crocodile's back and serves as a lookout, emitting shrill cries when danger seems imminent. The plover also digs parasites out of the crocodile's back. When the crocodile finishes its dinner, the big reptile opens up its mouth so that its small helper can hop inside, and pick its teeth clean of uneaten food.

* * *

The smallest of all birds is the bee hummingbird which is about 2¼" long, most of that length being the beak. It takes 18 of these creatures to tip the scale to one ounce.

* * *

The female cuckoo of Europe searches out the egg-filled nest of some hard-working bird and lays her single egg in that nest. Then the cuckoo picks up one of the eggs of its host, drops that egg to the ground, and flies away, never to return, hoping that the substitution won't be noticed. If the returning mother recognizes the strange egg as an interloper, she jabs a hole in it, and rolls it out of the nest.

* * *

Young puffins are fed and fed until they grow larger than their overworked parents. Then their parents fly away. The youngsters are too fat to start food-searching on their own, but well larded as they are, they don't starve. They live off their stored fat, gradually getting thin enough to go out on their own.

* * *

Ostriches feed unhatched eggs to their young. Several female ostriches often lay their eggs in a single nest during the mating season. They add a few each day until there is a total of two dozen. Some of these eggs hatch earlier than others. To feed their hungry babies who cannot eat the rough food of the adult ostrich, the parent birds crack open the unhatched eggs and feed them to their youngsters.

Wren House

North Carolina and Arkansas mountain people handcraft these bird habitations. Made of split red oak. $3.00. Shipped express collect. *Storehouse.*

Polish Bird House

This straw hut is 14" high and is attached atop a tree branch to make an over-all height of 26". $8.50. Postage $1.50. *Hall's.*

Birds

Bird Bath Lady

Carved by the famous Mexican sculptor, Licea, each piece is signed, and carries his distinctive primitive quality: a fluid, undisturbed shape emboldened by rough texture and deeply chiselled detailing. Cast of light grey pompeian stone. Naturally finished to preserve the hand-hewn quality. 27" high. Bowl is 11" in diameter. $65.00 postpaid. *Patio.*

Red Barn Bird Feeder

Miniature barn scene made of wood. $18.00. Postage $1.00. *Pappagallo Shop.*

Bamboo Cage

This sturdy cage, handcrafted in Mexico, is 14½" long by 11¾" wide by 12" high. Five-week delivery. $14.85. Postage $1.25. *Mexican Art Annex.*

The Owl Critic

"Who stuffed that white owl?" No one spoke in
   the shop.
The barber was busy, and he couldn't stop;
The customers, waiting their turns, were all reading
The "Daily," the "Herald," the "Post," little
   heeding
The young man who blurted out such a blunt
   question;
Not one raised a head, or even made a suggestion;
      And the barber kept on shaving.
"Don't you see, Mr. Brown,"
Cried the youth, with a frown,
"How wrong the whole thing is,
How preposterous each wing is
How flattened the head is, how jammed down the
   neck is—
In short, the whole owl, what an ignorant wreck 't is!
I make no apology;
I've learned owl-cology.
I've passed days and nights in a hundred collections,
And cannot be blinded to any deflections
Arising from unskilful fingers that fail
To stuff a bird right, from his beak to his tail.
Mister Brown! Mister Brown!
Do take that bird down,
Or you'll soon be the laughing-stock all over town!"
      And the barber kept on shaving.

"I've *studied* owls,
And other night-fowls,
And I tell you
What I know to be true;
An owl cannot roost
With his limbs so unloosed;
No owl in this world
Ever had his claws curled,
Ever had his legs slanted,
Ever had his bill canted,
Ever had his neck screwed
Into that attitude.
He can't *do* it, because
'Tis against all bird-laws.
Anatomy teaches
Ornithology preaches,
An owl has a toe
That *can't* turn out so!

I've made the white owl my study for years,
And to see such a job almost moves me to tears!
Mr. Brown, I'm amazed
You should be so gone crazed
As to put up a bird
In that posture absurd!
To *look* at that owl really brings on a dizziness;
The man who stuffed *him* don't half know his
   business!"
      And the barber kept on shaving.

"Examine those eyes.
I'm filled with surprise
Taxidermists should pass
Off on you such poor glass;
So unnatural they seem
They'd make Audubon scream,
And John Burroughs laugh
To encounter such chaff.
Do take that bird down;
Have him stuffed again, Brown!"
      And the barber kept on shaving.

"With some sawdust and bark
I could stuff in the dark
An owl better than that.
I could make an old hat
Look more like an owl
Than that horrid fowl,
Stuck up there so stiff like a side of coarse leather.
In fact, about *him* there's not one natural feather."

Just then, with a wink and a sly normal lurch,
The owl, very gravely, got down from his perch,
Walked round, and regarded his fault-finding critic
(Who thought he was stuffed) with a glance
   analytic,
And then fairly hooted, as if he should say:
"Your learning's at fault *this* time, anyway;

Don't waste it again on a live bird, I pray.
I'm an owl; you're another. Sir Critic, good day!"
      And the barber kept on shaving.

                              James Thomas Fields

Birds

The size of a parrot's vocabulary depends upon a variety of factors: the patience and perseverance of the trainer; the age at which the parrot is trained; and of course, the talent of the individual bird. Well-trained birds can accumulate a vocabulary of a few hundred words, but several birds have been taught to utter fairly complex sentences or passages.

There have been fairly reliable reports that a certain parrot was trained to recite the Lord's Prayer entire. According to the United States Biological Survey, there is no reason to doubt the claim on biological grounds.

*　*　*

There is one family of birds whose young can fly immediately after being hatched. These birds are the mound builders, natives of Australia and some South Sea islands, which emerge from the shell fully feathered.

*　*　*

The toucan's bill, which is bigger than its body, gives it an ungainly, comical appearance. But in spite of its large size, the thin-walled bill is lightweight and easy to carry.

*　*　*

The Arctic tern winters in the Antarctic and summers in Greenland and Alaska.

*　*　*

A hornbill must find just the right size hole in a tree for a nest. The female slips inside and there lays her eggs.

The male seals off the entrance with mud, leaving only a narrow slit. Inside, the female is both protected and imprisoned while incubating her eggs. She gets food from her mate by sticking her bill out of the slit. When the young are full grown, the seal is broken, and the young leave the home with their mother.

The largest bird on earth is the North African ostrich which weighs as much as 345 pounds, and whose height sometimes exceeds nine feet.

*　*　*

The grebe, the mute swan, some ducks, and the loon have a special way of caring for their young. Very often, especially at the first sign of danger, the crested grebe sinks until its back is level with the surface of the water. Its young climb onto its back. Then the parent grebe rises to its swimming position, and with strong strokes carries them across the water to safety.

*　*　*

The tropical man-of-war, or frigate bird likes a fish dinner. But it doesn't fish in the way most birds do. Instead, it waits until another bird has done the work. Then it swoops down and beats the bird with its wings. The unlucky bird, trying to defend itself, lets go of the fish. The swift man-of-war dives, snatches the fish, and zooms away.

Sometimes this robber does its own fishing in mid-air above the ocean. It dives down and grabs flying fish when they sail above water.

*　*　*

The brilliant pink flamingo goes to the unappetizing bottoms of lakes and bogs for its meals. Standing in fairly shallow water, it plunges its head and long neck straight down into the mud so that it seems to be standing on its head.

With the upper part of its beak, the flamingo scoops up the mud. Then it strains the mud through its specially built, immovable lower beak. What's left—small mollusks and other little creatures—it eats.

*　*　*

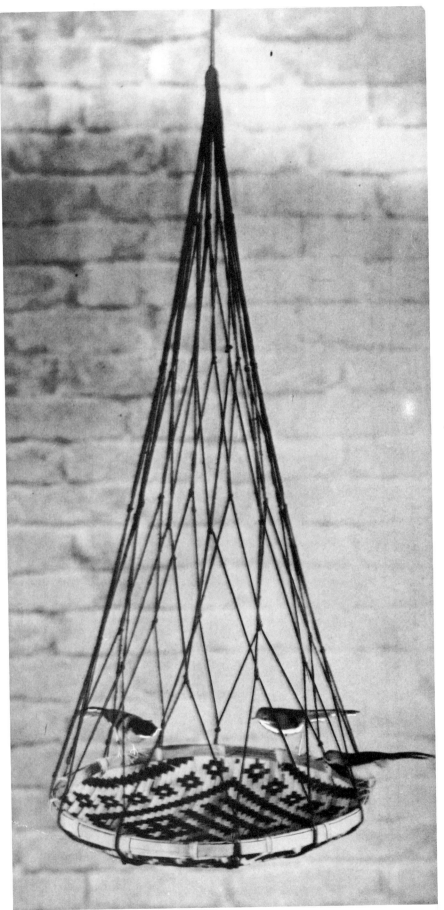

Netted Bird Feeder

A brown and tan handwoven bamboo tray, 13½" in diameter is set in a hand-knotted green netting, 40" long. Can be filled with two cups of seed and outfitted with two small tree branches to provide perches. Can also serve as a planter. $3.60 postpaid. *Duncraft.*

Birdville Hotel

Precision cut pieces of mahogany plywood come in a snap-together kit, requiring no tools, no nails, and no glue. 7" by 12" by 7¼". $3.45. Postage 78¢. *Suburbia.*

Dig These Cool Tools

> *Work is love made visible.*
> Kahlil Gibran (1883-1931), THE PROPHET

> *Work is the sustenance of noble minds.*
> Seneca (4? B.C.–A.D. 65),
> EPISTULAE AD LUCILIUM

> *All work, even cotton-spinning, is noble; work is alone noble. . . . A life of ease is not for any man, nor for any god.*
> Thomas Carlyle (1795-1881),
> PAST AND PRESENT, Bk. iii, ch. 4

> *Good work makes beautiful things, and good work lasts.*
> Lord Dunsany (1878-1957), MY IRELAND

> *Sweet is the memory of past labor.*
> Euripides (480-406 B.C.), ANDROMEDA

> *Toil, says the proverb, is the sire of fame.*
> Idem, LICYMNIUS

> *Work is no disgrace: it is idleness which is a disgrace.*
> Hesiod (c. 735 B.C.), WORKS AND DAYS

> *Employment is nature's physician, and is essential to human happiness.*
> Galen (130-201)

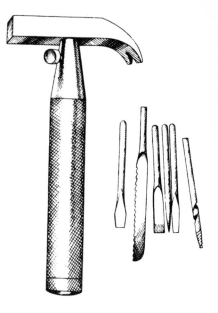

Magic Hammer

The handle contains two screwdrivers, a chisel, a gimlet, an awl, and a saw. Imported from Germany. $10.75. Postage $1.15. *Hoffritz.*

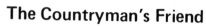

The Countryman's Friend

A versatile tool which cuts, hammers, and digs. It is 17" long, and weighs 1 lb. 7 oz. Very sharp, rustproof blade with hardwood handle. Comes with metal sheath and with belt clip. $19.95. Postage $1.50. *Vermont Country Store.*

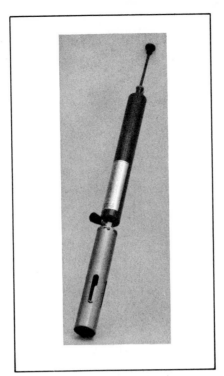

Microflame Torch

A self-contained miniature welding tool that utilizes gas. It produces a pinpoint flame which burns at 5000° Fahrenheit, using cylinders of oxygen and butane gas. Complete set includes torch, flame tips, torch tool, gaskets, two oxygen tanks, one butane tank, instructions, welding book. Size (less tube) 5¼" by 2" by 1¼". $21.95. Postage $2.00. *Gallery.*

Versa Drill

Powered by any 12-volt battery, this drill has power enough to work through wood, fiberglass, or metal. Because of a 20:1 ratio between motor speed and output shaft speed, its 15,000 rpm is geared down to a 750 rpm no-load speed; the drill, therefore, will draw no more power than your windshield wipers. $24.95. Postage 40¢. *Chris Craft.*

Power Flame

Weeds between flagstones are cleared fast, and ice melted off walks with this power flame apparatus. Uses kerosene, so there are no cords or batteries. $19.95. Postage $2.00. *Haverhill's.*

Rock Tumbler

Will process rocks, pebbles, shells, pieces of glass and metal to a gleaming finish. Set with attachments, supplies, and manual. $29.40. Postage $2.50. *J. D. Browne.*

Self-Priming Pump

This powerful, self-priming pump works off an ordinary electric drill. Pumps up to 200 gallons per hour on a ¼" drill motor. Attaches to any garden hose. $7.95. Postage 99¢. *House of Minnel.*

Electric Scissors

Cuts the thinnest paper or the heaviest fabric. $5.95. Postage $1.50. *Haverhill's.*

Dig These Cool Tools

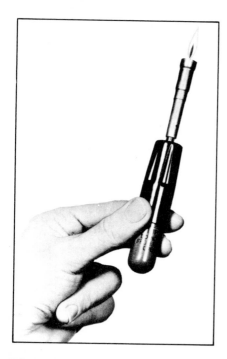

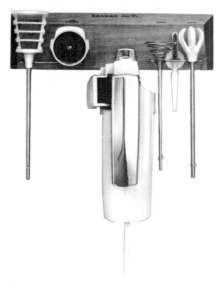

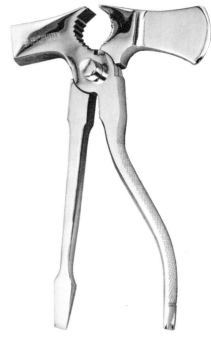

Mini-Torch

A pocket-size blow torch and soldering kit. Uses a tiny replaceable fuel cartridge that gives 30 minutes of heat at 3500°. Complete with soldering tip, wire, and two butane charges. $4.95. Postage 75¢. *Chris Craft.*

Can-Do

This portable electric tool opens cans of any size, sharpens knives, mixes drinks, whips cream, mashes potatoes, whisks, stirs, and beats a variety of foods. All the attachments store on a wooden wall rack. Runs on 110-volt AC current. With all attachments and rack $31.95. Postage 80¢. *Chris Craft.*

Hausmeister Tool

Extremely versatile, this tomahawk-like tool is a screwdriver, a wrench, a hammer, a nail lever, a wire cutter, and a hatchet all in one. Made of chrome steel. $15.95. Postage $2.00. *Invento.*

Stud Finder

If you want to hang something on the wall and avoid cracking the plaster, the best bet is to drive into the wooden stud. This gadget enables you to pinpoint the stud. $1.49. Postage 65¢. *Hanover House.*

Versa-Tool

Will cut, grind, polish, drill, deburr, buff, sand, rout and shape. The home hobbyist will find this a jack-of-all-trades. Can be used with plastic, wood, or metal. Has a 3000-RPM motor and a two-foot flexible shaft. $19.95. Postage $1.95. *Childcraft.*

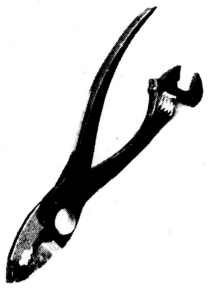

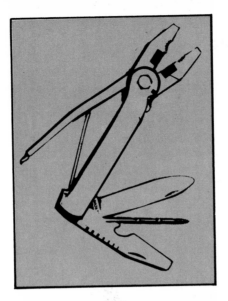

Electrician's Knife

Contains cutting blade, pliers, wire cutter, insulation stripper, screwdriver, cap lifter, gimlet, wire stripper for 7 gauges, and steel leader cutter. Imported from France. $13.50. Postage $1.15. *Hoffritz*.

Fortune Hunter

Want to go prospecting for gold? Or any other metal or mineral fortune? This dectector is equipped with a 5" search coil. 29" by 10" by 10½", 4½ lbs. Complete with instructions. $89.95. Postage $3.00. *Garrett*.

Combination Pliers

A tool that acts as pliers, wire cutter, wrench, and screwdriver all in one. 6" long, $4.00 postpaid. *L. L. Bean*.

Electric Pencil

Will engrave just as easily as you write with a pencil. Will permanently inscribe wood, plastics, metal, pottery. 110-volt motor. $7.99. Postage $1.20. *Sunset House*.

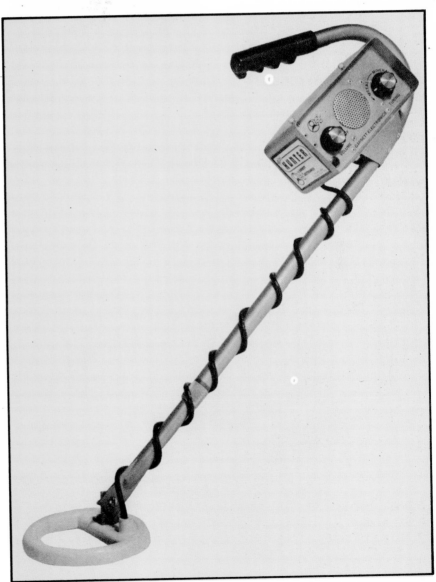

Dig These Cool Tools

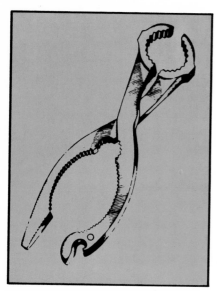

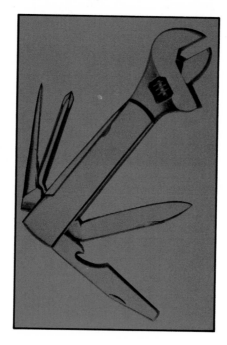

Multipurpose Wrench

One twist opens caps of jars, large and small. Hook pries open vacuum and anchor-type covers. And when it is not opening things, this chrome-plated tool can be used as ice tongs, a nut cracker, or to shell fish. $6.50. Postage 65¢. *Hoffritz*.

Combination Knife

Contains an offset wrench, cutting blade, screwdriver, cap lifter, Phillips screwdriver, awl. Imported from France. $17.00. Postage $1.15. *Hoffritz*.

Open-all Tool

Ten different sizes of wrenches in this one tool. Will fit 99% of all the nuts and bolts in the world. No adjustments needed. Small head on one end for hard-to-get-at-places. 4" long by 1" wide. $1.00. Postage 60¢. *Downs*.

Speedy Inflator

Only 6½" long, 4¾" wide, and 4¾" across, this air compressor provides up to 60 pounds of pressure. The 12-volt inflator uses the battery power of your boat or your car to blow out a clogged fuel line, inflate a rubber dinghy, a beach toy, or a bike tire. Comes with a cigarette lighter plug. 3 feet of cord, 10 feet of pneumatic hose, and an assortment of inflator nozzles. $29.95. Postage $1.00. *Chris Craft*.

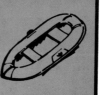

TOYS

If you've ever watched a father and son with a new set of electric trains, you might get the idea that it isn't just children who play with toys.

Toys, or miniature replicas of real things, were in many cases made by adults for use in religious rites. Likenesses of the animals man hunted for food, as well as personifications of his deities and the forces he feared, were used by primitive man to protect himself.

The rattles that infants love to drool over were originally meant to scare away devils, as well as to keep the tyke quiet. Even today, any toy that can keep a child occupied for more than a few minutes is considered by many harried parents to have magical powers.

Teeter Totter

Pre-tested to 300 lbs., the Teeter Totter ain't just for kids—second-childhood adults can play, too. This 2' high, 6' long seesaw adjusts to two heights. Made of rustproof metal. Comes in yellow, black, and white. Stop and Go seats are in red and green. $45.00. Shipped express collect. *Patio*.

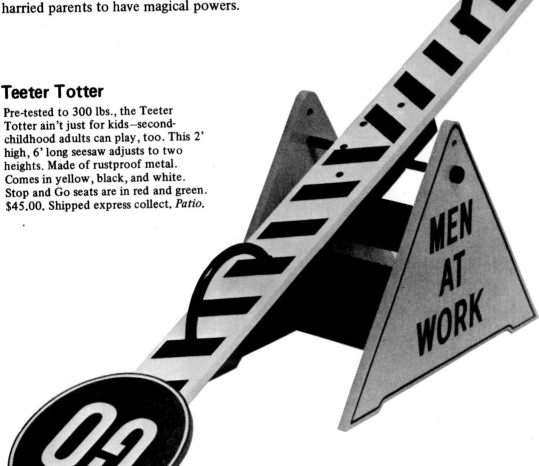

TOYS

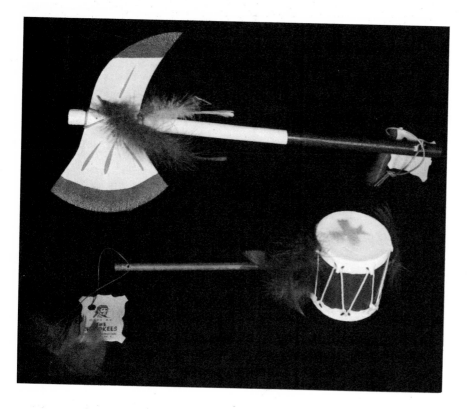

Tomahawk and Rattle

Brightly painted and mounted on a wood handle with ornamental feathers, this tomahawk has a soft rubber head for safety. The rattle, also decorated with ornamental feathers, has a leather head. Made by the Cherokees. $1.75 for both. Postage 75¢. *Casco Bay Trading Post.*

A little-known invention by Thomas A. Edison is a doll that talked, the first ever to do so. Built in 1888, the doll had a small phonograph in its body that enabled it to recite a dozen nursery rhymes. After making several hundreds of these dolls, Edison was informed that his company had previously sold the right to manufacture phonograph toys to another firm. Although that firm had never exercised its right, Edison stopped production and had the dolls destroyed. Of the few he saved and presented to friends, only two are believed to be in existence today.

Soda Fountain

This all-wood soda fountain is fun no matter which side of the counter you're on. Comes with plates, plastic tableware, ice cream scoop, soda glasses, flavoring, napkins, and battery-operated blender. 36" long, 41" high. $69.95. Shipped express collect. *F.A.O. Schwarz.*

Tree House

This solid wood tree house can be reached only by climbing the retractable rope ladder, and then closing the trap door. Measures 74" by 63" at the railing, and sits atop 10' poles which can be sunk into the ground or held by braces which are included. $250.00. Shipped express collect. *F.A.O. Schwarz.*

Sno-Star Skimobile

Utilizing 10" wide track skis, this steel and fiberglass Sno-Star can travel at 13 m.p.h. It is powered by a 4 h.p. gasoline engine with a 3-quart capacity. Brakes, throttle, and safety switch are mounted on the handlebars. 58" long, 24" wide, and 24" high. Can carry up to 135 lbs. $495.00. Shipped express collect. *F.A.O. Schwarz.*

TOYS

Mini-Bike Saddle Mate

One-piece aluminum mini-bike has coil spring. $79.00. Shipped collect. *Game Time Inc.*

Horse and Sulky

A plush-covered wooden horse with a bucket-seat sulky, and bicycle wheels with chain drive. $135.00. Shipped express collect. *F.A.O. Schwarz.*

Frontier Fort

Made of rough wood stained a leather brown, this fort is big enough for the neighborhood army. It's 6' sq., and stands 64" to the top of the wall and 73" to the top of the lookout turrets. A 30" ledge with mounting ladder runs along the length of the rear wall. The assembled sides hook together at the corners. $199.00. Shipped express collect. *F.A.O. Schwarz.*

Jerusalem

This model city arrives in rolls of paper, complete with walls, turrets, towers, mountains, and various religious pilgrims. When built, it is 12" high and 12" across. Imported from the Holy Land. $5.00. Postage 60¢. *Kenton Collection.*

Stockade

This 16" square, all-wood stockade comes with 20 cavalry defenders and attacking Indians. $19.95. Postage $2.55. *F.A.O. Schwarz.*

Besieged Castle

This exquisitely detailed castle consists of 43 plastic figures which make up the defenders and attacking forces, the scaling ladders, catapult, besieged tower, and moat drawbridge. The figures are 1¾" high and include archers and sword-bearing knights on foot and on horseback. 28½" wide by 24" high by 18" deep. $69.95. Postage $14.00. *F.A.O. Schwarz.*

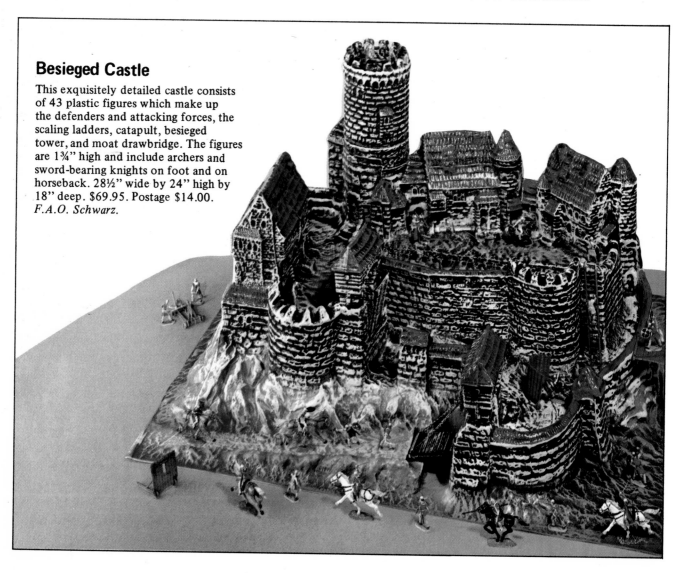

Sioux War Bonnet

This chief's bonnet is made of imitation eagle tail feathers. Each headdress is made to your order and your choice of colors for fluffies. Imitation beaded browband, mirror rosettes, white rabbit-fur side drops, and fluffies all over the back of the hat. $26.00 postpaid. *Grey Owl.*

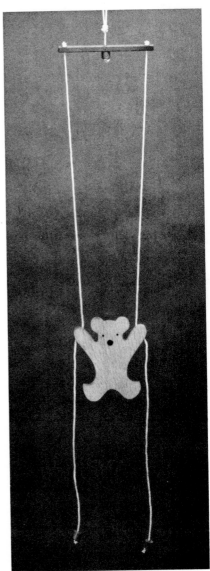

Climbing Bear

Pull the strings and the little wooden bear climbs to the top. Release the strings and he slides back down. Overall height, 4½'. $3.00. Postage 75¢. *Appalachian Spring.*

Limberjack

With a little help, this Early-American gentleman does a merry dance on the paddle. Made of softwood. $6.00. Shipped express collect. *Storehouse.*

TOYS

Spinning Fool Top

The early-American settlers used to carve a spinning fool top as a toy for their children. And it seems the children handle this instrument very well, indeed. Adults, on the other hand, have a bit more trouble. The record spinning time is 12 minutes. See if you can beat it. 7½" long, 5" high, handmade of Tennessee hardwood. $2.95. Postage 45¢. *The Spinning Fool Top.*

Indian Headdress

A colorful bonnet made by the Cherokee Indians. $1.95. Postage 75¢. *Casco Bay Trading Post.*

Caboose Toy Chest

The roof of this plastic toy chest lifts easily, revealing the toys stored inside. But this red and black caboose is a toy in itself. Well-hidden casters allow it to be ridden, pulled, or pushed. Large enough for a small boy to fit into. 14¾" by 10" by 33¼" long. $24.95. Postage $6.05. *Hammacher Schlemmer.*

Tug and Barge

This tandem really moves in the tub. Tug toots and pulls the barge behind it. Works on batteries (not included). $5.95. Postage $1.50. *Haverhill's.*

Camping

Funny, how the daily struggle of one generation becomes the leisure recreation of another. Time was, not so long ago, that Americans out on the western plains, or in the mountains or deserts, would have no choice but to sleep and eat under the stars. Their only concessions to comfort would be a bedroll, some eating utensils, and some preserved rations. For these pioneers, roughing it was not a weekend's diversion but a life's work.

Today, we are a great deal further removed from nature than were our forefathers. A week or a weekend away from the chrome-and-steel jungle or the pre-packaged utopia we call home affords an invigorating perspective on what life is all about. It links us to a past and to a future that are greater than our quotidian scuffling for survival. To modern man in this technological age, a week in the woods is perhaps a necessary diversion.

One-Man Pack Boat

This rugged neopryl boat weighs only nine lbs. Its two air chambers blow up to 65" long and 38" wide. Deflated, it rolls down to 9" in diameter, 19" wide. Complete with oars, pump, and carry bag. $39.50. Postage $1.00. *Orvis.*

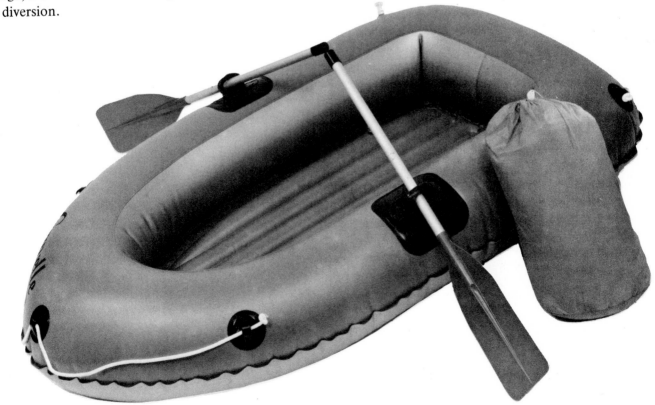

Camping

Survival Tent

Providing insulation from the cold and wind, the survival tent is a necessity on high altitude expeditions in the event of an enforced bivouac. Made of a proofed nylon material, it is fitted with retractable tube ventilators and drawcord closures, and may be slept in, if necessary. The cord along the ridge permits the sack to be hung, where terrain permits. More typically, it is supported by the two occupants who sit opposite one another with their heads at the extreme ends in the sack. Measures 6' by 6'6" open; folds to 8" by 11" by 1¼". $16.25. Postage $2.65. *Robert Lawrie Ltd.*

Wendy Bag

Two sleeping bags join together to make this roomy double, with 8' zippers down each side. Filled with 2 lbs. of prime goose down, this snug outfit should keep a family of three warm in any temperature above 10 degrees. Weighs 4 lbs. Made of nylon. Available in green, dark blue, and brown. 7' 8" long. $64.50. Postage $2.00. *Kreeger & Son Ltd.*

Portable Toilet

The light metal frame is of standard height and folds compactly. Uses disposable plastic bags. Weighs 4 lbs. Comes with 6 bags. $5.85 postpaid. *Gokey.*

Man is not as powerful as the bear, nor as swift as the deer, nor as agile as the cat, nor as wily as the fox. On purely physical terms, man is no match for the denizens of the wild. What evens the contest is man's ability to form and use tools.

With a few pieces of basic equipment, man can hold his own in the wild, even under the direst of circumstances. On these pages, you'll find a few items any outdoorsman might consider purchasing before venturing too far from civilization.

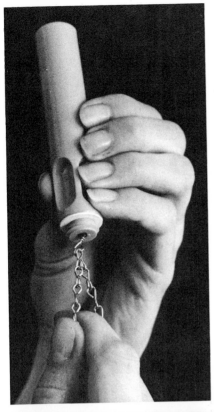

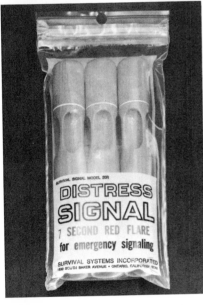

Explorer Minilantern

Sheds the equivalent of a 75-watt bulb light, and can be regulated from bright to dim. Uses a cartridge which lasts an average of eight hours. 11" high. 2¾" in diameter. Weighs 20 oz. with 9 oz. cartridge (not included). $11.95. Postage $2.00. *Triangle Stores.*

Ministove

This safe stove measures 12½" high. It is only 3" in diameter, and folds to 12½" high, 3" wide, and 3" deep. Nickel-plated anti-clog 4,800 BTU burner. Handles everything from a soup can to an 11" fry pan. Weighs 1½ lbs. with cartridge (not included). $9.95. Postage $2.00. *Triangle Stores.*

Survival Signal

Three complete self-contained signal flares come in a pocket pack. Each weighs only one oz. A flare shoots up hundreds of feet high, burning brilliant red for more than seven seconds, and visible for miles, even in broad daylight. Set off by putting a finger through the firing ring and pulling. Rustproof. Buoyant. Functions in any weather, including downpour and high winds. Dissipates high in the air; no danger of forest fire. $6.95. Postage $1.00. *Orvis.*

Camping

Thermal Mugs

These vacuum lined cups will keep coffee steaming hot, or will keep cocktails well chilled. Each comes with a tight-fitting insulated screw-top cap that makes carrying the beverage across a slanting deck or across an unpaved terrain somewhat less of an adventure. Beige plastic. $5.00 each. Postage 20¢. *Chris Craft.*

Ice-O-Magic

By adding water, you activate Ice-O-Magic, a dry chemical refrigerant. Once activated, the package will keep food and beverages cold for as long as 12 hours. And because salt water works as effectively as fresh water, the compound is as practical on boating and fishing trips as it is for camping, picnicking, and as a stand-by for refrigerator failure in the home. $1.25. Postage $1.50. *Chris Craft.*

Miniheater

An infrared radiation heater which provides instant heat indoors and outdoors using a cartridge (not included) which lasts about seven hours. The precision valve provides controlled heat between 500 and 2,000 BTU. Adjustable wire-guard heat reflector. 13½" high, 5½" in diameter. Weighs 20 oz. with 11 oz. cartridge. $13.50. Postage $2.00. *Triangle Stores.*

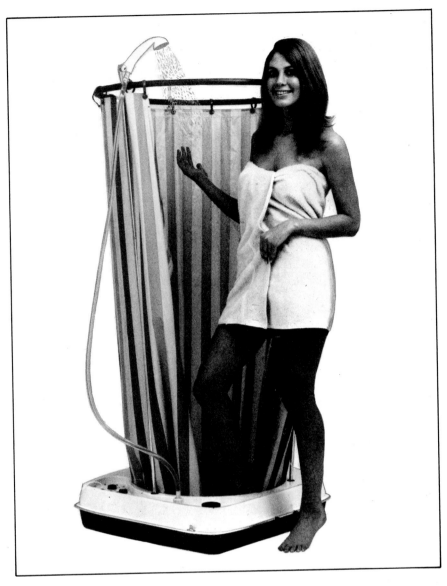

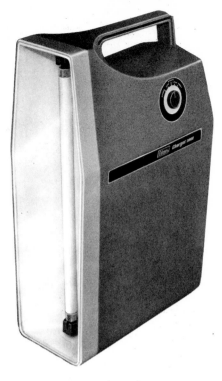

Electric Lantern

Probably the first portable lantern with rechargeable wet cell battery, this lantern provides up to 3,000 hours of brilliant light from a single 8-volt battery. Battery is spill-proof. Battery life begins only when tap water is added; does not deteriorate during storage. Full charge provides 20 hours of power. Battery can be recharged 150 times. Made of plastic. Fluorescent bulb. 13-1/4" by 8-7/8" by 4-3/4". $60.00. Postage $2.40. *Triangle Stores.*

Portable Shower

Just what the road-weary traveler might need to take the dust off: a portable shower. Loads to its six U.S. gallon capacity from the faucet—more than enough water to take a five-minute shower. Runs on 12-volts, 1.5 amps. Power sources may be a dry cell battery pack or 110-volt AC converter. Polished white styrene foot basin is 22" in diameter, 6" deep. Bottom and cover are plastic, and open to 5' high, with an upper ring 30" in diameter. Shower closes into a suitcase-like container, 30" long, 28" wide, and 6" high, weighing 20 lbs. $149.95. Postage $4.50. *Chris Craft.*

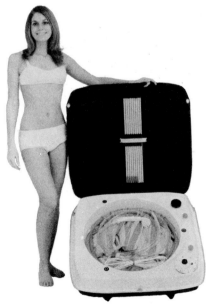

Camping

Net Hat

When bugs become unbearable, this chapeau will provide protection. The hat folds up into very small space. One size fits all. $3.50. Postage $1.00. *Orvis.*

Insta-Hot Water Heater

An instant and continuous flow of hot water is provided by this water heater. You simply press a button that automatically lights the burner. In no time at all, you are pumping a stream of 185-degree hot water with which to cook, shave, wash clothes, or wash dishes. Fully portable, the heater stands only 14" high, weighs but 7 pounds. Fueled by LP gas cylinders. $39.95. Postage $1.80. *Chris Craft.*

Two-Way Thermo Bag

Two containers inside this fiberglass insulated carrying bag permit food and drinks to be kept hot and cold at the same time. Watertight containers are made of vinyl. Rust-proof zippers. Outer pocket carries accessories. 21" long, 11" wide, 11" high. $13.95. Postage 95¢. *Gokey.*

Prairie Schooner

This water-repellent, mildew-resistant tent has an external frame of fiberglass ribs and stainless steel ferrules. Four cots fit easily into this 12' model. Zippered storm flap; screened rear window. 12' model weighs 37 lbs. $125.00. 9' model, weighs 33 lbs. $105.00. Both models 6'2'' high. Shipped express collect. *Triangle Stores.*

Jungle Hammock

Based on U.S. Army design, this hammock has a cotton seat and nylon-screened walls that are extra-strong, waterproof, and mildew-proof. A full-length zipper runs along one side to permit easy access. The vinyl-coated roof is waterproof. Easily converts to a one-man tent. Olive-drab color. Complete with two 5' lengths of 10 mm. sisal rope. Hammock is 107'' long, 27'' wide, 18'' high. Weighs 2½ lbs. $19.99. Postage $2.10. *Morsan.*

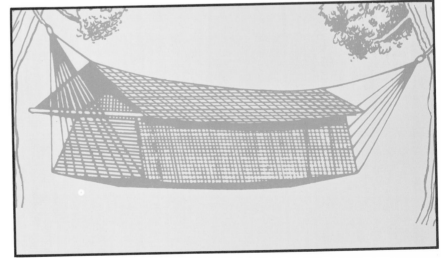

Camping

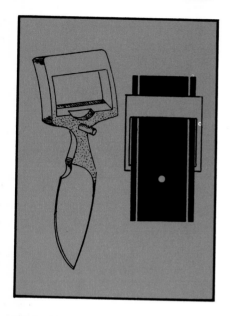

Propane Lantern

A built-in regulator controls light output and fuel flow; at any temperature, at any altitude, there is no wasted energy and no pressure build-up in the hose to reduce efficiency. The hose connection has a safety shut-off. Fueled from a 16.4 oz. disposable bottle, or with an adaptor, from a bulk tank. A Pyrex glove resists knocks and scratches, while a Silk-Lite mantle sheds steady, controllable light. $18.50. Postage $1.85. *Triangle Stores.*

Belt Knife

In an emergency, a knife is drawn from this belt and put into use in less than a second. This stainless steel knife, which also serves as a bottle opener, is an almost unnoticeable part of a top-grain leather belt. Black or brown. $30.00. Postage $1.00. *Collins Bros.*

Pop-up Tent

Water-repellent, canvas tent erects in a mere 90 seconds. Just remove it from bag, link the fiberglass rods together, hold it erect, and push down until lock clicks. The tent is up, and may be lifted into place. 9' diameter, 6' high. Sleeps four adults. Zippered storm flaps; two screened windows. Ground cloth is sewn in. Two poles for erecting canopy are supplied. Entire tent weighs 32 lbs. $105.00. Shipped express collect. *Triangle Stores.*

Solar Cooker

The sun's rays will cook skewered food in minutes without matches, charcoal, flame, or smoke. 12" by 12" by 4". $9.95. Postage $1.50. *Haverhill's.*

Portable Sink

Carrying its own 5-gallon water supply, this portable sink is great for washing clothes, dishes, and people. It also provides a reserve supply of pure drinking water. Made of rugged polyethylene, it has a leak-proof cap, a pump-action faucet, a drain plug, and a drain hose. Comes in avocado green. $13.95. Postage $1.00. *Chris Craft.*

Wonder Blanket

This great blanket was developed by the U.S. space program. It weighs only 12 ounces and folds into a compact carrying case, opens to 56" by 84". It will effectively insulate against cold and wetness in even severe weather. On the other hand, the silver-treated side which reflects sunlight can be used to promote a suntan. Its grommeted corners attach to uprights for use as a lean-to or a make-shift tent. $5.98. Postage 75¢. *Triangle Stores.*

Folding Camp Oven

Heavy-gauge steel oven measures 11 5/8" on a side when open, folds flat for transporting and storing. Works on Coleman stoves, electric hot plates, and gas burners. Easy-to-read thermometer; adjustable steel rack. $9.50. Postage $1.00. *Laacke and Joys.*

Camping

Dual Thermos

Independently insulated compartments enable you to carry both hot and cold beverages at one time. Each compartment holds two quarts. Unbreakable polypropylene liner. $6.95. Postage 75¢. *Chris Craft.*

Bleuet Stove

Gas stove requires no priming or pumping to start or maintain flame. Non-refillable Gaz C 300 butane cartridge burns up to 3½ hours. Not recommended for extreme cold, unless cartridge can be kept above freezing (inside a sleeping bag). Cartridge not included. $7.45. Postage $1.25. *Taylor Gifts.*

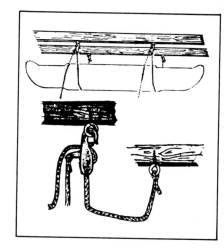

Boat Trick

Stores duck boat, canoe, or fishing boat easily, safely, and out of the way, suspended from the rafters of your garage. Self-locking pulley enables you to quickly lift boat from top of car. Release mechanism permits lowering. $13.95. Postage 75¢. *Laacke and Joys.*

Lightweight Stove

A complete unit enclosed in a metal box that measures 5" by 5" by 3". Easy-fill tank pops out when box is opened. Stove has built-in self-cleaning device. Primed with white gas or alcohol. No pumping necessary to start or maintain flame. Weighs only 1¾ lbs. $12.95. Postage $1.25. *Taylor Gifts.*

Gems for the Precious

Whether true beauty lies without or within, a
jewel is a rare and a precious thing. The most
precious stone today is the ruby, which after
1955 became increasingly rare as supplies from
Ceylon and Burma dwindled. Carat for carat
(one carat equals 200 milligrams), a flawless
natural ruby of good color is more valuable than
a diamond. An excellent six-carat ruby, for instance, recently brought $30,000 on the open
market.

If rubies have topped diamonds in the gem
hierarchy, diamonds nevertheless remain a girl's
best friend. The diamond is the most durable of
all gems—90 times harder than the next hardest
mineral, corundum. Commercially, the diamond
is used to cut other stones.

If heated sufficiently, diamonds will burn.
Although an ordinary fire will not ignite them, a
blow torch will do the job easily. Diamonds are
not affected until the temperature reaches from
1,400 to 1,607 degrees Fahrenheit, depending
on the diamond's hardness. Such high temperatures are not common in ordinary fires, but they
were achieved in the great 1906 fire which destroyed San Francisco.

The largest diamond ever found was the 1½-
pound Cullinan diamond, unearthed in South
Africa in 1905. Other notable diamonds: the
Koh-i-noor, now among the British crown
jewels; the Hope diamond, the largest known
blue in existence; the Star of Africa No. 1, cut
from the Cullinan; the Tiffany, an orange-yellow
diamond; and the Dresden, a greenish diamond.

The green variety of beryl is known as
emerald; the blue is aquamarine. Highly prized

in antiquity, the emerald was a particular favorite in pre-Columbian Mexico and Peru. An
11,000-carat emerald was reportedly found in
South Africa in 1956.

Sapphire is a variety of transparent blue
corundum. It is mined primarily in Asia and
Australia, though some sapphires are to be
found in Montana. The "Black Star Sapphire of
Queensland" is the largest cut gem-quality
sapphire. Between 1953 and 1955, this huge
gem was fashioned to form a bust of then President Dwight D. Eisenhower.

If you are fervidly fond of some female, the
thing to remember is that no woman is so beautiful that a lustrous gem will not make her more
so.

Medallion

18-carat gold medallion is 2½" wide.
$1,295.00 postpaid. *Mayors.*

Gems for the Precious

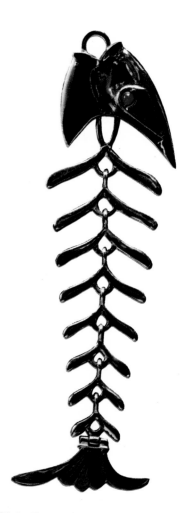

Kitten Brooch

Tiger eyes in enamel and 14-carat gold are the elements that make up this attractive 1 3/8" high, 1 1/8" wide pin. $289.00 postpaid. *Mayors.*

White Owl Brooch

Made of yellow gold, studded with diamonds. Made in England. $1,200.00 postpaid. *Garrard.*

Elephant Brooch

Made of 18-carat gold. From Amsterdam. $215.00 postpaid. *Bonebakker.*

Pooch Brooch

A diamond bow is the outstanding feature of this piece of 14-carat gold jewelry. 1¾" high, 1" wide. $350.00 postpaid. *Mayors.*

Fish Brooch

Made of 18-carat shiny yellow gold with green and blue enamel. Made in Venice. $220.00 postpaid. *Gherardi and Ghilardi.*

Donkey Brooch

18-carat platinum. Made in England. $537.50 postpaid. *Garrard.*

Today, most jewelry adorns the hands, faces, and necks of women. But in ancient Rome, men sported more baubles and bangles than their mates. In fact, unmarried Roman girls were actually prohibited by law from wearing pearls. The pearls were worn instead by young men, who placed the pearls in tiny bells which, hanging from their ears, tinkled gaily.

* * *

The ancient Incas of Peru were masters at decorating their teeth. Unlike primitive tribesmen today who often grind their teeth down to fine points, the Incas inlaid their teeth with gold and semi-precious jewels. When an Inca maiden smiled, it was a very bright smile indeed. The custom was adopted briefly in the west; some wealthy women who had more diamonds than they knew what to do with inserted genuine sparklers in their front teeth.

Koala Bear Brooch
14-carat gold, 1¾" high, 2¼" wide. $269.00 postpaid. *Mayors.*

Owl Brooch
Made of 18-carat gold and rhodolite. Made in England. $180.00 postpaid. *Garrard.*

Bird Brooch
This Georgian bird of blue enamel, studded with diamonds, holds a diamond drop in its beak. $975.00 postpaid. *Bloom and Son.*

Cat Brooch
Made of 18-carat gold and quartz. Made in England. $280.00 postpaid. *Garrard.*

Chicken Brooch
With rubies, diamonds, and 18-carat gold, this has just gotta be the best dressed chick in town. $275.00 postpaid. *A.E. Köchert.*

Flexible Fish
Flexible fish with green crisophrase stone eyes. Made of 18-carat gold. Made in Venice. $110.00 postpaid. *Gherardi and Ghilardi.*

Gems for the Precious

Bee Brooch

Victorian in style, this pin has diamond wings, a cabochon amethyst body, and opal eyes. $1,625.00 postpaid. *Bloom and Son.*

Fish Brooches

Striped agate brooch with a ruby eye set in 18-carat gold. $330.00 postpaid. Pair of Fishes. Blue enameled fish set with rubies on 14-carat gold. $100.00 postpaid. Striped agate with ruby eye set in 14-carat gold. $290.00 postpaid. *A. E. Köchert.*

Mayan Brooch

Made of 18-carat gold, this attractive pin, studded with emerald eyes, is styled in the manner of the ancient Mayans. 2¾" high, 1¾" wide. $379.00 postpaid. *Mayors.*

Dog Brooch

18-carat gold. Made in England. $61.25 postpaid. *Garrard.*

Fish Brooch

From London comes this 18-carat gold diamond and enamel brooch of a spiny fish. $1,287.50 postpaid. *Garrard.*

Of the many collectors of glittering jewels down through the ages, Emperor Jahangir, the noble ruler of India who died in 1627, is the most noted who ever lived. It is reported that he owned a total of 2,235,600 carats of pearls, 931,500 carats of emeralds, 376,600 carats of rubies, 279,450 carats of diamonds, and 186,300 carats of jade.

For his time, Jahangir was an enlightened monarch. During his reign, architectural masterpieces rose throughout India.

One of the emperor's hobbies was fishing, but Jahangir never killed a fish he caught. Instead, he would place a string of pearls through the fish's gills and throw it back into the water.

If nothing else, the man was extremely vain, for his name itself, Jahangir, means "Conqueror of the World." In addition, he had other glorious titles such as "Possessor of the Planets," "Mirror of the Glories of God," and "King of Increasing Fortune."

* * *

The world's largest gem reposes not in a wealthy dowager's vault but in a glass case on the fifth floor of the American Museum of Natural History in New York City. A topaz of 1.38 million carats, taken from Brazil's Minas Geraes, it weighs 596 pounds. It is rather dull-looking, and few of the visitors who make it up to the fifth floor pay this huge gem any mind.

* * *

There was a time when jewelry boxes were equipped with devices that killed anyone who attempted to open them without knowing the secret. One such case, sold at auction in New York several years ago, stood about 14 inches high by 20 inches wide and 10 inches deep. It had a bottom lock for the box, and a top lock for the protective mechanisms. If the top lock was open when the case was opened, the four doors instantly flew open, a pistol sprang into position behind each door, and all four pistols fired automatically.

Leather Jewelry Box

Hand-tooled sole leather is fashioned into a jewelry box, 3" deep, 4¼" wide, 6" high. Black or natural. $6.00. Postage $2.00. *Akios.*

Puzzle Ring

Devised from a clever design created in the Orient, this ring consists of four interlocking bands, each of a different pattern. When properly arranged, these four bands form a ring. However, putting them together properly is quite a challenge. Specify ring size. Sterling silver, $4.50 postpaid. 14K gold, $40.00 postpaid. *Postamatic.*

Gems for the Precious

Primitive Icon

This hand-sculptured white ceramic pendant, which has a length of 2½" and is 1¾" wide, has a sort of mystical religious quality. Hung at the end of a black leather tie, it depends to a length of 16". No two exactly alike. $20.00 postpaid. *Fritzie Abadi.*

Hand-Painted Miniature Portrait

Enclosed in a metal scroll frame of either gold or silver finish. The colors of the face are warm flesh tones against a black background. No two exactly alike. 2" wide by 2½" high. $25.00 postpaid. *Fritzie Abadi.*

Aztec Necklace

This primitive necklace, which is styled along Aztec lines, is 11½" long. The blue-green, antiqued, hand-sculptured medallion has a 2½" diameter, and is followed by a miniature cow bell which has a charming tinkle. The flat-toned beads are consonant with the basic color scheme. $50.00 postpaid. *Fritzie Abadi.*

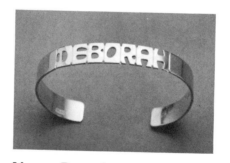

Name Bracelet

Made of sterling silver, this 3" wide bracelet can serve as a lovely memento of your affection. $11.00. Postage $1.15. *Sleepy Hollow Gifts.*

Brass Jewelry Box

This octagonal brass box imported from India was originally made to be used for betel nuts, but will serve very well for rings and bangles. 4½" by 6¼". $10.00. Postage $1.50. *Gump's.*

All These Are Radios

Reports of the death of radio are, like those about Mark Twain, greatly exaggerated. More radios were sold in the U.S. in 1971—18,579,000—than in any previous year. And this was more than twice the number of radios sold in 1937, in the "golden age of radio." Today, there are approximately 630 million radios being listened to all over the world. About 354 million of these are in the United States and its possessions—about one and a half sets for every man, woman, and child.

The history of radio begins before Marconi with the studies of electromagnetic waves conducted by Heinrich Hertz and James Clark Maxwell. But it was Guglielmo Marconi who, in 1895, gave the first demonstration of radio-telegraphy. During the following year, he secured a patent for his system of communication; and in 1901, he accomplished the first transatlantic transmission.

The first advertised broadcast was transmitted from Brant Rock, Massachusetts on Christmas Eve of 1906 by Professor Reginald Aubrey Fessenden. But the first radio station with a regular broadcasting schedule—KDKA of Pittsburgh, Pennsylvania—did not come on the scene until 1920. Today, there are more than 4,370 A.M. stations and 2,350 F.M. stations broadcasting in the U.S.

Fire Engine Radio

This replica of a Mississippi pump engine, circa 1869, in shiny red and gleaming brass, is also a transistor radio. Batteries included. $29.50. Postage $1.20. *Game Room.*

All These Are Radios

French Phone Radio

Rather good-looking, don't you think? 7¼" high. Comes with batteries. $25.00. Postage $1.25. *Game Room.*

Wrist Radio

Attaches to wrist, leaving both hands free. Comes with earpiece, wrist strap, and batteries. $19.95. Postage $1.95. *Childcraft.*

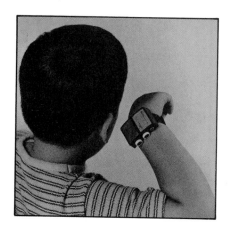

Paddle Wheel Radio

Accurate replica of the old Mississippi river boat immortalized by Mark Twain. Made in Japan. 11" long; 7" wide. With batteries. $25.00. Postage $1.25. *Game Room.*

Baseball Radio

A regulation-sized plastic baseball turned into a transistorized, solid-state radio. Complete with 3-bat stand and 9-volt battery. Good tone. $15.00. Postage $1.90. *Hammacher Schlemmer.*

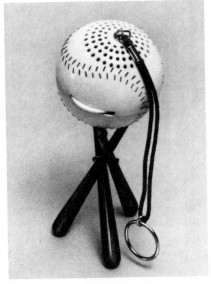

Radio Puppy

This soft plush button-nosed puppy is a six-transistor radio. The volume and tuning controls are in its tummy. 10½" long. Batteries included. $10.95. Postage $1.05. *F.A.O. Schwarz.*

Country Music Radio

This 5½" structure houses a powerful 6-transistor radio, with good tone and a wide range selection. No good outhouse should be without one. $12.95. Postage $1.25. *Game Room.*

Rolls Royce Radio

This gold-plated replica of the Rolls Royce Phantom II with white sidewalls houses a 9V transistorized radio. 9¾" by 4¼". Battery included. $25.00. Postage $1.20. *Game Room.*

Furniture

After a hard day at the pyramids, the Egyptians knew, nothing could beat a cold Pepsi and a snooze on the couch. They didn't have the Pepsi, so they invented the couch.

Their early couches were ornately styled and carved; the legs imitated the clawed feet of wild animals or the hooves of cattle, and the frames were often elaborately decorated with representations of the popular deities. The Egyptians pioneered seats made of woven rope and woven reeds, much like the wicker and caning still done today. Tables, benches, and boxes were used to such an extent that King Tut's tomb had everything in it but the kitchen sink.

While the Greeks, like most ancient cultures, used wood as the principal material in their furniture, bronze and marble couches from that period have been excavated.

As they had plenty of slaves to do the dusting, the Romans, in their turn, began to use more and more furniture. With the riches they gathered from all parts of the world, the Romans adorned their furniture with gold, silver, tortoise shell, bone, and ivory, and often painted their pieces with scenes from Roman life.

With the fall of the Roman Empire, furniture design sank into the Dark Ages. Europe's artisans made only the most basic and rudimentary stools, tables, benches, and chests. Few pieces of this era have survived.

During the 14th and 15th centuries, new types of furniture emerged in Europe. The cupboard, literally a board with holes in which cups could be placed, became commonplace. Desks, too, appeared.

Furniture of the period was constructed so as to be easily transported, so that noblemen who had more than one residence but who had only one set of furnishings could carry these things along with them, from home to home. This fact is illustrated by the French and German words for furniture, *meubles* and *mobel*, both of which mean movable. During that era, furniture was so scarce that it was not unusual for a visitor to bring along his own bed. There was so little furniture that the chair—if there was one in a house—was reserved for use by the lord or magistrate, resulting in our use of the phrase *chairman* to denote someone in authority.

For most people, the basic piece of furniture was a chest which could serve as seat, table, and cupboard—and as a writing desk, too, for those fortunate few who were literate. From this wide-ranged use of the chest, there evolved many variations such as the armoire, the dresser, the credenza, the highboy, the lowboy, the breakfront, and the bureau.

It was during the Renaissance that all those ornate, high-priced antiques, now seen only in museums, castles, and auction galleries, were created. Provincial pieces developed from the characteristic national styles: in France, the Louis period styles, the Directoire style, and the Empire style; in England, the Elizabethan,

Lounge Table
A rectangular smoked glass top on chromium-finished spiral legs. 48" long, 24" wide. $280.00. Shipped collect. *Harrods.*

Jacobean, William and Mary, Queen Anne, and Georgian styles. Among the famous English designers were Chippendale, Hepplewhite, Robert and James Adam, and Sheraton.

In the later years of the 19th century, machine-made furniture began to be mass-produced in bastardized versions of earlier period styles. A new attempt to redefine period style was made in England and France in the early 20th century, and both countries produced well-designed pieces. But the German and Italian emphasis on simplicity and functionalism became dominant. Bleached woods, tubular steel, glass, and synthetic materials came into prominence. Body-contoured chairs and long, low, horizontal lines characterize the new functionalism which remains the style most expressive of our times.

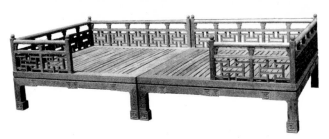

Korean-Style Bed

Handmade in Hong Kong, this rosewood bed is composed of two sections. Two muslin-covered 2" foam rubber seat pads and two muslin-covered foam rubber bolsters are included. 78" by 40" by 12". $516.00. Sea freight to New York, $120.00. *Charlotte Horstmann Ltd.*

Roll Top Desk

This solid maple desk has two drawers above and two below the roll top, and a rack of pigeonholes. 35" wide, 20" deep, 45" high. $104.00. Shipped express collect. *Ephraim Marsh.*

Adjustable Folding Bookstand

This library stand adjusts to three positions, and folds out when not in use. The table top is 18½" by 24", ample enough to hold the largest book. The book is secured by a 1" lip. Made of pine with birch legs. Choice of honeytone or antique finish. $32.50. Shipped express collect. *Yield House.*

Red Pinewood Cabinet

An antique patina has been created on the red pinewood of this good-sized cabinet. It has three drawers in the middle section, two lattice doors at the top, and two solid doors at the bottom. Hinges and drawer pulls are of wrought iron. 71" by 49" by 16". $704.00. F.O.B. Madrid. *Abelardo Linares, S.A.*

Furniture

Betsy Ross Desk

Made of solid pine, this desk measures 31" high, 21" wide, and 21" deep. Four drawers. $98.50. Shipped express collect. *Bryan Robeson.*

Ben Franklin Desk

A large pine surface allows plenty of room for papers and lamp. Three front drawers. $179.95. Shipped express collect. *Bryan Robeson.*

Wagon Seat Chest

For storage, this quaint relic may fit the bill. 31" high; 38" wide; 20" deep. The seat, which opens up, will hold a lot of stuff, and is 18" high when closed. The tweed cushions come in red, green, gold, or black vinyl. The wood is pine. Price $99.95. Shipped express collect. *Templeton Colonial Furniture.*

Mini Love Seat

Only 40" long, the elegant styling of this love seat is just right to make a small empty space a source of elegance. Upholstered in A-grade fabrics. Diamond-tufted at back and sides. The solid mahogany frame is enhanced by a hand-carved rose and leaf design. $199.95. Shipped collect. *Magnolia Hall.*

Fainting Sofa

The design for this Victorian sofa was introduced in 1847. Fainting was a popular activity of the day, but ladies always had to maintain a graceful position. As a result, the fainting sofa provided just the place for a lady-like swoon. With its extra length and gracefully curved back it has a regal beauty. Solid mahogany, all hand-carved; 82" long, 26" deep; 38" high. The upholstery, in A-grade fabrics, is biscuit tufted at back and sides by hand. $489.95. Shipped collect. *Magnolia Hall.*

Grain Cutter's Table

Solid pine in a dark antique tone. Porcelain knobs. 26" high, 25" wide, and 12½" deep. $69.95. Shipped express collect. *Old Guilford Forge.*

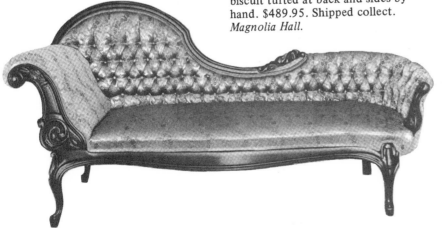

Furniture

Ming Four-Poster

The frame and the canopy of this attractive Chinese bed are made in Hong Kong. The outside measurements are 88" by 54" by 88" high. To complete the canopy, buyer should supply 12 yards of Thai silk. The entire bed can be collapsed. $1,140. Shipped express collect. *Charlotte Horstmann Ltd.*

Dining Table

Sculptor-designer Paul Evans created this dining table made with a base of walnut burl and polished chrome. The ¾" thick glass top is 8' long and 4' wide. The table is 29" high. $2,140.00. Shipped express collect. *Directional Furniture Showrooms.*

Campaign Table

Evidently politicians have the same needs all over the world, and this table made in Hong Kong apparently would be useful to a campaigner anywhere. The trestles fold, the campaign literature is taken off the table and put into the drawers, and the whole outfit is put compactly together while the speaker and his aides move on to the next assignment. 64" by 30" by 31" of solid wood. $240.00. Shipped collect. *Charlotte Horstmann Ltd.*

Adjustable Sofa

This sofa, created by Danish designer Borge Mogensen, adjusts at the right arm to five positions by means of leather straps. Frame is light beech, 32" high, 29" deep, 63" long, extending to 75" long. Foam rubber cushions. Upholstered in woolen fabric. $322.00. Shipping $175.00. *Asbjorn-Mobler A/S.*

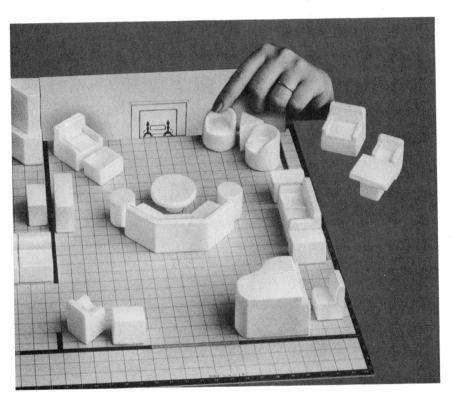

Furniture Arranging Kit

How to arrange the furniture can knock the daylights out of domestic tranquillity. This kit may restore a measure of reason. It contains about 150 different pieces of furniture scaled to 1/24 actual size. Pieces are made of lightweight styrofoam. Walls of sturdy cardboard, windows and doors with gummed backs. Included are graph paper, and an 8-page illustrated book. You can paint the furniture and wallpaper, lay out your color and fabric choices. $7.98 postpaid. *Plan-It-Kit.*

Gout Rest

Happily, gout is not a necessary prerequisite for enjoying this footstool, made of solid mahogany with hand-carved trim. 19½" by 16" by 11½" high. $69.95. Shipped express collect. *Martha M. House.*

Susan Reference Stand

This space-saving table top reference stand is a handy arbitrator in those Scrabble confrontations because it swivels—everyone can use it without wasting a lot of time or energy. The solid pine reference stand holds one book on top, and two more underneath. The table is 14" high, 14" wide, and 13" deep. $14.95. Postage $2.50. *Yield House.*

Furniture

Gossip Bench

A quaint hand-carved telephone bench with diamond-tufted back. White with brushed gold. 39" long, 23" deep, 33" high, in choice of cover. $179.95. Shipped collect. *Martha M. House.*

Spanish Cabinet

Handcrafted in Spain, this imposing pinewood side piece has many hand-carved panels. The upper spindels are hand-carved of walnut. Hinges and drawer pull are made of wrought iron. Stands 78" high, and is 49" wide and 19" deep. Fine patina. $880.00. F.O.B. Madrid. *Abelardo Linares, S.A.*

Dictionary Stand

These people go all the way. When you buy the stand, a Webster's Unabridged Dictionary comes with it. Width 23", depth 15", height 37½". Finished in fruitwood, maple, or antique. $89.95. Shipped express collect. *Martha M. House.*

Trundle Bed

A real space-saver, a 74" long drawer opens out from the bed on either side. Bed is 78" long; headboard is 42" high; footboard is 32" high. Finished in solid plantation pine. Spring and mattress not included. $169.50. Shipped express collect. *Bryan Robeson.*

Hand-carved Table

This Spanish handcrafted walnut table with central drawer has an antique patina. 31" high, 27" wide, 20" deep. $352.00. F.O.B. Madrid. *Abelardo Linares, S.A.*

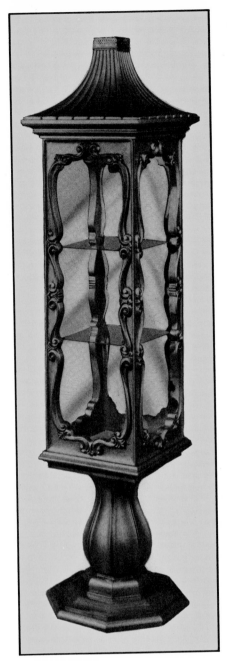

Bible and Dictionary Stand

Made of solid cherry and finished in dark forslund cherry, or light buckwheat honey. 44" high in back, 40½" high in front, 15" deep, 23¾" wide. Space above top shelf is 6"; above bottom and middle shelves, 11½". $154.95 postpaid. *Forslund.*

Curio Case

Your artifacts gathered from around the globe may be displayed on the two glass shelves of this cabinet, lit by two lights, one from the top and the other from the bottom. The wood is a combination of maple, hardwood, and urethane, and comes with an antique brown fruitwood, white, or gold finish (gold finish is $20 extra). The richly carved structure, standing 55" high on a heavy pedestal, frames the art pieces precious enough to be placed inside. 15" square. $159.95. Shipped express collect. *Magnolia Hall.*

For the Compleatest Angler

. . . God never did make a more calm, quiet, innocent recreation than angling.

Izaak Walton (1593-1683)
THE COMPLEAT ANGLER

When Izaak Walton wrote those words in 1653, the sport of fishing was in its infancy. No one had yet experienced the turbulent excitement of deep-sea fishing, or the thrills of underwater spear-fishing. Nonetheless, the idyllic pastime of Walton was not without its demands for imagination and precision. "As no man is born an artist," he wrote, "so no man is born an angler."

Today, the fisherman has many aids—everything from an electronic fish locater to an electrically operated reel. What's more, he can buy his worms by mail, and scale the fish he has caught on a marvelously clever contraption. It· has all become so highly sophisticated. Some fishermen's catalogs are 100 pages long, and dangle a myriad of flies in front of the buyer. One might say that it is the angler who is tantalized rather than the fish.

It is just because the science of angling has all been worked out in such detail that there's so very, very much to do and know. "Innocent recreation," says Walton. My left eye! It's a wearisome trial!

Knot Tyer

One simple knot ties mono to mono, mono to fly line, and mono to fly. Will also tie needle knots, blood knots, and barrel knots. Clipper is attached to 14" nickel steel chain coiled inside pin-on retainer. Comes with instructions and diagram. $5.50. Postage $1.00. *Orvis.*

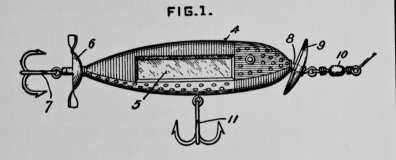

FIG.1.

FIG.2.

UNITED STATES PATENT OFFICE

ARTIFICIAL FISH-BAIT

1,180,753   Specification of Letters Patent   Patented Apr. 25, 1916

Application filed April 23, 1915. Serial No. 23,851

. . . My invention relates more particularly to artificial baits for trawling, and its primary objects are to make the bait more attractive to the fish, to secure its proper position in the water, to provide a convenient and effective hanging of the hooks, and to generally improve the structure and operation of trawling baits. . . .

The attractiveness of the bait for the fish is increased by making the disks 6 and 9 of highly polished metal. The glitter and flashing lights occasioned by these and by the mirror are well known attractives; but the mirror 5 is an additional feature that insures the effectiveness of the bait in the following manner: A male fish seeing his image upon looking therein will appear to see another fish approach it from the opposite side with the intent to seize the bait, and this will not only arouse his warlike spirit, but also appeal to his greed, and he will seize the bait quickly in order to defeat the approaching rival. In case the fish is suspected of cowardice I may make the mirror of convex form, as shown at 5ª, in order that the rival or antagonist may appear to be smaller. In the case of a female fish the attractiveness of a mirror is too well known to need discussion. Thus the bait appeals to the ruling passion of both sexes, and renders it very certain and efficient in operation. . . .

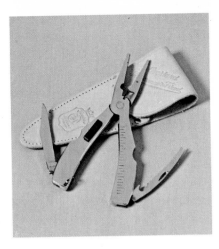

Fisherman's Friend

Seventeen jobs can be performed with this tool. It can be used as a crimper, a shot pincher, a wire twister, a measure, a screwdriver, and a fish scaler. Made of rust-resistant chrome. Comes in leather sheath. $13.50. Postage $1.75. *Abercrombie and Fitch.*

Fisherman's Knife

A steel powerjaw on the top of the grooved working surface of this filet board leaves both hands free to scale, skin, filet, and cut fish. The 6" by 24" hardwood board holds the fish firmly in place by head, tail, or side in a heavy clamp. The knife has a curved, flexible 6" Swedish stainless steel blade. $15.95 postpaid. *IPCO.*

For the Compleatest Angler

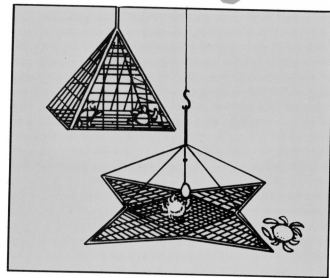

Star Crab Trap
This galvanized wire trap baits up in seconds. Spring-loaded sides cock open. Crabs caught with a jerk of the trap. 16" square. $3.98. Postage $1.00. *Netcraft.*

It was Saturday, April 17, 1937. The papers reported that the Wagner Labor Relations Act had been upheld by the Supreme Court, that President Roosevelt was shaping a new fiscal plan to avoid a tax rise, that Minsky's had been fined $500 in a strip-tease case, and that the first "Flying Fortress" was nearing completion in Seattle. On that same bright and sunny morning, four fishermen set out from Dallas. According to their own allegation, they too made history.

It seems that when they got into a small boat on the Dallas dock, they were determined to catch themselves some of the giant tarpon that lounge around the Gulf of Mexico. Out they sailed, far beyond the jetties, out to the sea where the tarpon run. There they settled down, let out their lines, and got all slouched in for a good bull session. These here tarpon don't bite so quick so that a coupla gents can't set back with a good cigar and take it easy-like, and—

Strike! One of the boys was practically jerked out of his seat as he whipped everyone to attention. The other 3 hurriedly began to reel in their lines to get out of his way. But it wasn't exactly free reeling. It was darn tough pulling, for each fisherman found *his own line* hooked up to a tugging tarpon.

The 4 Texans landed their 4 babies one after the other, each fish within a minute of the other. They could hardly believe what had happened. And if they couldn't, who would?

So they quickly sailed ashore and betook themselves to a notary, who for a proper fee, memorialized the day by certifying that this was "the most remarkable fishing expedition in the annals of Southern waters!"

And that's that!

Electric Fishing Reel
Holds 450 yards of 50 lb. Dacron line. Metal case resists corrosion. Retrieves at the rate of three feet per second. 12 volts. $199.95. Postage $2.75. *Abercrombie and Fitch.*

One of the oldest—and strangest—methods of fishing is practiced by the Maoris of New Zealand. The Maori fishermen wade out into the clear stream or lake, moving very quietly so as not to create ripples. Here fish swim in and out of clumps of rock or coral, sometimes stopping for a quick nap. Half of the fish may be hidden by the rock, but the rest of the fish juts out into view.

Wading up behind the fish, the silent Maori will reach down and tickle the fish's sides. In trying to wriggle away, the fish backs out of his hiding place and lands right in the fisherman's hands. The stealthy tickler must be very adept to hold onto his slippery supper.

*   *   *

Fish can be caught in the Sahara Desert. Strangely enough, there are many underground streams in the Sahara where, by digging through the sand, a desert angler can obtain fresh-water fish.

*   *   *

To escape its many enemies, a flying fish shoots out of the water and glides as far as 500 feet on its greatly enlarged fins. Some of the most powerful of flying fish can even jump over the deck of a small ship.

*   *   *

The crawling fish of Asia can live for a week out of water. In fact, this fish will instinctively leave a stream that is going dry and head for the nearest water, often traversing a mile or more of dry land.

The smallest fish in the world is the *Pandaka pygmea,* found in certain creeks in the Philippines. It reaches an average length of six-sixteenths of an inch, and an average width of seven-sixteenths of an inch. It is no bigger than an ant, and it is probably the tiniest creature with a backbone that has ever been isolated. The slender body of this fish is virtually transparent, and the only clearly visible features are its comparatively large eyes.

*   *   *

Ever wonder why some fish come to the surface, or at least stick their noses out for a breather? Well, they usually will not come up unless the water is polluted and deficient in oxygen. Since sediment sinks to the bottom, the upper layers of water are generally richer in oxygen.

Although fish have an air bladder, it is not that organ which needs periodic refilling, for the air bladder is not a part of the piscatorial respiratory system. Fish breathe through their gills alone, except in the rare cases of the bowfins, the fresh-water gars, and a few other species. These fish will occasionally protrude their snouts into the open air to gulp down some oxygen, which becomes mixed with the water passing through their gills.

*   *   *

The big fish fight, and fight hard, so game fishing is usually considered a man's sport. But on May 6, 1950, Mrs. H. A. Bradley took her boat out to Cape Charles, Virginia, and brought to gaff the largest drum fish ever caught—an 87-pound, 8-ounce giant!

Fish Gripper

For the Compleatest Angler

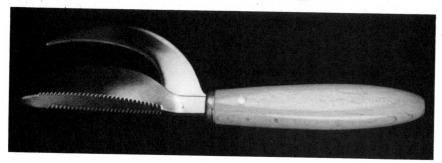

Fish Knife

Designed to facilitate cleaning fish. Made of Swedish steel. $2.50. Postage 75¢. *Casco Bay Trading Post.*

Fish Locating Glasses

These glasses are designed to eliminate bright water reflections. Locate your fish visually before casting. Also useful for skin divers who might not see underwater rocks before diving. Shadowproof polarized lenses. $7.95. Postage 75¢. *Hunting World.*

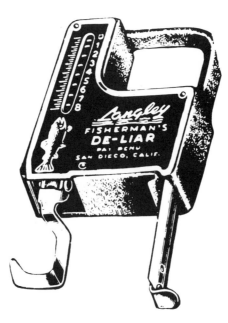

De-Liar

This stainless steel tape measure with automatic rewind and folding hood weighs fish up to 28 lbs. and measures fish up to 36". $1.65. Postage 77¢. *Netcraft.*

Worm Farm

All the equipment, bedding, and food for storage and breeding squillions of worms are included in this kit. You get a 4-quart container with carrying handle, a cover, 10 ventilation plugs, a 1½ lb. bag of bedding, and a 4 oz. bag of worm food. Instructions included. $3.75. Postage $1.00. *P. & S. Sales.*

SECURE GRIP...

FOR REMOVING HOOK...

STRINGING OR BOATING...

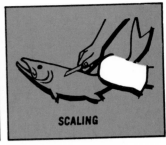

SCALING

Fish Mitt

Fish don't slip away quite so easily with this durable plastic glove. Gripping cleats built right in. Gives a secure grip for removing hooks, cleaning, etc. One size fits all. $3.00. Postage 50¢. *Deluxe Saddlery*.

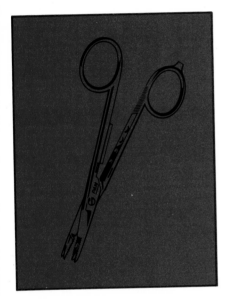

Fishing Pliers

A combination of pliers and scissors. As a fishhook degorger and remover, it prevents unnecessary damage to small fish, and offers no danger when removing hooks from big fish. Useful for close work in attaching leader line to small flies or hooks. Capable of cutting steel leaders. Equipped with a knife and holes to split lead shots, to change lead shots from wet to dry fly fishing, and to remove sinkers from line in bait fishing. A file sharpens fish hooks. A screw driver repairs fishing reels. Nickel-plated, $4.95; chrome-plated, $5.95; stainless steel, $6.95. Postage 35¢. *PAM Products*.

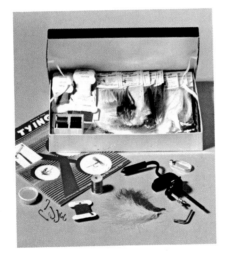

Fly-Tying Kit

A complete assortment of feathers, wools, chenilles, quills, floss and instruction booklet included. $26.00. Postage $2.00. *Abercrombie and Fitch*.

Instant Fish Skinning

This implement skins all sizes and types of fish without tearing the meat. It is designed so that the user's hands are safe. Made of stainless steel and aluminum alloy. Directions included. $5.95 postpaid. *IPCO, Inc.*

For the Compleatest Angler

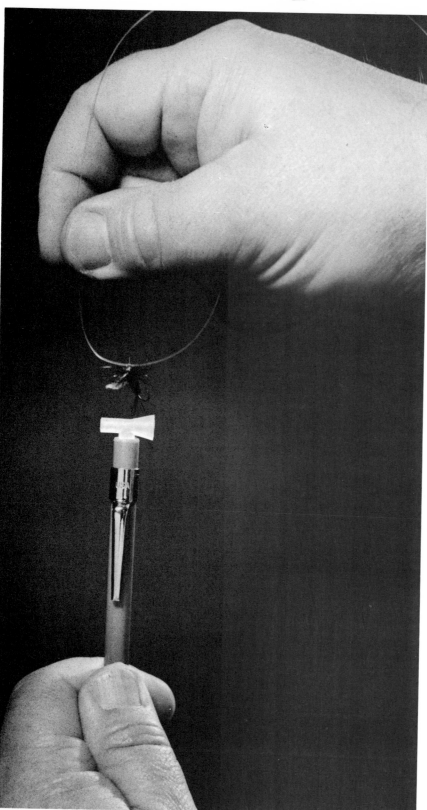

Fly Threader

Puts a fly on a leader instantly. Any size fly fits into the flexible top slot and stays there. Leader is inserted into the wide cone, and cone guides it through the hookeye. Once leader is picked up from the slot, the fly is on. In the dusk of an evening, even those gentlemen who have 20/20 vision may appreciate this threader. Threader is about the size of a ballpoint pen, and has a pen's pocket clip. $3.95. Postage $1.00. *Orvis.*

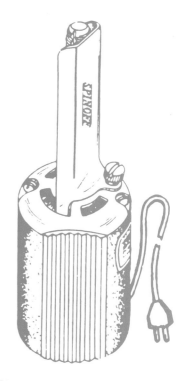

Electric Fish Scaler
Does exactly what it's supposed to. $13.75. Postage $1.98. *Netcraft.*

The largest fish ever caught by any method was a 17-foot-long, 4,500-pound white shark, harpooned by Frank Mundus off Montauk Point, Long Island, New York in 1964.

The largest fish ever caught by rod and reel was a white shark measuring 16 feet 10 inches long and weighing 2,664 pounds. It was brought in by Alf Dean at Denial Bay, near Ceduna, South Australia, on April 21, 1959.

* * *

In 1946, casting for distance, Wilbur Brooks of Indianapolis set his toe in the dirt, took a deep breath, and sent 5/8 of an ounce of bait 427 feet for a world's record. Out Wilbur's way the fish never knew what hit them!

* * *

When Robert Glen Gibson of Cape Breton, Nova Scotia, came home from his fishing trip on November 1, 1970, an awful lot of people had tuna fish salad. Gibson landed the largest tuna ever caught—a leviathan weighing 1,065 pounds!

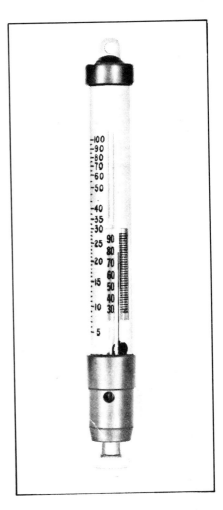

Depth-o-Plug
Because water pressure is in direct proportion to depth, this instrument measures depth by letting down a plug to trap water. Depth is indicated on one scale, water temperature on the other. Used to determine the best fishing areas. Instructions included. $2.35. Postage 85¢. *Netcraft.*

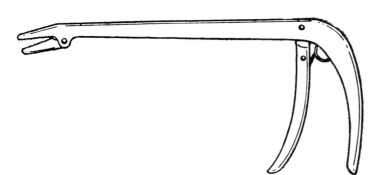

Hook Disgorger
Designed for safe removal of lures. Gives clean view and firm grip on hook. Made of corrosion-resistant steel. 9½" long. 5 oz. weight. $1.75 postpaid. *Netcraft.*

PUZZLES

Why do we enjoy puzzles? What's the fun in being stumped, frustrated, maddened? Maybe it's man's love of a challenge, and maybe it's mere masochism. In either case, a good puzzle is hard to resist.

Perhaps the oldest of all puzzles is the riddle, and perhaps the most famous of all riddles is that asked by the Sphinx:

> *What goes on four legs in the morning, on two at noon, and on three at night?*

Oedipus answered the riddle correctly, and thus became Oedipus Rex. His solution: "Man. In infancy he crawls; in his prime, he walks; and in old age, he leans on a staff."

Another famous riddle is one that is reputed to have stumped Homer. Someone propounded these two lines to the bard:

> *What we caught we threw away;*
> *What we couldn't catch, we kept.*

The answer to this one is fleas.

Another early puzzle which continues to per-plex us in its various forms is the labyrinth, an intricate arrangement of chambers and passages designed to befuddle the unfortunate person trying to navigate it. The great labyrinth of ancient times was built by Amenemhet IV of Egypt near Lake Moeris; its purpose is unknown. More renowned was a labyrinth built, according to Greek myth, in Crete by Daedalus to house the voracious minotaur.

In comparison, a crossword puzzle or jigsaw may seem pretty tame. But anyone who has been stuck on a real toughie knows what a victim of King Minos must have felt like as he wended his way through the cul-de-sacs of the labyrinth, heading toward his death.

The Nine of Swords

This attractive sculpture—a snow white cube, intersected by nine jet-black swords, displayed on a chrome column—poses a devil of a puzzle. Taking the swords out is easy. Putting them back may keep you up all night. $9.95. Postage $1.50. *Childcraft.*

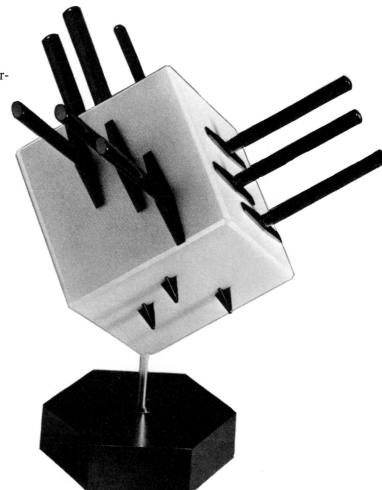

Third Dimension Puzzle

This 36-piece puzzle reflects and refracts light while its interlocked construction poses a challenge in reassembling. But first, you have to get it apart. That's a bit of a puzzle in itself. A cube of 3-3/8". $5.00. Postage 50¢. *Brentano's.*

Gravity Trap

Strictly for the physically alert! The objective of this puzzle is to trap three metal balls in the interior of a block of wood. Unless they are put in just right, gravity will cause them to fall out. Wood is black walnut. $4.00. Postage $1.50. *Childcraft.*

Chaotic Cube

There are twelve possible ways that the six panels and the 21 pegs, in four different lengths, can be assembled without blocking yourself out. But there are thousands of ways to wind up wrong. Made of plastic. $3.95. Postage 65¢. *Game Room.*

PUZZLES

Contura Puzzle

All surface contours of 64 pieces—each an exact square of the same size—must be matched to form the 7½" finished square of this sculptured jigsaw. The real teaser is that individual pieces were randomly selected, so the wood grain offers no clue. Crafted of finished hardwood. $12.50. Postage $1.29. *House of Minnel.*

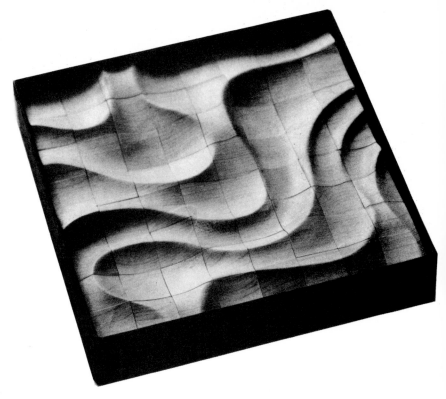

Wreck-Tangle

This tantalizing puzzle is made of six pieces of wood, each one 1" by 1" by 2". All the pieces are permanently connected by bolts, but each piece can swivel around in almost any direction. Only an educated flip of the wrist arranges the parts into a single rectangular block. Solid polished aluminum. $20.00. Postage $1.00. *Bloomingdale's.*

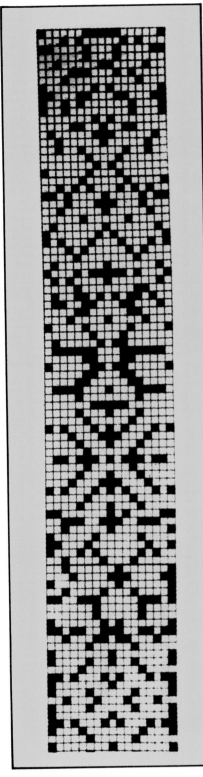

Loony Loop

The idea is to remove the nylon loop from the four wire loops. Eight moves are all that is required, but figuring them out could take you hours. Instructions included. $2.50. Postage $1.50. *Childcraft.*

Confusing Cubes

Here are the last seven letters of the alphabet—T to Z—plus one extra cube. They interlock to create two boxes. One is flat, and the other is four cubes high. To arrange these eight pieces into a cube may take minutes, days, or weeks. Cubes are 3 3/8" high. $15.00. Postage 75¢. *Austin Enterprises.*

Magic Marble

The steel marble is dropped into the hole in this black walnut block. To get the ball back, you use your sense of touch, your sight, and your hearing. It will take all your patience to keep from sawing the block in half. $4.00. Postage $1.50. *Childcraft.*

6-Foot Crossword Puzzle

Measuring 6' by 18", the puzzle is printed on a plastic coated, washable fabric, so you can hang it on the wall for posterity. Definitions are modern, and come on separate sheet, as do the answers. $5.00. Postage 50¢. *Deluxe Saddlery.*

SLEEP

How much sleep does one need? Answer: Anywhere from five to ten hours. Science has come up with no explanation as to why one individual requires more sleep than another. An infant sleeps most of the day because he is growing at a faster pace than at any other period in his life.

As we age, the quality of our sleep tends to gradually deteriorate. The sleep of older people is sometimes so fragmented that it is little more than a series of catnaps. Winston Churchill managed to turn his handicap into an advantage. He took short snoozes throughout the day to rejuvenate himself; and he insisted that his daily nap in the afternoon turned one day, in effect, into two. Still, medical evidence suggests that sustained sleep is more helpful; "to sleep like a baby" is an apt description of ideal slumber.

However, not even the sleep of infants is always tranquil. In the 1950s, psychologists Eugene Aserinsky and Nathaniel Kleitman observed a regular pattern in the sleep of in-fants: intervals of quiet slumber alternated with periods of body activity. Extending their discovery to a study of adult sleep, these scientists noticed recurring periods of rapid eye movements (*REMs*) beneath the closed lid, alternating with periods of peaceful sleep. These REMs, the psychologists learned, signaled the onset of dreams.

Dreams are similar to hallucinations in that they are not usually caused by sense impressions. To be sure, a toothache or indigestion may affect the form of the dream, but it will not determine the content of the dream. While the duration of a dream is a matter of dispute among scientists, many believe that even the most image-crowded dream lasts but a few seconds. All dreams occur in living color.

What gives the dream its restorative power? Little is known for certain about the dream world, but Freud believed that dreams provide a safety valve for suppressed desires, and that dreams actually protect sleep by draining off the emotional turmoil that would otherwise cause a person to wake up.

So many of us have so much trouble getting to sleep in the first place that nearly half a billion dollars are spent annually in the United States on sleeping pills.

Sleep Sound

Here's an instrument that induces sleep by recreating relaxing sounds. You will hear the wave pattern of the surf, and the sound of rain. The instrument also screens out other noises. $75.00. Postage $2.10. *Invento.*

> *When they are asleep you cannot tell a good man from a bad one, whence the saying that for half their lives there is no difference between the happy and the miserable.*
> Aristotle (384-322 B.C.), NICHOMACHAEAN ETHICS
>
> *No small art is it to sleep: It is necessary for that purpose to keep awake the whole day.*
> Friederich Wilhelm Nietzsche (1844-1900), THUS SPAKE ZARATHUSTRA

Sleep Pillow

The pre-shaped cradle and side wings are designed to support the neck. The zipper arrangement enables the height fullness to be varied. Filled with urethane foam, 26" long, 11" wide. $7.98. Postage 60¢. *Better Sleep, Inc.*

Measuring Devices

The two systems of measurement now in use are the Metric and the English system. Oddly enough, the English have recently converted to the metric system.

The meter is defined in terms of lightwaves. According to this definition, one meter is equivalent to 1,533,164.12 wave lengths of the red light emitted by cadmium.

According to legend, Henry I established the yard as the distance from the point of his nose to the end of his thumb when his arm was outstretched. In the U.S., the foot and the yard are defined in terms of the U.S. prototype meter, the foot equaling 1200/3937 meter. This measurement is known as the "survey foot"; otherwise, countries on the English system use a yard of .9144 meter.

The English system has always been rather messy, and may well vanish by the next century. The system is burdened with three different kinds of weight: avoirdupois weight, used for common purposes; troy weight, used for weighing gold, and silver; and apothecaries' weight, used in making up medical prescriptions.

There are other measurements for special purposes:

KARAT   A measure of gold, indicating how many parts out of 24 are pure. For example, 18 karat gold is ¾ pure.

ELL   1¼ yards or 1/32 bolt; used for measuring cloth.

FATHOM   6 feet or 1.8288 m. Derived from the distance to which a man can supposedly stretch his arms. Used for measuring cables and depths of water.

PICA   1/6 inch or 12 points; used in printing.

BALE   A large bundle of goods. In the U.S., the approximate weight of a bale of cotton is 500 pounds. The weight varies in other countries.

MICRON   .01 millimeter; used for scientific measurements.

Thommens Altimeter

The large dial of this Swiss-made pocket altimeter registers 20-foot graduations up to 3,000 feet. A small dial records multiples of 3,000 feet. Measures 2½" square; ¾" thick. Comes in leather case. $65.00. Postage $1.75. *Taylor Gifts.*

Tapeless Tape Measure

A skid-proof, mar-proof wheel that glides along surfaces measures distances on a digital counter. Works more effectively and faster than a yardstick or a folding ruler. Lightweight and compact, this measurement gadget provides magnified readings up to 99 feet, 11 inches. Simply skim it over walls or floors. Inner gears require no lubrication. $8.95. Postage $1.25. *Gallery.*

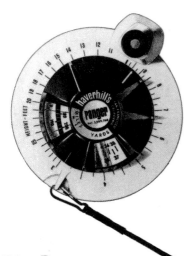

Disc Ranger

Measures distances from 6 feet to almost as far as the eye can see in yards, nautical miles, and statute miles. $24.95. Postage $1.50. *Haverhill's.*

Pocket-Size Ruler

A retractable ruler with a magic pad and pencil for jotting down measurements. Measures up to 118". Comes in a leather case 3¼" by 2½". $10.00. Postage 90¢. *Kenton Collection.*

Measure Meter

Tells you just by looking how far you've walked. $9.95. Postage $1.50. *Haverhill's.*

Digital Pedometer

You can easily measure the length of your room, your golf drive, or the land your house is on with this meter. The 4" wheel, calibrated to read from 1" to 1,000', is attached to a high handle. You roll the wheel around curves, or from wall to wall. You can roll vertically or horizontally. Adjustable handle extends from 20" to 36". Meter has a push-button reset. $14.95. Postage $1.25. *Game Room.*

Measuring Devices

An altimeter, as you might have guessed, measures altitude. Used primarily in airplanes and balloons, the device is generally a type of barometer. But the altimeter differs from the barometer in that it can indicate the distance that one is above the surface of the ground.

Some altimeters, such as an airplane's terrain-clearance indicator, utilize radio waves. The altimeter measures the time taken for a wave to be sent from the plane to the ground and back, converts this time into feet, and thus indicates the distance between the plane and the ground.

* * *

Chicago may be the windy city, but it can't compare to Adelie Land, in the Antarctic region. The *average* wind velocity there is 50 miles an hour, and hurricanes of 100 mph or more are regular occurrences.

The highest wind velocity ever recorded in the United States was 231 mph, on Mount Washington, New Hampshire, in 1934.

Wind-Speed Indicator

Every lull and every gust, from dead calm to 100 mph, is registered on the 6" dial of this instrument. A spinning cupwheel on your roof or on your TV mast transmits the reading to the indicator inside your home. Comes with 50 feet of wire. $80.00. Postage 80¢. *Chris Craft.*

Wind Direction Indicator

The appropriate compass points of this polished brass instrument, indicating in what direction the wind is blowing, light up on a silver dial. Comes with wind vane for rooftop mounting and 50 feet of wire. $60.00. Postage 80¢. *Chris Craft.*

Tape Measure

Encased in gleaming chrome-plate, this 10-foot tape measure permits direct reading through the window on top. A built-in compass enables you to describe a perfect circle, and another device lets you draw parallels and perpendiculars. $7.50. Postage 75¢. *Chris Craft*.

Perpetual Calendar

The entire area of this calendar is composed of raised, labeled circles. Snap-on rings encircle the date, the month, and day of week, and tell you at a glance what you want to know. The clock operates on a 1½ volt flashlight battery. Overall size is 12" wide by 24" high. $29.95. Postage $1.99. *House of Minnel*.

Portable Anemometer

When you hold it up in any wind current, this electric anemometer accurately registers wind velocity. The easy-to-read dial is calibrated in knots and miles per hour. Weighs 7 oz. 1¾" long. Needs no batteries. $44.50. Postage $1.00. *Chris Craft*.

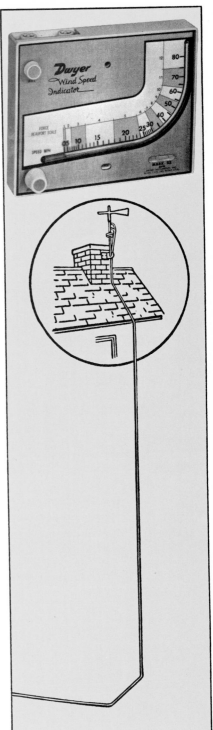

Wind Speed Indicator

You read it as you read a thermometer. Tells the wind velocity in miles per hour and in Beaufort scale designations. 7 3/4" wide, 7 5/8" high, 1" thick. Comes with 50-foot length of weatherproof tubing. $29.95. Postage 75¢. *Gokey*.

For Sailors

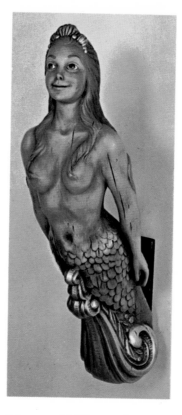

Jolly Roger

Roughly 19" high, this simulated carving is made of latex, and is hand-painted. Weighs 5 lbs. $25.00. Postage $2.10. *Artistic Latex.*

Blown Glass Lamp

This hanging light in oxidized copper with blown amber-colored glass is 15¾" high and 11½" wide. $82.90. Postage $3.20. Comes with chain and ceiling plate. *Preston's.*

Mermaid Figurehead

This hand-painted latex figurehead has the appearance of wood. It is 32" high and weighs 20 lbs. Wood bracket included. $45.00. Postage $5.00. *Artistic Latex.*

Thermo-Coasters

These thermo-coasters keep your drinks cool, leave no moisture rings on woodwork. Fit standard beverage cans, bottles, and drinking glasses. Nautical design in red and blue, with color-coded rims so you'll know which drink belongs to whom. Set of six, $2.00. Postage 20¢. *Chris Craft.*

Bosun's Brush

A nautical conversation piece, as well as a functional brusher-upper. Hand-fashioned from a length of golden manila rope, accented with colorful whipping. 10" high. $2.50. Postage 75¢. *Chris Craft.*

Non-Slip Tray

How dreadful to have all the drinks tilt over when the sea gets rough. But don't cry over spilt liquor; just avoid the catastrophe. This non-slip tray is 16½" by 12½". Non-skid surface will keep all glasses on an even keel. $8.00. Postage 95¢. *Game Room.*

Vacuum Cleaner for Liquids

Designed for portability, power, and the ability to drink up liquids, this vacuum cleaner is made of rust-resistant steel. An easy-glide dolly allows it to trail after the hose. The air-cooled one horsepower motor is fully protected from moisture. 18 3/7" high, 14" in diameter. Weighs 17 lbs. Comes with 8' grounded three-wire cord, hose, and nozzle. $59.95. Postage $4.40. *Chris Craft.*

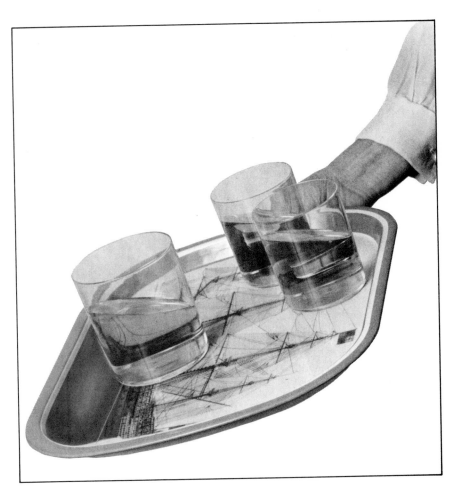

For Sailors

Sportsman's Magnet
Measuring only 4" long, this powerful magnet retrieves anything of iron or steel. Will even locate an outboard motor, should it happen to go overboard. $2.25 postpaid. *Gokey.*

Electric Rope Cutter
Simultaneously seals and fuses ends. Operates off a 12-volt battery current. Draws only 4.8 amps. 1¾" high; 3¼" wide; 3½" long. Can handle lines up to 1" in diameter. $19.95. Postage 20¢. *Chris Craft.*

Rope Coil Lamp
A coil of No. 1 marine manila forms the base for this lamp, which comes shaded in gold, green, and aqua tones. Solid brass stem, three-way switch. May be bolted to ship's table. 21" tall. $40.00. Postage $2.25. *Bluejacket.*

Fender Lines
These 4" fender lines are made of first-grade ¼" nylon line, with an eye splice at one end. Pair for $1.00. Postage 75¢. *Chris Craft.*

For a Blaze of Glory

For many years, fires just burned wherever they happened to be. Somewhere, back in the dim past, a disgruntled homeowner who had just lost his house to a wandering fire decided that something must be done. He reasoned that fires got out of control because they had nothing to call their own. In his new dwelling, he built something he called a "fireplace," and put his fire in it to live. The fire liked the idea so much, it immediately adopted a cheery glow, something which fires in fireplaces exhibit to this day.

The earliest fireplace was a stone hearth built in the center of a hut; the smoke would course upwards through a hole in the roof. The hearth of the Roman patricians was located in the middle of the atrium or court, the center of domestic life.

In the medieval European castle, the hearth still remained at the center of things, smack in the middle of the great hall. But from the 13th century on, rooms were built above the hall, and the fireplace was moved from the center of the room to an outer wall. By the mid 1400s, the fireplace-and-chimney assembly looked pretty much as it does today.

Some time later, an early cigarette smoker, tired of singeing his hair by bending over the hearth for a light, developed the match.

Hearth Stand

Reproduced from an early American style, this solid brass hearth stand has Queen Anne legs and intricate designs on both top and sides. 11" high, 16" wide, 11" deep. $90.00. Shipped collect. *Vroubel.*

For a Blaze of Glory

Fireplace Grate

The manufacturers of this patented fireplace grate say it is a new kind, unavailable elsewhere, and that it is designed to cure most smoking problems, will make fire-starting easier, will cut down firewood costs, will diminish air pollution, increase safety, and permit easier ash removal. $27.50. Shipped express collect. *Garden Way Research.*

Pine Tree Andirons

A young craftsman in Maine makes these graceful and sturdy andirons of black wrought iron with cutouts to let the fire show through. 18½" tall, 11½" wide, 18" deep. $55.00. Postage $3.50. *Adirondack Store.*

Ecuadorian Bellows

This pair from Ecuador is decorated with Indian designs. 8" by 18". $9.00 postpaid. *Akios.*

Logs from Newspapers

Newspaper logs burn as long and evenly as dried wood. They won't smoke either, because this device creates passages for air circulation as the logs are made. 12 log ties for $1.49. Postage 60¢. *Sunset House.*

Tennessee Brooms

A mountain family in Tennessee has been making these brooms for three generations. They grow the grass, dry the straw, and cut the laurel handles. 35" high: $3.50; 16" high whisk: $2.50. Shipped express collect. *Storehouse*

Charcoal Keg

This 17" by 10" pine keg holds 20 lbs. of charcoal, dispensing the coal as the keg is tipped to pour. Charred finish, black steel bands. Two hemp handles. $15.00. Postage $1.50. *Deluxe Saddlery.*

Fireside Bucket

In this wooden fireside bucket, with hand-stenciled decoy, you can store a bundle of Georgia fatwood. Only two sticks will start a roaring blaze—without kindling or newspaper. 9-lb. bundle of 7½" sticks, $7.75; 11-lb. bundle of 14" sticks, $13.50; bucket, $13.50. Postage $1.00. *Orvis.*

SOUPERLATIVES

Homoeopathic Soup

Take a robin's leg
(Mind, the drumstick merely);
    Put it in a tub
Filled with water nearly;
    Set it out of doors,
In a place that's shady;
    Let it stand a week
(Three days if for a lady);
    Drop a spoonful of it
In a five-pail kettle,
    Which may be made of tin
Or any baser metal;
    Fill the kettle up,
Set it on a boiling,
    Strain the liquor well,
To prevent its oiling;
    One atom add of salt,
For the thickening one rice kernel,
    And use to light the fire
"The Homoeopathic Journal."
    Let the liquor boil
Half an hour, no longer,
    (If 'tis for a man
Of course you'll make it stronger).
    Should you now desire
That the soup be flavoury,
    Stir it once around,
With a stalk of savoury.
    When the broth is made,
Nothing can excell it:
    Then three times a day
Let the patient *smell* it.
    If he chance to die,
Say 'twas Nature did it:
    If he chance to live,
Give the soup the credit.

Electric Tureen

This gleaming white glazed china bowl
has a heating element in it to keep
soups hot. Holds 3 quarts. $11.95.
Postage $2.80. *Hammacher
Schlemmer.*

UNUSUAL SOUPS

Bird's Nest	$2.75	15½ oz.	*Maison Glass*
Bisque of Crawfish	$1.50	14 oz.	*Maison Glass*
Bisque of Deep Sea Lobster	$1.50	14 oz.	*Maison Glass*
Bouillabaisse	$1.98	14 oz.	*Colonial Garden*
Charisse, Crab	$1.00	14 oz.	*Maison Glass*
Fromaut (Cheese & Tomato)	$0.90	14 oz.	*Maison Glass*
Kangaroo Tail	$0.90	15 oz.	*Maison Glass*
Masalah (Shrimp)	$0.90	14 oz.	*Maison Glass*
Oyster with Guinness	$1.00	12/15 oz.	*Maison Glass*
Romaine	$0.90	14 oz.	*Maison Glass*
Sea Scallop (Coquille)	$1.00	14 oz.	*Maison Glass*
Snail	$1.25	14 oz.	*Maison Glass*
Ventura (Crab & Mushroom)	$1.00	14 oz.	*Maison Glass*
Wild Duck (Jellied)	$1.25	15 oz.	*Maison Glass*
Wild Duck with Orange	$1.00	12 oz.	*Maison Glass*

The Ballad of Bouillabaisse

A street there is in Paris famous,
    For which no rhyme our language yields,
Rue Neuve des Petits Champs its name is—
    The New Street of the Little Fields.
And here's an inn, not rich and splendid,
    But still in comfortable case;
The which in youth I oft attended,
    To eat a bowl of Bouillabaisse.

This Bouillabaisse a noble dish is—
    A sort of soup, or broth, or brew;
Or hotchpotch of all sorts of fishes,
    That Greenwich never could outdo:
Green herbs, red peppers, mussels, saffron,
    Soles, onions, garlic, roach, and dace:
All these you eat at Terré's tavern
    In that one dish of Bouillabaisse.

Indeed, a rich and savoury stew 'tis;
    And true philosophers, methinks,
Who love all sorts of natural beauties,
    Should love good victuals and good drinks.
And Cordelier or Benedictine
    Might gladly, sure, his lot embrace,
Nor find a fast-day too afflicting,
    Which served him up a Bouillabaisse.

I wonder if the house still there is?
    Yes, here the lamp is, as before;
The smiling red-cheeked *écaillère* is
    Still opening oysters at the door.
Is Terré still alive and able?
    I recollect his droll grimace:
He'd come and smile before your table,
    And hope you liked your Bouillabaisse.

We enter—nothing's changed or older.
    "How's Monsieur Terré, waiter, pray?"
The waiter stares, and shrugs his shoulder—
    "Monsieur is dead this many a day."
"It is the lot of saint and sinner,
    So honest Terré's run his race."
"What will Monsieur require for dinner?"
    "Say, do you still cook Bouillabaisse?"

"Oh, oui, Monsieur," 's the waiter's answer;
    "Quel vin Monsieur désire-t-il?"
"Tell me a good one."—"That I can, Sir:
    The Chambertin with yellow seal."

"So Terré's gone," I say, and sink in
    My old accustom'd corner-place;
"He's done with feasting and with drinking,
    With Burgundy and with Bouillabaisse."

My old accustom'd corner here is,
    The table still is in the nook;
Ah! vanished many a busy year is
    This well-known chair since last I took.
When first I saw ye, *cari luoghi,*
    I'd scarce a beard upon my face,
And now a grizzled, grim old fogy,
    I sit and wait for Bouillabaisse.

Where are you, old companions trusty
    Of early days here met to dine?
Come, waiter! quick, a flagon crusty—
    I'll pledge them in the good old wine.
The kind old voices and old faces
    My memory can quick retrace;
Around the board they take their places,
    And share the wine and Bouillabaisse.

There's Jack has made a wondrous marriage;
    There's laughing Tom is laughing yet;
There's brave Augustus drives his carriage;
    There's poor old Fred in the *Gazette;*
On James's head the grass is growing;
    Good Lord! the world has wagged apace
Since here we set the claret flowing,
    And drank, and ate the Bouillabaisse.

Ah me! how quick the days are flitting!
    I mind me of a time that's gone,
When here I'd sit, and now I'm sitting,
    In this same place—but not alone.
A fair young form was nestled near me,
    A dear dear face looked fondly up,
And sweetly spoke and smiled to cheer me
    —There's no one now to share my cup.

I drink it as the Fates ordain it.
    Come, fill it, and have done with rhymes:
Fill up the lonely glass, and drain it
    In memory of dear old times.
Welcome the wine, whate'er the seal is;
    And sit you down and say your grace
With thankful heart, whate'er the meal is.
    —Here comes the smoking Bouillabaisse!

William Makepeace Thackeray

If You're Traveling Incognito

If you think that incognito is the class just below economy, you've never heard of the Mardi Gras. In a week of bacchanalian festivities the folks in Rio and New Orleans parade and cavort, protected from disapproving stares by—masks.

The masks depicted on the walls of prehistoric caves, as well as in the tombs of ancient Egypt, prove that false faces evolved universally. From the earliest of times, man has attempted to endow himself with the essence of certain animals. A Stone Age cave painting depicts a man wearing the skull of a deer over his head, with the attached skin covering the rest of his body. Certain Indians living in New Mexico celebrate festivals by having a man cover his own head with that of a deer, using the real skin and the antlers.

That the mask was indispensable in the evolution of theatre is obvious, but even dance itself can be traced to man's attempt to imitate the animals he depended on for food, with his masks and movements intended to somehow conquer these animals symbolically. In fact, tracing the development of masks in a society, as much as that of stone tools, metalwork, and ceramics, provides the anthropologist with an accurate measure of the society's evolutionary process.

Every primitive tribe has, to some degree, developed an indigenous mask culture—from simple face painting to elaborate false faces, with eyes that can be rolled, and mouths that can be opened and closed. In North America, the most elaborate masks can be seen among certain Canadian and Alaskan tribes who fashion and wear large wooden masks. Apache and other tribes of the American Southwest make their masks of highly colored wood and textiles to personify supernatural forces.

Masks were widely used in warfare, both by the American Indians and by African tribes, to help terrify the enemy.

In the Middle Ages, the passion plays of the Church used masked figures to depict God and his angels, as well as representations of the Devil and his legions. This custom was carried on by the court jesters of the period, who dressed as clowns, as well as by wandering minstrels of the day.

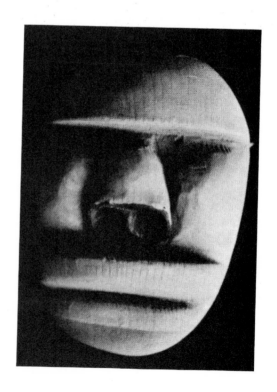

Ceremonial Mask

This spirit mask from King Island, Alaska is made of driftwood, tinted with cinebar. $55.00. Postage $1.50. *Arctic Trading Post.*

Stebbins Mask

Owl feathers 9" long decorate this Alaskan ceremonial mask. Made of driftwood. 7" by 10". $55.00. Postage $1.50. *Arctic Trading Post.*

Greek Mask

Dionysus, the God of Wine, is represented in a wall mask of terra-cotta, with a green antique finish. 9" by 6½". Imported from Greece. $6.50. Postage 45¢. *Vassilios Rallis Co.*

Alaskan Ceremonial Mask

This whalebone ceremonial mask has ivory eyes, teeth, and labrets. It comes from Point Hope, Alaska. $55.00. Postage $1.50. *Arctic Trading Post.*

If You're Traveling Incognito

Mask of Tragedy

This terra-cotta wall mask from Greece shows the face of Tragedy. Green antique finish. 9" by 6½". $6.50. Postage 45¢. *Vassilios Rallis Co.*

Aktuvuk Mask

Masks of caribou skin and hair, trimmed with wolf, sewn together with sinew, take on male or female form. 10" long. No two are alike. Each $29.95. Postage $1.50. *Arctic Trading Post.*

Wall Masks

Balsawood wall masks in Incan motifs. Each is 12" by 7½". $2.50. Postage $3.00. *Akios.*

Giant Wall Mask

This hand-carved wall mask from Ecuador measures 30" long, 10" wide. Depicts various Incan motifs in high relief. $23.00. Postage $3.00 *Akios.*

The Modern Bathroom or Johnny-Come-Lately

The ancients are believed to have washed themselves with ashes and water, which was followed by an application of oil or grease to relieve the irritation caused by its ashes. The first mention of soap, as we know it today, was made in the first century A.D. by Pliny, who wrote that some Germanic tribes washed their hair with a mixture of tallow and ashes of wood.

Subsequently, soap became popular in Rome, but fell into decline when the Roman Empire fell in 476. Some 300 years later, soap was "rediscovered" by the Italians.

Oddly enough, soap did not reach France until the early 13th century. For many years, the English—like the French—favored perfumes as a means of, if not keeping themselves clean, at least seeming to. But by the 17th century, soap became common in England, and in its North American colonies as well. In colonial America and Canada, many housewives made their own soap from waste animal fats and lye.

Although soap may be made of many substances, all methods of manufacture are based on the same principle. Fats and oils are heated, an alkali introduced, and the mixture stirred. When salt is added, the brew forms a curd which floats to the top. This curd is the soap. To produce a purer soap, the curds may be washed with a salt solution and allowed to settle. The upper layer thus formed is the pure soap, which is then churned, perfumed, colored, poured into huge frames, cut, shaped, and stamped.

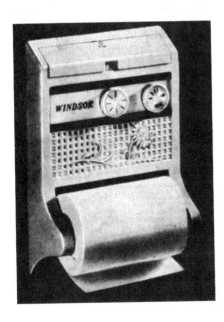

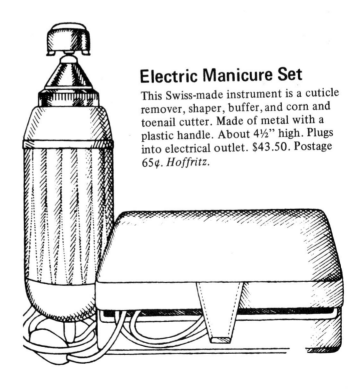

Electric Manicure Set

This Swiss-made instrument is a cuticle remover, shaper, buffer, and corn and toenail cutter. Made of metal with a plastic handle. About 4½" high. Plugs into electrical outlet. $43.50. Postage 65¢. *Hoffritz.*

Bathroom Radio

This solid-state transistor radio attaches to bathroom wall in seconds with the adhesive strips furnished. Built-in antenna gives excellent fidelity on A.M. stations. 3" deep, 6¼" wide, 9¼" high. Weighs only 15 oz. Choice of colors. Operated by 9-volt battery (included). $9.95. Postage $1.00. *Electronics International.*

The Modern Bathroom or Johnny-Come-Lately

Chaise Percee

This is unquestionably the snazziest
john extant. Designed to fit over a
water closet, this hand-carved wooden
caned seat with caned back and caned
sides, is finished in antique white,
gold, fruitwood, or walnut. Specify
make and model number of water
closet. $544.50. Shipped express
collect. *Sherle Wagner.*

Digital Scale

Shows weight on an illuminated
screen. Battery operated. $25.00.
Postage $1.00. *Haverhill's.*

Uncommon Soaps

Almond Oil	3 bars	5.00	*Caswell-Massey*
Astral Cream	3 bars	4.50	*Caswell-Massey*
Auguri Cuore	3 bars	6.50	*Caswell-Massey*
Blueberry	3 bars	1.65	*Vermont Country Store*
Brown Sugar	3 bars	3.50	*Caswell-Massey*
Buttermilk	3 bars	3.00	*Vermont Country Store*
Ca' d'Oro	1 bar	2.00	*Caswell-Massey*
Cranberry	3 bars	1.05	*Vermont Country Store*
Cyclamen	3 bars	3.75	*Caswell-Massey*
Devon Violet	3 bars	3.00	*Caswell-Massey*
Dutch Garden	2 bars	3.50	*Caswell-Massey*
Ginseng	3 bars	4.50	*Caswell-Massey*
Hammam	3 bars	3.75	*Caswell-Massey*
Khus-Khus	2 bars	2.50	*Vermont Country Store*
Lemon Oil	3 bars	5.00	*Caswell-Massey*
Maharani Sandal	3 bars	3.00	*Caswell-Massey*
Malabar Glory	3 bars	4.50	*Caswell-Massey*
Margo Hygienic Toilet	3 bars	1.80	*Caswell-Massey*
McClinton's Barilla	3 bars	3.00	*Caswell-Massey*
Moloy Sandalwood	3 bars	4.25	*Caswell-Massey*
Neca 7	3 bars	3.75	*Caswell-Massey*
Oatmeal	3 bars	4.00	*Vermont Country Store*
Pine Needle Oil Soap	4 bars	.99	*Herter's*
Pino Silvestre	3 bars	3.00	*Caswell-Massey*
Rain Water	3 bars	3.75	*Caswell-Massey*
Savon Huile de Vison	1 bar	2.50	*Caswell-Massey*
Savon Surgras	3 bars	6.00	*Caswell-Massey*
Spanish Seaweed	1 bar	3.00	*Caswell-Massey*
Strawberry Juice	3 bars	3.75	*Caswell-Massey*
Violettes de Toulouse	3 bars	5.00	*Caswell-Massey*
Waterloo	1 bar	2.00	*Caswell-Massey*
Witch Hazel	3 bars	6.00	*Caswell-Massey*
Wright's Coal Tar	3 bars	6.00	*Caswell-Massey*
Zignago	3 bars	1.50	*Caswell-Massey*

Blue Belle

Made of latex, this simulated carving is hand-painted. Weight 5 lbs. $25.00. Postage $2.10. *Artistic Latex.*

Decorative Plaque

Inspired by early advertising art, this plaque is hand screened on wood. 15¼" by 24¼". $13.00. Postage $1.00. *Yorkraft.*

The Modern Bathroom or Johnny-Come-Lately

Although the Romans took baths and had excellent plumbing facilities for hot and cold water more than 2,000 years ago, the habit of bathing died out during the Middle Ages. Baths were usually taken only on a doctor's request. The result was a lack of hygiene that encouraged infection. Even the United States did not get its first bathtub until 1840.

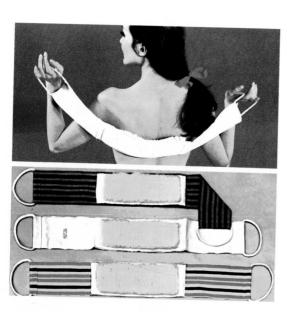

Austrian Back Scrubber

The Austrian firm that makes these has been in the business of manufacturing back scrubbers since 1827. The brush area is 3½" by 10½", and is made of sheared bristles, permanently woven into a heavy canvas belt. Large grippers assure ease of arm motion. Natural color, $5.50. Red with black stripes, or yellow with red and blue stripes, $6.50. Postage 89¢. *House of Minnel.*

Book Rack

If you don't read in the bathroom, you're wasting a helluva lot of good time. This rack holds reading matter along with two rolls of toilet tissue. 18" high; 11¾" wide; 4½" deep. Honeytone finish or antique finish. $9.95 postpaid. *Yield House.*

Gum-Tinting Toothpaste

The manufacturer claims that this toothpaste, imported from France, tints gums pink, making the teeth look whiter by comparison. It is also a dentifrice, of course. $2.00. Postage 60¢. *Caswell-Massey.*

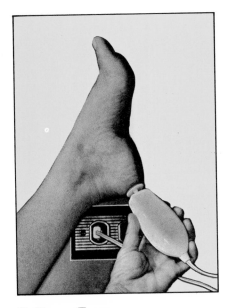

Callous Eraser

Removes pedal uglinesses. Hand-size, lightweight. Made of white plastic. 5½' cord. $3.98. Postage 70¢. Disc refills, $1.49. *Walter Drake.*

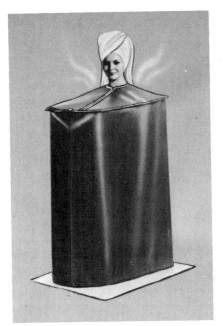

Poor Girl's Sauna

This steam bath can be set up with ease and then folded away compactly. It plugs into any outlet. Vinyl floor mat. Built of durable vinyl. Complete with steam generator, instruction booklet, and stall cover. $12.98. Postage $1.75. *Hanover House.*

Rich Girl's Sauna

Step into this sumptuous Finnish bath which has a low humidity and a temperature which ranges up to 200ºF. Operates on 110 volts, 2,000 watts. A thermostat controls the heat. There's also an interior light and a thermometer. Made of Luan plywood with solid redwood flooring, ceiling, and benches. 4' square and 6½' high. Prewired for easy assembly. $599.50. Shipped express collect. *Hammacher Schlemmer.*

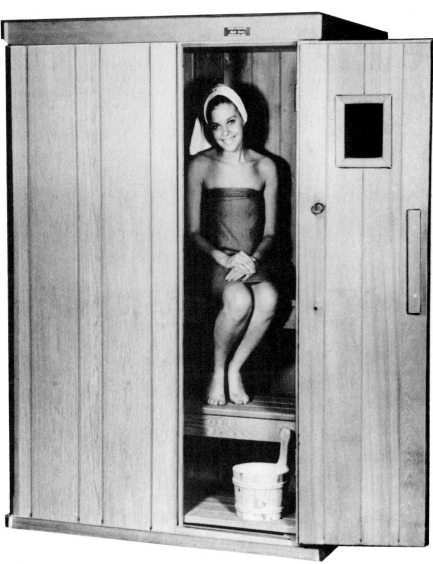

Treat Your Ford Like a Rolls

If in 1600, you happened to be walking along a Dutch canal, you might have been surprised to see a two-masted ship bearing down on you. Not in the canal—on the road. There was one such ship that was said to have reached a speed of 20 mph while carrying 28 fear-stricken passengers. In his notebooks, Leonardo da Vinci had envisioned some sort of self-propelled vehicle; and some Dutchman, quite naturally, had modeled such a vehicle after a sailing vessel.

About 1700, a Swiss inventor mounted a windmill on a wagon. It was hoped that as the windmill wound up a huge spring, the vehicle would lope along under its own power.

But even before then—as far back as 1668, to be exact—someone had built a steam-powered carriage. In 1769, one Nicholas Joseph Cugnot of France was credited with the invention of the first automobile. He built himself a steam-powered tricycle which attained a speed of 2 mph while carrying four people. This machine was the forerunner of the famous Stanley Steamer of 1906, an automobile which utilized steam as the motive force, and which established the then world land-speed record of 121.52 mph.

The early steam engine, however, was found to be impractical on ordinary roads, for it required great engineering skills on the part of the driver. So other sources of power were investigated. Over the latter years of the 19th century various electric cars were introduced with some frequency, but these never quite caught on with the public because they had to be recharged regularly. Gasoline and the internal-combustion engine proved to be the final answer, at least until the 1970s. Today, there is much talk of reviving the steam or electric engine, or converting from the piston-driven car to a Wankel, or rotary, engine.

In 1864, an Australian named Siegfried Marcus was experimenting with the lightbulb, and he wasn't very successful. He ignited a mixture of gasoline and air, believing he would at last be producing illumination. He was right. But

he also produced a violent explosion, jolting him into the discovery that his mixture could be a method of powering a vehicle. The drawback, however, was that his contraption required a strong man to lift the rear end of the vehicle while the wheels were being spun to get the engine going. Like almost all inventors, Marcus was a bit crazy; and after 10 years, he lost interest in the automobile, calling it "a senseless waste of time and effort."

By this time, the steam vehicle was already coming under public pressure because of the noise it engendered. Moreover, the steam engine was considered downright dangerous, and so it was common for early motorists to find the roadway blocked with barricades. Back in 1865, in response to an outcry against trains, England had passed an act which limited steam-driven vehicles to 4 mph in the country and 2 mph in the city.

One of the men most responsible for the development of the gasoline-powered engine was Carl Benz of Munich, who also supplied one of

Personalized License Frames

Silver-toned custom license frames accommodate two lines of lettering to add personality to your car. Top line holds ten letters and spaces; bottom holds 18 letters and spaces. Fits all license plates. One: $4.95 postpaid; two: $9.50 postpaid. *Bruce Bolind.*

the first traffic accident statistics. During an exhibition of his 1885 three-wheeled model, he lost control of his car and smashed into a wall. Undaunted, he went on to refine automobile mechanics.

Gottlieb Daimler, a compatriot of Benz, independently arrived at his own version of the internal-combustion engine. Although the two never met, the firms which succeeded their enterprises merged and formed the present Mercedes-Benz company.

Perhaps the first truly practical gasoline-powered automobile was the Panhard, designed, in 1894, by a Frenchman named Krebs. The French had begun to produce autos a few years earlier, after Levassor purchased the French rights to Daimler's engine of 1887.

In the United States, several inventors get high marks for pioneering efforts in the field. Among them were the Duryea brothers, who won the first automobile race in America in 1895. One year earlier, an American named Elwood Haynes had gained the patent for a gasoline-powered car that was developed at the Apperson wagon works in Kokomo, Indiana. The first car manufactured in Detroit was made by Charles King in 1896. By 1898, there were no fewer than 50 automobile manufacturers in the U.S.

Preceding Henry Ford by two years, Ransom Olds commercially produced a three-horsepower Oldsmobile. He produced over 400 cars a year before the turn of the century.

Henry Ford's ideas were as brilliant from the standpoint of marketing as they were from the standpoint of mechanics. Ford perceived the need to transform the automobile from a luxury to a necessity by making cars cheap and making them simple to operate. His was a car everyone could afford. In its heydey, the flivver sold for about $400. Ford's concept succeeded beyond his wildest dreams, and the Tin Lizzie transformed the face of America. Its success enabled Ford to retire at an early age, whereupon he took up sailing to avoid the traffic jams he had created.

Key Holder
A powerful magnet holds metal key case to any steel surface so you can keep a spare key hidden away on the outside of your car. Holds the largest keys. 79¢. Postage 39¢. *Walter Drake.*

Wheel Cover
Ends steering-wheel slippage by giving you a warm grip in winter and a cool grip in summer. Textured vinyl cover fits snugly over any steering wheel. Soft foam lining; leather-grain effect. Won't crack or stain. $2.98. Postage 60¢. *Holiday Gifts.*

Treat Your Ford Like a Rolls

It wasn't enough for Sir Malcolm Campbell to be the first man to drive a car faster than 250 miles an hour. He wanted to beat 300!

And so on the morning of September 3, 1935, the flying Englishman checked the tires and wiped the windshield on his mighty 2,500-horse-power *Blue Bird,* which stood at the starting mark of the Bonneville Salt Flats at Great Salt Lake, Utah.

Adjusting his goggles, Sir Malcolm hopped aboard. He had 6 miles in which to pick up speed before hitting the timing tape. Screaming along at 280 with 2 miles to go, he closed his radiator front to streamline the face of the car—and got trouble.

Blotches of oil blacked out his windshield just as the *Blue Bird* snapped the timing tape. In his rocketing prison, Campbell continued to torture the accelerator, and covered the required mile in 12 seconds. But as he slowed down to 280 miles per hour, the left front tire blew and the *Blue Bird* went crazy. With the skill that comes at near death, Campbell spun the wheel furiously in order to right the skidding car, and 5 miles later he stopped—with flames eating up the bad tire!

But Campbell had done only half a day's work. To establish a record he had to make the return trip.

Squirting out the fire, his mechanics threw on new wheels, and before he waved goodbye again the timers informed him he had run the course at a bit over 304 miles an hour. He could already see the newspaper headlines!

Only this time he had to let the car breathe. The radiator was left open, to push against a brick wall of wind. As he sped by the mark again, his speedometer read 290. Feeling his blood becoming a part of the car's circulation, he begged more speed out of it . . . and was timed at just under 296 for the return trip.

His average was 299.9—a new world's record, but a miserable tenth of a mile short of his goal!

He was already starting to think about next time as he walked unhappily away from the car. But the fates were having their little joke, because suddenly an official shouted, "Wait, there's been a mistake!"

Sir Malcolm actually hit 298.013 on the second trip. His average speed was a neat 301.1291 miles per hour!

Auto-Mate

This styrene compartment clamps tightly over the center hump of your car. It includes: full-size tissue dispenser and tissues, highway flares, wastebasket, first-aid kit, map holder, cigarette holder, flashlight, notebook and holder, hand towel, and a tray for snacks. 8" by 11". $12.50. Postage $1.25. *Gallery.*

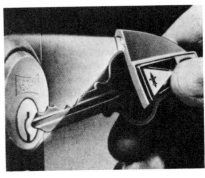

Key Beam

No more fumbling for house or car keyholes. This clip, powered by a self-charging cell, fits instantly over any key. No bulbs needed, no battery needed. Virtually indestructible. $3.95. Postage 90¢. *Carriage Shed.*

Warning System

This unit is placed on the rear window ledge. The remote control box is plugged into the cigarette lighter socket. A flip of the switch warns drivers behind to "Dim Lights" or "Stop Tailgating"; in the event of emergency, an "SOS" brings help. $9.95. Postage $2.00. *Lewis & Conger.*

Warning Triangle

The red reflective surface of this international danger signal is visible for more than a quarter of a mile, day or night. Sets up in seconds and cannot be blown over. No bulbs, no batteries. Lasts for years. Comes folded in a case 3" by 19". When opened, it is 16" high and 18" at the base. $3.50. Postage $1.35. *Clymer's.*

Change Carrier

If you travel a lot and need coins ready at hand for tolls, this chrome-plated holder will handle $7.00 worth of quarters, nickels, and dimes. Opens with a key; two keys are provided. Chrome. $10.95. Postage $1.29. *House of Minnel.*

Treat Your Ford Like a Rolls

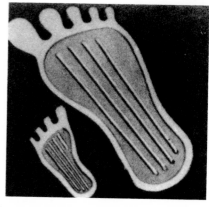

Fog-Proofing Stick

Eyeglasses, ski goggles, car windows, gun scopes, bathroom mirrors—any glass or plastic becomes fog-proofed and stream-proofed with one application of this stick. At least, that's what the manufacturers say. Smear a line every couple of inches across a window, or smear a stroke on each side of your lenses. Then buff with a soft dry cloth. One stick, the blurb says, provides a full year's supply for car windows, or a five-year service for glasses. $2.50. Postage $1.00. *Orvis.*

Foot-Shaped Car Pedals

Made of cast aluminum, these phoney pedals clamp right over the existing pedals, so that you can drive your car barefooted. $4.98 a pair. Postage 95¢. *Holiday Gifts.*

The first President to ride in an automobile was Theodore Roosevelt, but he didn't much care for it and seldom allowed the Secret Service chauffeur to take him out for a spin.

The next President, William Howard Taft, made more regular use of his brougham, but he didn't drive the car himself—perhaps because his enormous girth would not allow him to squeeze beneath the steering wheel.

Warren G. Harding was the first man elected President to drive a car himself.

* * *

A car runs more smoothly at night or in damp weather simply because the air is cooler, not because it contains more oxygen; the amount of oxygen in the air is a constant. Cool air is more dense than warm air; and therefore, an engine takes in a greater weight of air when it is damp and chilly. This accounts for the increased power and the freedom from engine knock which so many motorists notice when they drive at night or in the rain.

What's the most popular make of American car? Well, if we take the 1971 figures, it's the Chevrolet, with 2,320,777 in sales. The next most favored car is the Ford, with 1,761,112 cars sold. A distant third is the Oldsmobile, which sold 775,199 cars.

* * *

What country boasts the safest drivers? Surprisingly, the Philippines have the lowest traffic fatality rate of any nation, 1.5 deaths per 100,000 population. Though you might guess that the U.S. is plagued with the most reckless drivers in the world, four other countries show a worse record. Who these are is likely to surprise you—Canada, Australia, West Germany, and Austria. Austria, at the bottom of the barrel, has a rate of 31.9 traffic deaths per 100,000 population. The United States averages 26.7.

Automobile enthusiasts were aghast. The world's speed record was held, not by one of their pet gasoline-powered cars, but by an automobile with a steam engine in the nose. And the honor of being first to travel faster than 2 miles a minute had gone to this traitorous device.

It happened in January, 1906, when the Frenchman Marriott took his steam-powered Stanley to Daytona Beach, Florida. On the sands outside Ormond, Marriott sped over a measured mile at a rate of 121.52 miles per hour!

Not until 1908 did the gasoline engine return unto its own. Then a huge Fiat named *Mephistopheles* zoomed to a new record, searing the cinders at the rate of 121.64 mph.

* * *

Believe it or not, the first automobile race ever held was won by a car that was powered by a steam engine. On June 22, 1894, Paris was bub-bling with excitement as 20 horseless carriages lined up for the 80-mile race from Paris to Rouen and back again to the big town.

Could these new-fangled things run at all? And if they did, would they prove as fleet and as dura-ble as a few changes of horses?

Less than 5 hours later, a De Dion Bouton lumbered down the boulevards of gay Paree. The steamer had covered the distance at the dare-devil rate of 17 miles per hour.

* * *

Chicagoans were out in force on Thanksgiving Day, 1895. They came to see a new-fangled con-traption called an automobile. A few of the gasoline-powered horseless carriages were going to race.

The route lay from the heart of Chicago to a nearby suburb and back. The road measured exactly 54.36 miles. The winner would have to cover that terrific distance without breaking down.

J. Frank Duryea busted the tape 7 hours and 17 minutes after the start of the race. He had covered the distance at an average speed of 7.5 miles an hour!

The crowd went wild!

Portable Electric Vacuum

Because it is cordless, it goes any-where. For use in cars or hard-to-reach areas in the house. Comes with utility pickup, crevice tool, and soft foam-rimmed pickup. All three attachments fit right inside the case. Plastic. Weighs 1½ lbs. Uses four batteries (not included). $6.98. Postage $1.15. *Lillian Vernon.*

Auto Altimeter

Know how high you are as you motor along. Altitude from 0 to 15,000 feet is measured with this instrument. The grey plastic case is 3-3/8" in diameter. The pointer is bright red. A pressure sensitive plate permits mounting on glass or any hard surface. $10.95 postpaid. *Gokey.*

Back Supporter

Have you ever driven in a car and found that after four or five hours' driving, your back started to ache? This supporter can be inflated to render it firmer or softer. Folds flat. Neutral shade vinyl. 14" x 17½". $2.89. Postage 30¢. *Better Sleep, Inc.*

Poolside

One of the unique properties of water is its ability to fit any container, no matter what size or shape. And perhaps in no other manner is this carried to such an extreme as in the construction of swimming pools. Limited by the restraints imposed by poured concrete, for years the blue rectangle was the prime shape in the backyards of a privileged few.

Evolving technology brought concrete-spray and steel skeletons, fiberglass, and malleable plastic. These new materials took care of all the mutations the imagination of every dilettante dipper-designer could conceive. Fly over almost any city in the U.S. that has a temperature above freezing, and you will see giant water-filled instruments, rabbits, Mickey Mice, kidneys, organs of all types, musical as well as vital, flowers, fish, and profiles of the owners.

One beautiful specimen, in the now defunct Palisades Amusement Park in New Jersey, came complete with salt-water and waves.

Turn-of-the-Century Swim Suits

Made of stretch jersey cotton with bright 1½" wide stripes, these hilarious bathing outfits will cause raised eyebrows. HIS is an exact replica of a Gay 90s outfit with its ¾-length sleeves, knee-length pants, boat neck and draw-string waist. Sizes range from small to extra large. HERS has elastic and lacy ruffles at the sleeves, divided ruffles at the shirt waist. Comes in sizes small through large. HIS: $10.95; HERS: $11.95. Postage $1.00. *Patio.*

Underwater Slalom

Four giant plastic rings tied to four weighted plastic pylons are held by ropes which adjust to the depth you want. $15.00. Postage $2.00. *Patio.*

Aqua-Chaise

Buoyant arms support you while the seat strap lets you sit or lie flat in the water. Permits complete freedom of motion, and helps keep hair dry. Separate valves for arm and back sections. $6.98. Postage 60¢. *Better Sleep, Inc.*

Pool Badminton or Volleyball

Break the tedium of swimming laps, and get everyone into the pool for games. A 6' net attaches to an aluminum frame which floats 36" above the water on ethafoam pontoons. There'll be fun when the whole family taps around the 8½" molded volleyball. Comes with four badminton rackets made of plastic, and four waterproof shuttlecocks. $25.00. Postage $1.00. *Patio.*

Floater-Loafer

An unsinkable 4' wide horseshoe float of expandable polystyrene has recessed holes for cup, ash tray, etc., and floats a blue-webbed aluminum chaise. Chaise adjusts to body position. $32.95. Postage $1.00. *Patio.*

Let There Be Light!

Man is not a nocturnal creature; his eyes do not adjust to darkness as well as do those of an owl. When early man discovered the secret of fire, he soon thereafter discovered how to brighten his night with a torch or a candle.

The candle probably evolved when a piece of wood, or rush, or cord fell into ignited fat. How astounding it must have been to realize that the foreign body was not immediately consumed.

In the late 18th and early 19th centuries, candles were made of tallow, beeswax, and vegetable wax, such as bayberry. During the past decade, there has been a great revival in candle-making, especially of the organically scented varieties.

The first lamp was probably a dish which contained oil and a wick. The next development, thought to have originated in Egypt, was the float-wick lamp; here the wick was supported *above* the oil.

Early European lamps were always smoky, because the center of the round wick received too little air for proper combustion. But this drawback was overcome in the 18th century with the introduction of the flat-wick lamp. In that era, the most popular lamp fuel was whale oil; but by the 1840s, kerosene had come to the fore. The kerosene lamp is still in sporadic use today, where gas or electricity are not available.

The first electric lamp was the arc lamp, developed from the electrochemical principle demonstrated by Humphrey Davy in 1801. In 1879, Cleveland, Ohio, became the first city to use the new carbon-arc street lamps devised by C. F. Brush. Although an impracticable incandescent electric lamp appeared as early as 1858, it was not until 1879 that this type of illumination was perfected by Thomas A. Edison.

Neon lamps were invented by Georges Claude in 1911, and came into wide use within a decade. Different colors could be obtained by using different gases—argon for blue, neon for red, helium for yellow, carbon dioxide for white; and these gases could be mixed to produce virtually any color.

Among the more recent developments in lighting are the fluorescent lamp, a tube coated with a fluorescent powder and filled with traces of argon and mercury. The sodium vapor light, which represents the new trend in highway illumination, gives off a pinkish or yellowish aura which offers very little glare.

"The thing to do," Woodrow Wilson once said, "is to supply light and not heat." Though men of reason would wish always to do so, nature is not reasonable, and heat always accompanies light. For light is energy—particles, photons, or waves traveling at 186,000 miles per second.

Cable Car Lamp

This perfectly scaled model of San Francisco's famed cable car is a lamp, handmade of dark solid walnut, hand-rubbed to a glistening luster. 12" long, 6¾" wide, 5½" high. $45.00. Postage $6.50. *Cable Car Clothiers.*

Poly-Optics

With Poly-Optics, you're in the land of magical lighting. The crystal-like floral quality of the five delicate blossoms makes this unit enchanting. 15-watt bulbs are used to light the sprays which, in turn, radiate mystical beams. Base is black and walnut acrylic. $100.00. Postage $1.99. *House of Minnel.*

Solartronic Spiral

As long as the sun keeps radiating energy, the Solartronic Spiral will transform that energy into beautiful motion. As this instrument spins, enchanting reflections of the sun's rays are created. $13.00. Postage $1.65. *Childcraft.*

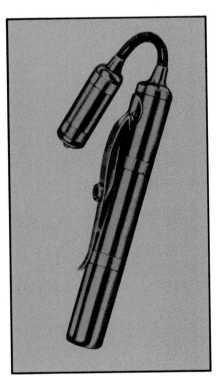

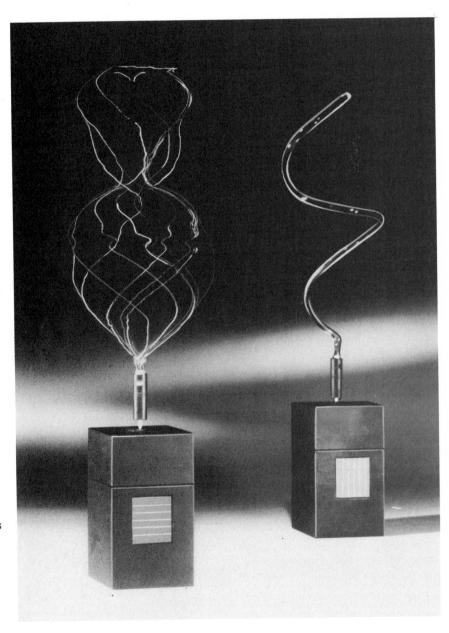

Flexible Light

Very useful when both hands are occupied, this battery-operated light provides a bright beam. It clips and locks onto a pocket or onto a belt. A flexible goose neck permits redirecting light as needed. Bright metal finish. 9½" long with 3¾" swivel neck. Batteries not included. $5.95. Postage $1.00. *Orvis.*

Let There Be Light!

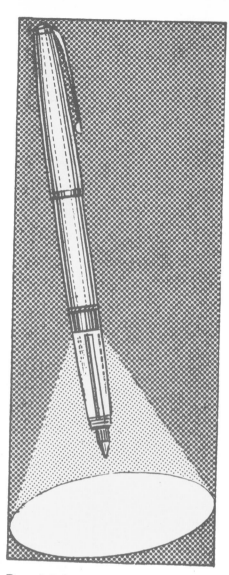

Creole Wall Bracket

Two black cast iron arms extend 11½" from wall. Can be spread open to 180°. Arms support two 5" cast iron cups. $9.50. Postage $1.70. *B. Altman.*

Pen Light

This aluminum flashlight pen may aid in finding your house lock or your car lock. Also effective for reading a theater program. $3.75. Postage 40¢. *Henningham's.*

Cordless Lamp

Powered by two C cell flashlight batteries, this cordless lamp can be used anywhere. It sets down securely on its own battery-weighted base, and has an arm which extends to 9". Its adjustable reflector will throw light exactly where needed. Chrome-finished, with base of simulated leather. Batteries not included. $6.95. Postage 40¢. *Chris Craft.*

Lift-a-Light

This night-light torch turns on when it is lifted, off when it is set down. 7½" high. In green, black, or blue velvet with beige brocade and floral tapestry. $12.50. Postage $2.00. *Three New Yorkers.*

Switchless Lamp

A touch of the hand at the "on" panel and the 6" cube glows. Another touch on the "off" panel and the light is extinguished. Perfect for an encounter group or for the kids' room. $14.95. Postage $1.20. *Game Room.*

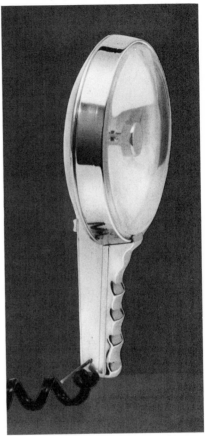

Powerlight

Capable of projecting a brilliant beam more than three-quarters of a mile, this powerful lantern employs a quartz-iodine bulb that is three times brighter than the conventional beam. Moreover, its life expectancy is much greater. Corrosion proof. Operates on 12-volt DC system, either by plugging into a cigarette outlet, or by direct battery hook-up. $29.95. Postage 40¢. *Chris Craft.*

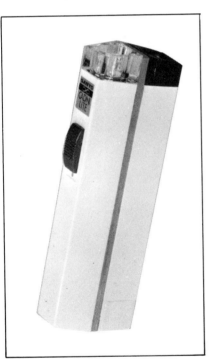

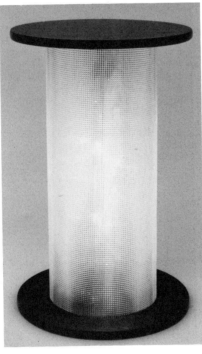

Rechargeable Flashlight

Only 4 3/8" long, 1 1/2" wide, and 3/4" deep, this flashlight will serve for pocket use. It will easily fit into the glove compartment of your car. The batteries may be recharged by reversing the end cap and plugging it into any 110 volt AC outlet. Batteries are never replaced. For emergency signaling, you slide the switch forward and a brilliant white light shines at one end, and a red light shines on the side. Comes in a white case with silver trim. $7.95 postpaid. *Gokey.*

Light Column

A four-color light display constantly changes in response to music and voices. In addition, the light column has an additional black light which shows off day-glo posters and gives the column's outer shell a bluish tinge. Walnut-like top and base. 18" by 12". $59.95. Postage $2.00. *Haverhill's.*

Let There Be Light!

Five-Year Light
How exasperating to find that the flashlight you need in a hurry is dead. Such a catastrophe is not likely to happen with this light since there is absolutely no power drain when it is not in use. This flashlight will stay alive for five years. Aluminum finish. $6.95. Postage 90¢. *Sleepy Hollow Gifts.*

Portable Fluorescent Lantern
Provides a bright, smooth flood of light, spread over a wide area for eight hours of steady illumination, on one set of batteries. Because it operates on eight self-contained standard flashlight D cells, this lantern goes anywhere. A bright 4" flourescent tube and an efficient reflector are housed in a chip-proof, water-resistant plastic case. Batteries not included. $19.95. Postage $1.00. *Chris Craft.*

Fantasia Musical Lamp
This music box plays the theme from "Love Story," while hidden lights create patterns on the highly polished plastic surface. 4¾" by 4¾" by 6¼" high. Battery operated. $25.00. Postage $1.95. *Hammacher Schlemmer.*

Illuminated Magnifier
Permits you to read fine print. A 3½" lens enlarges the type, and the light illuminates it. Takes two C batteries (no batteries included). $3.98. Postage 50¢. *Collier's.*

Pop Art Lamp

Featuring a beer can as a shade, this is a modern version of a high intensity gooseneck lamp. Stands 15" high. Complete with high intensity bulb. $5.95. Postage 95¢. *Artisan Galleries.*

Antiqued Lamp

This Spanish handcrafted lamp is made of tin, gilded to have an antiqued patina. Measures 44" by 24". $88.00. F.O.B. Madrid. *Abelardo Linares, S.A.*

*And this I know: whether the one True Light
Kindle to Love, or Wrath consume me quite,
One flash of It within the Tavern caught
Better than in the Temple lost outright.*

Edward Fitzgerald (1809-1883),
RUBAIYAT OF OMAR KHAYYAM

The two noblest things, which are sweetness and light.

Jonathan Swift (1667-1745),
THE BATTLE OF THE BOOKS

And the light shineth in darkness; and the darkness comprehended it not.

New Testament: John, i, 5

To give light to them that sit in darkness and in the shadow of death, to guide our feet into the way of peace.

Ibid. Luke, i, 79

The Home Barbershop

It was, of course, the hippies who started the current style of long hair, beard, whiskers, and sideburns—more properly called burnsides, after the Confederate general who sported this particular brand of hirsute adornment. The hippies, and their forerunners, the beats, who rebelled against the foppery of fancy duds and the time-wastefulness of trimming away the indicia of manliness, can be said to have become a social force just around the time Jack Kerouac wrote *On the Road* in 1957. The hippy paean struck its high note with the presentation of "Hair," which celebrated the most visible aspect of hippiness.

Yet it is now being bruited about that the beard has reached the heydey of its current vogue, and may well be on the way out—or off, as the case may be. Indeed, love for the beard has been very fickle. During the first part of this century—between 1910 and 1960—facial foliage in the United States was indeed a rarity.

Through the centuries, man has made a great to-do about his hair. Some of the ancients went to great extremes in caring for their beards. The Lords of Nineveh oiled and curled their beards. The Kings of Persia plaited their hirsutulous draperies with golden thread. Early French kings daintily tied their whiskers with silken ribbons. Even today, the Sikhs of India dye their beards, for it is only a flaming red patch that will establish a Sikh as a man among men.

Let's pull a few threads out of the tangled mass of facts concerning hair. The growth of beards varies considerably among the peoples of the earth. The Celts and the Slaves have most luxurious appendages; the Chinese, but a few hairlets; the Ethiopians, a curly beard; and the American Indians, hardly any tuft at all. The Lombards derived their names from the shagginess of their faces; originally, they were called Longobards (long beards).

In connection with the American Indians, we recall to mind the sad plight of Daniel Boone, who was captured by the redskins and granted life on condition that he would turn Indian

brave. In order to effect initiation into the tribe, he had to submit to becoming whiskerless through the grand old Indian method of having the hairs of his face plucked out. Dan, when he grew old, used to say when referring to the incident, "I simply loved to play Indian . . . but it took a lot of pluck!"

"Oh, they're always in the way;
They're always in the way;
    My mother eats them in her sleep,
    She thinks she's eating shredded wheat.
They're always in the way;
The cows eat them for hay.
    They hide the dirt, on father's shirt,
They're always in the way!"

Time was when the way a beard was sculptured caused a nation to gird up its loins and do battle. The terrible Tartars actually declared war against the perfumed Persians because those effeminates trimmed their tassels in a manner

1890s Ad
Inspired by early advertising, this fiberboard sign extols the virtues of Samson's Onguent, whatever that was. 11-7/8" by 15-7/8". $9.00. Postage $1.00. *Yorkraft.*

which offended the religious feelings of the orthodox Tartars.

Time was, too, when a beard could pluck at the heart of a king—and soften it. Ivan the Terrible, a tyrant who terrified a nation, was mesmerized by the five-foot, two-inch beard of George Killingsworth, ambassador of Queen Elizabeth; and while his subjects quailed and quaked at his gruesome edicts, Ivan sat in the throne room, docile as a doe, lovingly caressing the envoy's whiskers.

But a successor, Peter the Great, had no use for whiskerandos. In order to occidentalize his Russian subjects, he compelled shaving by laying a tax on beards, assessed according to the rank of the offender.

Alexander the Great was likewise famed as a capillary killer. Ingenious general that he was, he commanded his men, according to Plutarch, to hack off their capillose extensions so that the enemy should not be able to plant their hands in his men's whiskers and win through pull.

From Alex's time on, the Greeks severed all connections with beards and started in to shave. The Romans began to gather in their spinach crop in 296 B.C. when a certain Ticinius Mena, a barber from Sicily, introduced the fashion. Pliny tells us that Scipio Africanus was the first man who shaved every day. The initial leveling of the face of a young Roman was celebrated on the day on which he reached his majority, and the hairs planed off were sacrificed to his patron god. The fashion lasted until the Emperor Hadrian discovered that his countenance had a most unfortunate habit of growing warts. In order to camouflage the pesty protuberances, he promptly re-introduced the fashion of wearing long beards. But the new-fangled, old-fashioned style was short-lived; and pretty soon, facial underbrush found no refuge under a Roman nose.

Then came the barbarians, each one hiding a sinister scowl behind a voluptuous Visigothic visker. When Rome fell, hair arose on the cheeks and chins of all who would curry favor with the hairy Huns. The barbarians put the shush on shaving for a few hundred years. But in 1084, Pope Gregory the 7th bullied the clergy into becoming shavelings. From then on, it was heresy for a priest not to practice hairicide.

In the middle of the 14th century, in Spain, there arose a vogue of wearing false beards. In the morning, a grandee dandy would drape his

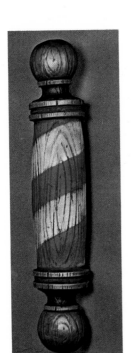

Medicine Man Memento
You might get a kick, but you'll get no Kickapoo out of this wood sign which is 6½" by 32¼". $11.00. Postage $1.00. *Yorkraft.*

Barber Pole
This decorative bit would fit into any man's shaving premises as a sort of imprimateur of what he was doing there. Made of latex, painted by hand, and antiqued, it stands 35" high, weighs 12 lbs. $30.00. Postage $4.00. *Artistic Latex.*

The Home Barbershop

chin in a crimson beard; in the evening, he serenaded his senorita in an adjustable, long, black hanging. Soon the country resembled a huge masquerade party. No one knew who was who. Creditors could not catch up with debtors. The police arrested the innocent while villains hid behind hair. Wives were conjugal with the wrong husbands, whereupon the price of horsehair skyrocketed. King Peter of Aragon had to end the farce by forbidding the wearing of false beards.

Beards have been useful not only for seduction but for health. As a matter of fact, many physicians of the 19th century used to prescribe them for persons with delicate throats. These savants reasoned that a good substantial beard was nothing more or less than a permanent muffler; and pursuant to their recommendations, many a person beat a cold by a whisker.

Some years back, the favorite sport of bus riders in London was a game called "Beaver." For sighting a bearded man, an ordinary "Beaver," one received 10 points; and for sighting a Red Rex, or "King Beaver," one chalked up 50 points. Many color blind Britishers went bankrupt.

In 1922, when the city of Sacramento wanted to arrange a celebration commemorating the swashbuckling era of the forty-niners, they passed an ordinance compelling "all male citizens over the age of consent to grow whiskers and thus make the town look like it used to." Loyalty to their fair and sentimental city won over gallantry toward their wives and sweethearts; and all and sundry males became so enthusiastic over the idea, they even formed a Whiskerino Club, offering a prize for the longest pair of whiskers. A natty gent, sporting passementerie some 17 feet in length, won the first prize. In keeping with the whole idea, and feeling quite hellish, the Sacramento Club also awarded a prize for "the most impressive cootie garage." There are no further statistics.

Probably the most interesting single fact about beards is the respect with which some peoples regarded their hairy herbiage. The Bible records the story of how David's ambassadors had their beards spitefully shaved off by a defiant heathen. The king covered their shame, saying, "Tarry ye at Jericho until your beards be grown"—but war answered the insult.

Livy relates that when the barbarians overran the Golden City, the Roman senator sat still, unmoved at everything, until the Goth touched his beard—then he struck, although he died for the blow.

The early kings of France, for a long time, stuck three hairs plucked from their beards in the seal of official papers to lend the documents greater sanction.

Today, the custom of the Mussulman is to carry a comb with him to manicure his whiskers. He does so immediately after prayer, while still on his knees, and any strands of hay that fall out of his beard are carefully picked up and preserved for burial with the owner. Two hundred million Mohammedans still swear by the beard of the Prophet.

In medieval times, a banker accepted from Baldwin, Count of Edesse, a pledge of his lordly beard as security for the repayment of a substantial loan. This was considered collateral of the first water.

An old source sponsors the story that an Italian called Filefo and a Greek philosopher named Timothy got into a violent dispute concerning a most important problem. The question was whether a certain Greek syllable was long or short. The seriousness of the issue caused Filefo to wager a considerable sum of money. Timothy matched the stake by hazarding his long beard. It was a terrific chance to take with the winter coming on. When Timothy was declared vanquished, he offered Filefo his wife as accord and satisfaction, if only he could keep his beard. But Filefo scoffed: "A woman for a beard?" and a scornful laugh laughed he. Then Timothy offered Filefo his home, including the new radio; then all his money; and finally a mortgage on a certain plot in Paradise. But Filefo was inexorable! He would have nothing but *the beard*. Accordingly, the unfortunate Timothy, mid pomp and circumstance, was deflowered of his chinly raiment. Filefo gathered his spoils and carefully wrapped the whiskers in cellophane. When he died, it took two monks two years to catalog his private capillary collection.

Commercializing their foliage occurred to the House of David. They went to bat with their whiskers and made a hit.

Here's one Ripley overlooked: In Rumania, beards were once put under government control. They could only be worn if the owner got an official permit, which had to be paid for.

Coming down to modern times, there's no doubt that beards have played a great part in American politics. This, at first, might sound like a piece of extravagant absurdity, but in the presidential campaign of 1916, didn't Wilson beat Hughes by a close shave?

Shampoo, which to us means to wash your hair, comes from the Hindu word *shampu,* which means to press. A good shampoo is one where you press your fingers hard against your scalp, so our word still indicates part of the original Hindu meaning.

* * *

In Panama, a Guaymi Indian need never buy a razor. When he wants a shave, he just wanders to the edge of a grassy field and pulls one of the thick, high stalks. He removes one of the oatlike seeds that grow in bunches on each stalk. On the sides of each of these seeds are two slender blades that are as sharp as glass.

Holding the seed firmly by its tough filaments, the Guaymi draws it across his face, and off go his whiskers. He couldn't get a cleaner shave in a barber shop.

* * *

The pride and joy of Hans Lanoseth, a Norwegian-American farmer who lived in North Dakota, was his eleven foot, six inch beard. It took 36 years to grow it to that record length.

To shave or not to shave, that is the question:
Whether 'tis nobler on the face to suffer
The itch and torment of outgrowing bristles,
Or to take blade against a snarl of whiskers,
And by truncating end them? To hack: to scrape:
No more; and by a swish to say we end
The tickle and the thousand prickly pangs
That flesh is hair to, 'tis a consummation
Devoutly to be wished. To hack; to scrape;
To scrape: perchance to cut: ay, there's the rub:
For in that prick of flesh what blood may come
When we have struggled on this stubborn root,
Must give us pause. There's the tough beard
That makes calamity of so dull an edge;
For who would the frothy foaminess bear,
The electric's burn, the balm's perfumery,
The pangs of o'erus'd blade, the styptic's delay,
The insolence of jingles and the price
That patient patrons of the new product pay,
When he himself might his punishment stay
With beard and mustache?

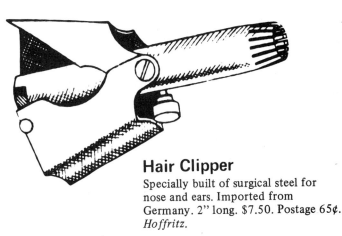

Hair Clipper
Specially built of surgical steel for nose and ears. Imported from Germany. 2" long. $7.50. Postage 65¢. *Hoffritz.*

Moustache Comb
From France. Small enough to fit into your pocket. 2¾" long. $2.75. Postage 76¢. *New Hampton General Store.*

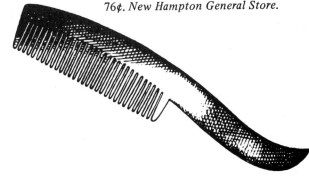

Finishing Touches

Every home, no matter how complete and opulent the basic furniture, requires finishing touches—a shelf to accent a dark corner, a little rug to set off a hearth, an umbrella stand to complete a foyer.

However, applying the Freudian principle of free association, the phrase *finishing touches* brings to mind the deft parry, the apt rejoinder, the mortal (or immortal) riposte, the bon mot that settles an issue definitively. In this connection, here are three incidents, each of which illustrates "the finishing touch," par excellence.

There was a great deal of bad feeling between William Pitt, First Earl of Chatham, and Robert Walpole, Earl of Oxford. After a particularly heated speech by Pitt, Walpole, who felt enormously aggrieved, met Pitt outside Parliament and furiously declared, "Sir, you will either die on the gallows or perish from some unspeakable disease."

"That, my lord," rejoined Pitt, "depends upon whether I embrace your policies or your mistress."

Two American statesmen who seemed to be in constant antagonism were John Randolph and Henry Clay. At one time, after these bitter enemies had not spoken to one another for quite a while, they chanced to meet in a narrow street. It was evident that one would have to step aside to let the other pass.

Randolph firmly held his ground. "I never give way to scoundrels," he said.

Clay then stepped into the muddy gutter. "I *always* do," he replied.

About a century later, Dorothy Parker sat at a dinner party laughing at the antics of a wit who was something of a clown. Her neighbor, an over-educated young snob, was particularly disdainful.

"I'm afraid I can't join in the merriment," he scornfully remarked. "I can't bear fools."

"That's queer," observed Miss Parker, "your mother could."

Fish Rug

This rug, imported from Dominica, is handmade of natural-color grass. 4' long by 15" wide. $14.95. Postage $1.30. *Elizabeth McCaffrey's.*

Victorian Umbrella Stand

An aluminum reproduction of a famed Victorian original. Stands 73" high, 26" wide. Weighs 33 lbs. Available in black, white, or moss green. $243.50. For any special color, add $15.00. Shipped express collect. *J. F. Day.*

Birds in a Gilded Cage

A pair of miniature tanagers—a lady in her yellows, olives, and blacks, and a gentleman in scarlet with black wings and tail-tip—trill and twitter as their tiny beaks open and close, and their tails flick. Works like a music box with a stop-and-go button. The cage, 12" high, is covered with genuine gilt applied to metal. $165.00. Shipped express collect. *Invento.*

Doorbell

This elaborate set-up involves eight different bells, a beautiful wrought-iron stand and a pull chain. $88.00. Shipped express collect. *Acme Hardware.*

Incense Burner

Made of pottery, about 3" by 3" by 5", this adobe home is suitable for burning incense. Comes with 18 sticks of pinon incense. $3.95. Extra packs of 40 incense sticks are $1.50. Postage $1.00. *Old Mexico Shop.*

Lavabo

Handmade ceramic lavabo from Portugal has a basin 12" by 10" by 8" high, and a water deposit 18" high. Comes in blue, violet, or multi-colored. $38.00. Postage $23.50. *Fabrica de Faiancas e Azulejos Sant'Anna.*

FinisHing TouCHes

Marriage Cup
Bride and groom toast their troth by
sharing their first cup of wine; the cup
tips to serve the bride, then tips to the
other side to serve the groom. Styled
as a bridal lace gown, the outside is
silver-plated, the inside is gold-color
lined. 8" high. $10.50. Postage $2.20.
Croydon's.

French Mailbox
The cover which bears a relief of a
nymph and child, is a faithful
reproduction of a European antique.
The 14" by 23" latched front is made
of cast aluminum and is hand finished
in white, black, or verde green. Mail is
collected in the wood container
attached at the back. Container is 12"
long, 8" wide, 4" deep. $35.00.
Postage $1.00. *Patio.*

Spoon Rack

This decorative wooden spoon rack is 18" wide and 19" high. $24.95 postpaid. *Forslund.*

Keyholder

This 14" long key rack is made of polished cherry wood. Comes with six keyrings, each 1" by 2¼", in unfinished cherrywood. $12.95 postpaid. *Forslund.*

Wheelbarrow Planter

Made of dark pine, this miniature planter is suitable for a centerpiece. It has a plastic liner. Water-resistant finish. 17" long. Bucket is 5" deep, has a diameter of 7¼". $7.95. Postage $1.75. *Sturbridge Yankee Workshop.*

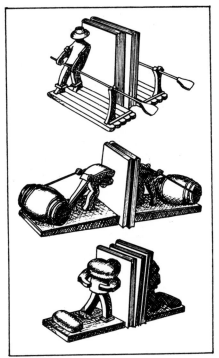

Ecuadorian Bookends

These wooden bookends are $7.00 for any pair, postpaid. *Akios.*

Violin Planter

Handcrafted mellowpine planter in the shape of a violin has a smooth finish. 19" by 7". $5.00. Postage $2.00. *Pohlson Galleries.*

Hitching Post

Black cast aluminum with brass rings. $99.50. Postage $5.00. *B. Altman.*

Scissors Candle Snuffer

Solid brass scissors snuffer trims wicks, pries out the candle stub, in addition to snuffing candles. Reproduction of Colonial Williamsburg model. 6¼" by 2". $12.50. Postage $1.00. *B. Altman.*

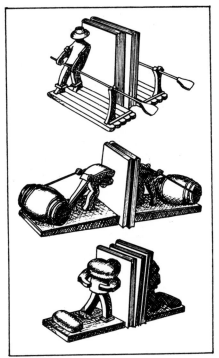

Wherever You May Roam

When Christopher Columbus chartered those three boats and kissed his mother goodby, he had no idea what he was starting. Otherwise, he would surely have set up the world's first travel agency.

Not only is the world's population growing—it's moving. At almost every major airport in the world, there are planes landing and taking off at the rate of nearly one a minute. If you've ever been stacked up over an airport, you know how many planes that is.

There are countless thousands of commuters who log more than 50,000 miles a year just driving from their homes in the suburbs to work. Then there are all those miles millions of people travel just on the elevators that carry them to their office skyscrapers.

With all this traveling going on, probably the only thing that keeps us moving is the myriad of devices which have been devised to speed the

traveler on his way. Of course, when you arrive at your destination, you find that claiming your baggage may seem to take more time than getting there. It's a prime irony that you can fly 3,000 miles from New York to Los Angeles in just five hours, and then find yourself in a traffic jam on the San Diego Freeway which may force you to take up to two hours to traverse the 20 miles from the airport to Hollywood.

What with the new boom in travel, with hordes of people coming and going, and with buffeting your way through the security checks and worrying your way through the customs checks, and with traffic backing up almost to your front door—there may be only one way left to avoid the hassle, the delay, and the utter, utter confusion—DON'T GO! But then again, you may wind up terribly lonely—the only one left in the neighborhood who's not out traveling.

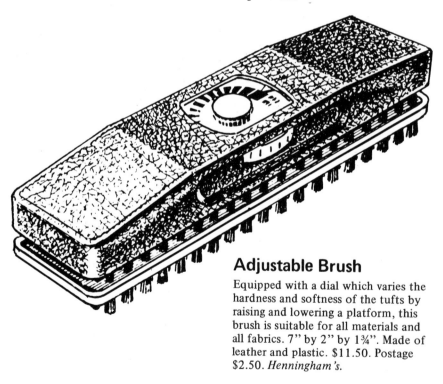

Adjustable Brush

Equipped with a dial which varies the hardness and softness of the tufts by raising and lowering a platform, this brush is suitable for all materials and all fabrics. 7" by 2" by 1¾". Made of leather and plastic. $11.50. Postage $2.50. *Henningham's.*

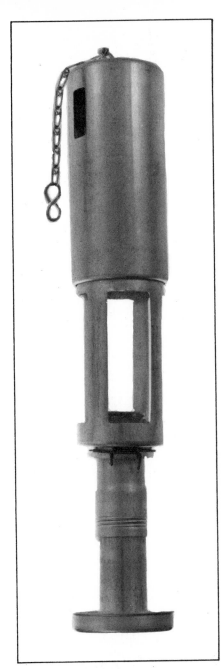

World-Wide Travel Iron

Light enough to carry in your luggage, this 2½ lb. iron is heavy enough to do the job. Works on either 110 or 220 volts, AC or DC. Comes with a set of world-wide adaptive plugs that you can use almost everywhere. Leather carrying case comes in red, black, or tan. $12.95. Postage $1.00. *Deluxe Saddlery.*

Electric Globetrotter

A set of conversion plugs to adapt American plugs to outlets in any foreign country. Comes in leather kit. $5.95. Postage $1.00. *Taylor Gifts.*

Candle Lantern

Aluminum, with a glass chimney, this French lantern telescopes to 2" by 4½". Has a chain for hanging. 4¾ oz. $3.85. Postage $1.00. *Taylor Gifts.*

Drip Dry Hanger

Contoured hanger holds front and back of shirt, and dress, and all drip dries apart so wrinkles can't form. Holder dries collars neat and crisp. Made of plastic. Folds flat for travel. Set of 3, $1.79. Postage 75¢. *Bevis Industries.*

Folding Hanger

This folding hanger also doubles as a brush. Fruitwood finish. 17" long. $1.50. Postage 50¢. *Triangle Stores.*

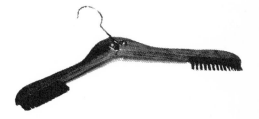

For Your Next Barbecue

Named by the Spaniards who first observed its practice in the New World, elevated to artistic and mythological fame by Charles Lamb's Dissertation, and raised to pre-eminence in a prestigious social occasion by LBJ, the barbecue is so well established today it's now even built *inside* many homes.

Cooking with hot embers is one of the oldest of culinary methods; and to a hungry group at the beach, it sometimes seems like the longest. Particularly when the first delicious-smelling sizzlings have begun to waft your way.

While waiting for the charcoal to turn white in your transistor-sized hibachi, it may be some consolation to consider the backyard parties of certain tribes in New Guinea. They dig a pit, 20 feet long, 15 feet deep, and 10 feet wide, burn logs in it till it's half-filled with glowing coals, and then toss in wet leaves, followed by upwards of 50 whole pigs. They cover the whole shebang with sand, and go away to dance for two days, until they hear the words so dear to all barbecue stand-bys: "C'mon and get it."

Patio Bar

This wicker tote-bar from Europe stores four large bottles or eight soft drinks in a bottom compartment. The top compartment, 3½" deep, holds nuts, crackers, sandwiches, glasses, etc. 18" high, 10½" in diameter. Easy to carry. $9.95. Postage $1.40. *Clymer's.*

Electric Char-B-Que

Permanent self-cleaning briquets make charcoal broiling without charcoal possible. No flames, no sparks. Starts at a turn of the dial. Special control sets heat at proper temperature; heat stays even throughout. Rust-proof aluminum housing. Large cooking area grills, bakes, broils, and roasts. Plugs into 110-volt outlet. Tangerine finish. 22½" by 14" by 10" high. $60.00. Postage $4.00. *Chris Craft.*

Ice Keg

This pine barrel holds 3½ gallons of ice cubes. Has yellow liner. Charred exterior is fitted with steel bands. Sturdy hemp handles. 16½" by 11". $16.00. Postage $1.50. *Deluxe Saddlery.*

Poultry Available

Bob White Quail (5 to 6 oz. each)	$4.00 pair	*Maryland Gourmet*
Chukhar Partridge (14 to 16 oz. each)	4.50 each	*Maryland Gourmet*
Norwegian Ptarmigan (14 to 16 oz. each)	5.95 each	*Maryland Gourmet*
Norwegian Ryper (pair weighs 1½ lbs.)	31.50 a box of six	*Maryland Gourmet*
Scotch Grouse (¾ lb. each)	6.75 each	*Maryland Gourmet*

All items listed above are packed in dry ice and shipped via air mail. Delivery in good usable condition is guaranteed by the supplier.

For Your Next Barbecue

Meats Available

Bear Steak	$3.75 lb.	*Maryland Gourmet*
Beaver	1.25 lb.	*Maryland Gourmet*
Buffalo Steak	3.90 lb.	*Maryland Gourmet*
Colorado Beef	27.00	*Daniel's of Denver*
(Eight 6-oz. fillets)		
Elephant Steak	3.75 lb.	*Maryland Gourmet*
Elk Boneless Rump	2.95 lb.	*Maryland Gourmet*
Hippopotamus Roast	3.75 lb.	*Maryland Gourmet*
Llama Roast	3.50 lb.	*Maryland Gourmet*
Mouflon Legs	2.25 lb.	*Maryland Gourmet*
Possum	.89 lb.	*Maryland Gourmet*
Raccoon	.89 lb.	*Maryland Gourmet*
Wild Boar Backs	2.75 lb.	*Maryland Gourmet*

All items listed above are packed in dry ice and shipped via air mail. Delivery in good usable condition is guaranteed by the supplier.

Spanish Bar Cart

This solid wood, hand-carved Spanish cart holds six bottles and set-ups. 30" wide by 42" high. Wheels are 19" in diameter. $50.00. Postage $15.00. *Herley Imports.*

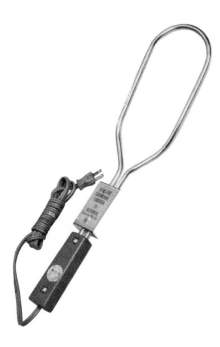

Fire Starter

This electric unit gets coals red-hot in 10 to 15 minutes, without kindling, fluid, flame, or smoke. It must be removed before using the grill. The mechanism operates on 115 volt, 60 cycle AC only; has a 500 watt element. Heating element sheathed in nickel steel. 18½" long, with a 6' rubberized cord. U.L. tested and approved. $6.50 postpaid. *Gokey*.

Hot Dog Cart

Comes with everything but the girl. 8' tall, 5½' long. Under the red, orange, and yellow circus-striped umbrella, there's a cooking area heated by propane gas, a 40-lb. ice storage box, and a compartment for bottles, glasses, buns, beer, and sauerkraut. Two side counters are of stainless steel. There's a carving board, too. Wooden wheels are rubber tired. 55" long, 33" wide working surface. $1,395. Shipped express collect. *Hammacher Schlemmer*.

Kalahari Grill

This wondrous grill will broil four steaks or six hamburgers in six minutes, using a match, some suet and four sheets of newspaper. No other fuel needed. Folds flat into a case 22" by 14" by 1-5/8". Two forks included. $18.95. Postage $2.00. *Hunting World*.

Chestnut Pan

This 10" steel pan has holes in the bottom for roasting chestnuts over an open fire. $3.00. Postage 95¢. *Bazar Francais*.

For Your Next Barbecue

Standing Salad Bowl

Made of pure maple, this imposing salad outfit stands 30" high. The bowl itself is 20" wide, fork and spoon each 18" long. $110. Shipped express collect. *Rosalind Light Ltd.*

Tub on Wheels

This hand-rubbed walnut keg has solid brass rings, hoops, and name plate. Metal lining. 23½" by 14½" wide. Holds 10½ gallons. $99.50. Shipped express collect. *Hammacher Schlemmer.*

Spark Gun

A squeeze on the trigger and a fat spark instantly lights alcohol, sterno, or gas fuel. Will work in any weather. No flints, no batteries, nothing to wear out or be replaced. Lasts for years. $4.95. Postage 75¢. *Chris Craft.*

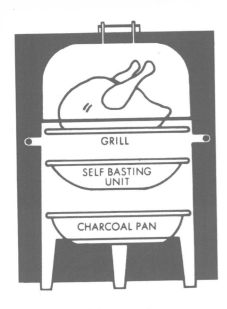

Smoke N' Pit Barbecue

This patented pit barbecue guarantees moist, tender roasts every time. Will handle up to 25 lbs. of meat at once. The grill and the charcoal are separated by water. As the water evaporates, it combines with the smoke and the drippings to do the cooking. There is no hand-basting here, no turning, no watching is required. Constructed of heavy steel, rust-proof enamel finish, wooden handles. 27" high, diameter 17", weight 27 lbs. Black. Instructions included. $39.95 postpaid. *L. L. Bean.*

Weber Barbecue

By providing a hood to cover what's cooking, this barbecue allows the food to cook in its own juices, thus allowing the food to remain moist and tender however well done. Dampers permit charcoal to be put out so that it may be reused. Heavy porcelain finish on inside. 13½" diameter; 13" high. $16.95. Postage $2.72. *Colonial Garden Kitchens.*

Electric Smoker

Hickory chips, furnished with smoker, impart a delicious flavor to fish and game. 1' square by 23" high. Capacity of 20 lbs. of meat. Has a sliding inspection panel. $24.40. Postage $3.40. *Netcraft.*

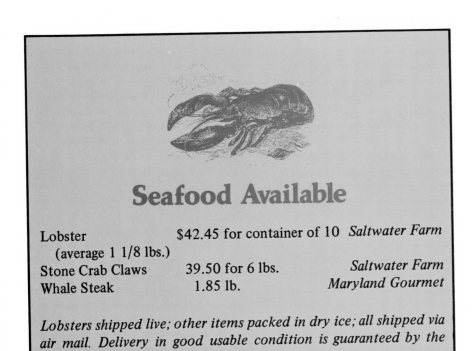

Seafood Available

Lobster (average 1 1/8 lbs.)	$42.45 for container of 10	*Saltwater Farm*
Stone Crab Claws	39.50 for 6 lbs.	*Saltwater Farm*
Whale Steak	1.85 lb.	*Maryland Gourmet*

Lobsters shipped live; other items packed in dry ice; all shipped via air mail. Delivery in good usable condition is guaranteed by the supplier.

For Your Next Barbecue

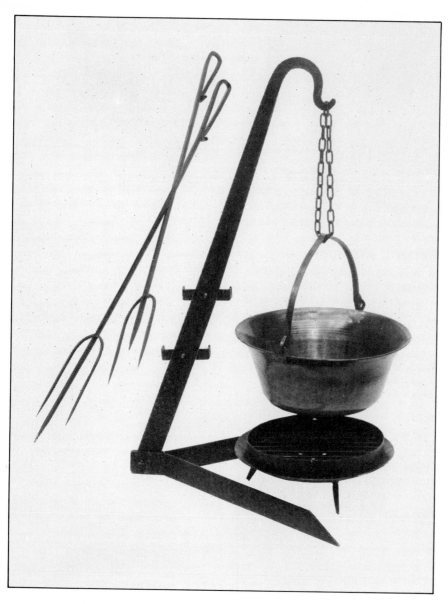

Cauldron Set

An imported wrought iron set which includes a four-quart steel cauldron, two long-handled forks, and a grill. 27" high. $29.95. Postage $1.50. *H. Roth & Son.*

Charcoal Igniter

With this lighter, charcoal is ignited in 90 seconds, and becomes red-hot in six minutes. One sheet of crumpled newspaper sets the gadget off; lighter fluids are not needed. Fill the starter with briquets, light the newspaper, and when the coals are red-hot, lift the lighter off with the handle and coals will dump out automatically. Aluminum-coated steel. 10½" high; 6" diameter. Doubles as camp stove. $4.63. Postage 80¢. *Walter Drake.*

Meat Thermicator

An electronic heat-sensing probe tells instantly and exactly when cooked foods are ready. This instrument converts the internal heat of food to an electric signal. Set tip to penetrate depth you want it to read, prick it into food, and read the exact internal temperature on a large dial. $119.50. Postage $1.00. *Orvis.*

Ball-B-Q

Here's a two-grill design which provides 340 square inches of cooking surface. Food on top grill cooks at same temperature as the bottom grill. Heat circulates inside the sphere, maintaining an even temperature. Drip pan keeps fat from fire, so grill cooks smokelessly. Leg is removable for tabletop use. Made of heavy steel covered in flame-orange baked enamel. $34.95. Postage $2.00. *Gallery.*

Wire-Wheel Cart

A movable feast can be compactly contained on this butcher block serving cart which holds a six-bottle wine rack, two removable oak trays, a two-way pull drawer, two fixed storage shelves and an 18" by 29" by 2" thick oak butcher block top. The aluminum spiked disc will, of course, hold a roast. 37" high, 37" long. $300.00. Postage $10.00. *Patio.*

Candy

Liquor may be quicker, but candy is still dandy. In the ancient Orient, sweets took the form of preserved fruits laced with honey. These not only delighted the children, but were an invaluable aid to doctors, who could disguise an unpleasant-tasting medicine by encasing the nostrum in a candy. For this purpose, medieval European physicians often used sugarplate, a sweet consisting of gum dragon, sugar, and rosewater, beaten into a paste.

One of the earliest confections made—still eaten today—is marzipan, a blend of nut paste, sugar, and egg white. Sugarplums, those objects of a child's vision on Christmas Eve, appeared in England in the 17th century. But it was not until the Crystal Palace Exhibition of 1851, where the boiled sweets of England were on display for the world, that fine candymaking became extensive on the continent.

Even today, the British eat almost eight ounces of sweets per person per week, more than any other people. But Americans, too, love their candy.

In the middle of the 19th century, while Europe was in its greatest candymaking boom, the United States had only 380 or so small factories making lozenges, jujube paste, and stick candy. Most fine candy was imported.

Chocolate, the bane of adolescent complexions and bulgy midriffs, is a preparation made from the seeds of the cacao tree. The Aztecs favored a chocolate beverage which they introduced to the Spanish explorers in the 16th century. This beverage found its way to Europe, where it soon become all the rage. Many chocolate shops became centers of political discussion, such as the famous Cocoa Tree in London.

Chocolate for eating was not perfected until 1876. M. D. Peter of Switzerland turned the trick. Today, Swiss milk chocolate is universally renowned for its flavor, color, and texture. But the most popular eating chocolate in the world is the plain old Hershey Bar, produced in Hershey, Pennsylvania, in the world's largest chocolate factory. The Hershey Factory turns out well over 200 million candy bars a year.

Now that your sweet tooth has been tickled, look through these pages, and then make an appointment with your dentist.

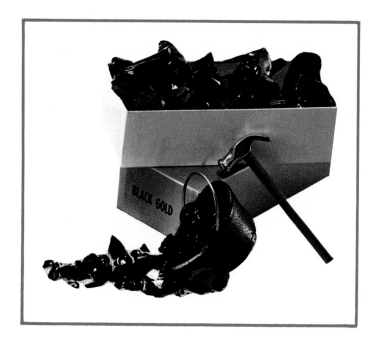

Coal Candy

This anise-flavored confection has the appearance of coal. A miniature coal scuttle, 2" by 2", and a hammer are included to crack the black coal candy. 1 lb. box. $4.95 postpaid. *Bachman.*

At many a fiesta held in rural Mexico, one of the treats enjoyed by the guests is ant candy. This unusual confection consists of the bodies of ants which gather honey from a species of oak leaf. The ants swell enormously until they are about the size of gooseberries. After the ants' legs and heads are removed, their bodies are piled on dishes and served as candy. The taste of these insects is very similar to that of a sweet, juicy fruit.

Milk Glass Candy Dish

Finely modeled cat tops a traditional lacy-edged Westmoreland candy dish. 8" by 5" by 6" high. $9.95. Postage $2.05. *Sturbridge Yankee Workshop.*

Cotton Candy Machine

An apparatus which turns out cotton candy. Operated by battery or through an electrical outlet. 14" in diameter, 10" high. Comes with batteries. $16.00. Postage $2.00. *Hammacher Schlemmer.*

Music! Music! Music!

Hurdy Gurdy

An old-fashioned music-maker reproduced here in function as well as appearance. Made of metal, hand-crafted in Spain, the 25" by 32" by 50" high instrument plays music from a roll of six tunes. Roll included. $650.00. Shipped express collect. *Hammacher Schlemmer.*

"Jazz will endure," complained John Philip Sousa, "as long as people hear it through their feet instead of their brains." Though he didn't realize it, Sousa was prophesying.

Rhythm, the prime ingredient of jazz, is the fundamental element of musical communication, for rhythm originates in the motor impulses of the human body.

Melody is a product of the capacity of the human voice to produce tone; and singing is likewise a motor reaction of the body. But harmony, although considered a basic element of music, is not at all present in Oriental music, and is a rather late development in the music of the West.

In reaction to the romanticism of 19th-century symphonic music, modern composers have relied increasingly on the use of atonality and dissonance, whose protagonists have been Paul Hindemith and Igor Stravinsky.

But one generation's avant-garde inevitably becomes the next generation's establishment. The concretist movement, led by John Cage, cut a swath of its own, with such baffling works as Cage's *4 Minutes 33 Seconds,* an opus of total silence. When asked what he thought of this trend among younger composers, Stravinsky said that he hoped subsequent compositions in this vein would be "works of major length."

If compositions for the vacuum cleaner and the electric drill have not captured the imagination of the partisans of serious music, jazz has certainly managed to dominate the popular music of our time. The hot blasts of Louis Armstrong and Jelly Roll Morton, the sweet lilt of Paul Whiteman and Bing Crosby, the swing of Glenn Miller and Benny Goodman, the rock and roll of Elvis Presley and the Rolling Stones—all these sounds of the last 50 years represent the unchallenged ascendancy of jazz. We'd wager John Philip Sousa will have to put up with those tapping feet for some time to come.

Around 1850, one Don Jose Gallegos, of Malaga, invented a musical instrument which he called the *Guitarpa*. It combined a harp, a guitar, and a violin-cello, and had 35 strings. Twenty-six strings and 21 pegs acted upon thè harp. Six strings belonged to the Spanish guitar, while three silver strings and 18 pegs managed the violin-cello. The pedestal by which the instrument was supported was so constructed that the Guitarpa could be either elevated or lowered at the musician's pleasure.

The Apollonicon was a gigantic instrument which could be made to sound like a symphony orchestra. First played publicly in London in 1817, the Appolonicon was played automatically or manually. The brilliant arrangement of its five keyboards enabled five persons to play a composition together.

* * *

The largest stringed instrument ever constructed for a single player was a pantaleon played by George Noel in England in 1767. Played with wooden mallets like a xylophone, the instrument consisted of 276 gut and metal strings stretched over a horizontal soundboard which was 11 feet long by five feet wide.

* * *

Since the violin was introduced in the 1600s, several devices have been invented for playing the instrument automatically. But the only one to vibrate the strings with a bow was the *violonista,* which could be found in penny arcades in the early 1920s. The machine was about three feet long, two feet high, and two feet wide. It was electrically operated and controlled by air flowing through the perforations of a music roll.

* * *

Pianoforte comes from two Italian words: *piano* which means soft, and *forte* which means loud. So pianoforte actually means "soft-loud". The piano, which is what most of us call a pianoforte, was the first stringed instrument ever invented which could play both soft and loud.

Music! Music! Music!

An ingenious Californian by the name of Dr. Cecil Nixon constructed a robot in 1940 with uncommon abilities. The doctor, who named his creation Isis, fashioned the instrument in the form of the ancient Egyptian goddess. Isis rested on a couch with a zither on her lap.

The instrument could play any of about 3,000 tunes if asked to do so by anyone within a 12-foot radius. This came about because Isis was constructed so that voice vibrations touched off her complicated mechanism. Isis' right hand picked out the melody on the zither, while her left hand performed the accompaniment.

The machinery inside of Isis included 1,187 wheels and 370 electromagnets. There were numerous other parts. As a crowning touch, Dr. Nixon made Isis react to a warm temperature. When she got hot, she would remove the veil from her face all by herself.

It is not known what has happened to Isis in the 30-odd years since she was built. Apparently, she is not on exhibition anymore.

*   *   *

For more than 300 years, Allegri's famous "Miserere" has been sung during Holy Week in Rome's Sistine Chapel. The work was considered so sacred that, for well over a century after its completion, anyone who attempted to transcribe its score was subject to excommunication. But in 1769, a 13-year-old boy named Mozart wrote the composition down from memory after hearing it twice. Soon afterward, it was published in England. Nothing came of the Church's threat.

Ts'nats'el

The Ts'nats'el—Amharic for sistrum—is an instrument related to one used in ancient Egyptian ceremonies worshipping Isis. Today, this instrument is found only in Ethiopia where it is used exclusively as a liturgical instrument. Its brass or copper frame has metal discs which slide on wires to produce a jingling sound when shaken. About 8½" high. $3.91. Postage $3.00. *Ethiopian Tourist Trading Co.*

Masenk'o

The haunting, monophonic tones produced by the masenk'o have thrilled lords and peasants for centuries, and have been traditionally associated with the troubadors of Ethiopia. The instrument has one string made of horse hair, and a bow made of wood. The diamond-shaped sound box is covered with calf or sheep skin. $4.83. Sea parcel post $5.00. *Ethiopian Tourist Trading Co.*

Grandpa's Gramophone

This all-wood replica of an old-fashioned record player plays everything on 45s and 33s. Operates on 4 C cell batteries (not included). $35.00. Postage $2.85. *Childcraft.*

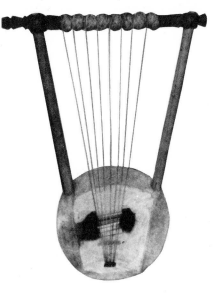

Nyatiti

Made of wood, string, beeswax, and pieces of reed, this eight-string Luo harp is a traditional musical instrument of a major tribe in Kenya. $31.50. Postage $5.00. *Kuja Crafts Ltd.*

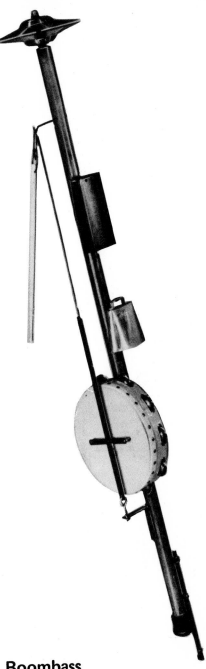

Finger Cymbals

These good-toned brass cymbals come from Syria where the instrument is an integral part of their dance. About 1¾" in diameter. Two pairs for $2.50 postpaid. *Clymer's.*

Boombass

With cymbals to clang, a cowbell to ring, a wooden clack-box to strike, and a drum-tambourine to beat, anyone who plays this one-man band can really turn himself on. Nearly 5' tall. Made of plastic, metal, and wood. $35.00. Postage $2.80. *Hammacher Schlemmer.*

Music! Music! Music!

About 525 songs and instrumental pieces were written about Abraham Lincoln, the largest number ever produced in honor of a secular individual. Approximately 450 of these compositions were published between his campaign in 1860 and his assassination in 1865. They comprise campaign and nomination selections, presidential hymns, emancipation songs, and minstrel and comic pieces. The other 75 consist of some 50 funeral marches and 25 memorial pieces.

* * *

Despite the fact that the jew's-harp has to be held between the teeth and its tone modulated by movements of the mouth, Charles Eulenstein of Germany could play 16 in different keys at one time. The 19th-century virtuoso accomplished this feat by fastening the instruments to a stand on a level with his lips.

* * *

Of the estimated 400,000 Christian hymns that have been published, fewer than 500 are in common use, and only 150 of them are well known by churchgoers. To determine their popularity in this country, a poll was made, not long ago, which disclosed that four hymns alone constituted the first choice of 20,384 of the 30,000 churchgoers questioned. And the relative popularity of these four outstanding favorites is shown by the following figures: For every 100 persons whose first choice was *Abide With Me,* the hymn that led, 75 preferred *Nearer My God to Thee,* 57 preferred *Lead, Kindly Light* and 47 preferred *Rock of Ages.*

* * *

The most spectacular musical event in the United States occurred at the World Peace Jubilee, held in Boston from June 17 to July 4, 1872, to celebrate the end of the Franco-Prussian War. An orchestra of 2,000 instruments, including a bass drum 25 feet in diameter, was bolstered by a chorus of 20,000. To lead this vast aggregation in a rendition of *The Beautiful Danube,* its composer, Johann Strauss, was brought from Vienna at a cost of $20,000—and in 1872, that was quite a sum.

Harpsichord

Despite its small size, this 52" German-made harpsichord produces a resonant sound. Available in walnut, elmwood, teak, mahogany, $1,800; or in cherry, maple, oak, rosewood, pear, $1,950. Shipping charges $110.00. *Kurt Wittmayer.*

Krar

This ancient Ethiopian musical instrument is similar to a lyre. It is made of either calf or sheep skin. Round sticks pass through the circular shape to form a triangle. The strings are made of gut. About 23" high. $14.49. Sea parcel post $5.00. *Ethiopian Tourist Trading Co.*

Kalimba

Plucking the metal reeds of this 17-note African instrument creates rippling musical sounds which resonate in the wooden box. 7½" by 5" by 1¼" deep. Instructions included. $16.95. Postage $1.40. *Clymer's.*

The Hindus of India are said to play more varieties of musical instruments than are found in all other countries combined. The Hindus have several thousand instruments, for virtually all of their early instruments remain in use. In fact, their most popular instrument is still the seven-stringed vina, which was invented more than 1,200 years ago.

* * *

A certain Austrian by the name of Karl Waetzel, who lived during the last century, had a particularly inventive turn of mind. He built a fabulous conglomeration of musical instruments which he called the *panomonico,* an instrument which could be played by a single person. The panomonico included 150 flageolets, 150 flutes, 50 oboes, 18 trumpets, 5 fanfares, three drums, and two kettledrums. The whole thing totaled 378 instruments. Waetzel's fantastic invention was purchased by Archduke Charles of Austria. The irony was that the Duke used the panomonico not to produce beautiful music, but for the purpose of annoying noisy courtiers of his royal household.

Music! Music! Music!

Handle Bell

Six bells attached by a leather strap to a 5½" long wooden handle. $4.00. Postage $1.50. *Childcraft.*

Pianola

You play roller music by pumping the pedals, or you can turn this fun box on electrically. When electrically operated, you can control the volume. Comes with a special attachment for rinky-dink sound. Finished in gold color. 39" high, 26" deep, 45" long. Piano bench has tilt seat. Complete with 25 rolls of piano music. $1,395.00. Shipped express collect. *Hammacher Schlemmer.*

Chord Organ

This electric floor model has 22 white keys, 15 black keys and 12 chords, a volume control, and a pilot light. 30½" by 12¼" by 30¾". The legs are removable. Made of shock-resistant plastic. $59.95. Shipped express collect. *F.A.O. Schwarz.*

Melodica

An instrument so easy to play, many educators use it to teach the rudiments of harmony, chord formation, and music theory. You can play chords and single notes, sharps and flats. Twenty chromatic keys from middle C up to G give it a range of an octave and a half. Interchangeable mouthpiece. $16.95. Postage $1.95. *Childcraft.*

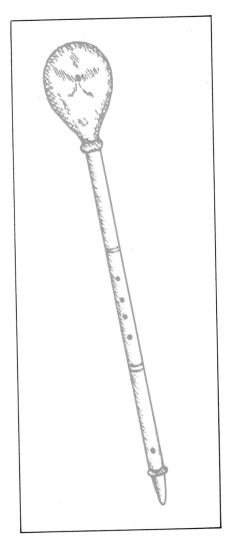

Ecuadorian Flute

Handcrafted in the original style of the Jibaros, this flute is 3" by 23" long. $1.50. Postage 80¢. *Akios.*

BREVES & SEMIBREVES,
JOBBERS IN
DULCET SYMPHONIES,
JEWS-HARPS AND BASS DRUMS.
Reference:—BOSTON JUBILEE.

Music is well said to be the speech of angels.
Thomas Carlyle (1795-1881), ESSAYS: THE OPERA

Music hath charms to soothe the savage breast,
To soften rocks, or bend a knotted oak.
William Congreve (1670-1729),
THE MOURNING BRIDE

Such sweet compulsion doth lie in music.
John Milton (1608-1674), ARCADES

Music! Music! Music!

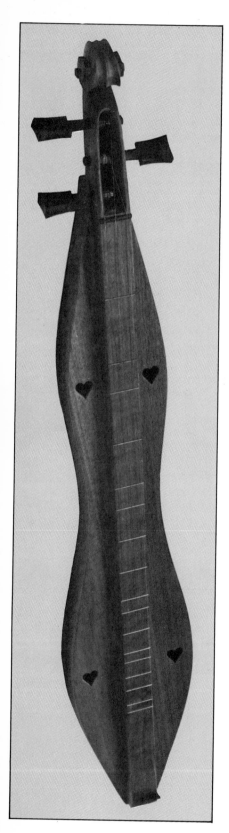

Dulcimer

The Latin word for *sweet* is *dulcis*—from which the dulcimer. This ancient three-stringed instrument was once very popular in Merrie Olde England. Handmade of walnut. $89.95. Shipped express collect. *Storehouse.*

Ankle Bells

Shake a leg, and make some music. Six jingle bells attached to a white leather strip. $2.00. Postage $1.50. *Childcraft.*

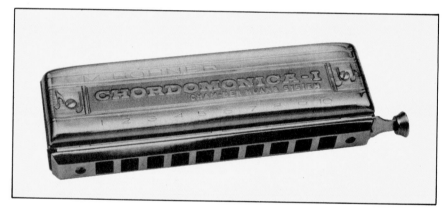

Chordomonica

It is impossible to produce a discord on this musical instrument, because any holes blown will play together in harmony. The upper note automatically carries the melody. Especially easy for the beginner. $12.50. Postage $1.65. *Childcraft.*

Stylophone

This battery-operated portable organ makes music anytime, anywhere. Has 12 white and 8 black keys. 4" by 6" by 4½" high. Instructions, music book, and battery included. $19.95. Postage $1.90. *Hammacher Schlemmer.*

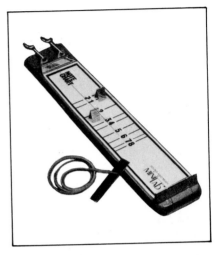

Sound and Music Lab

The scientific principles which explain sound are learned through experiments performed with this sound and music lab. The builder constructs and tunes a two-string musical instrument, and experiments with harmony and melody. $2.25. Postage 75¢. *The Gallery.*

Sidney Bechet was the first man to play a number of musical instruments in recording a song. He used six in making *The Sheik of Araby,* released in 1941. The feat was accomplished by recording the first instrument, re-recording it while the second was played in the studio, and so on until the disc contained the parts of all six instruments—soprano sax, clarinet, tenor sax, piano, bass fiddle, and drums.

* * *

In 1925, a staff composer for Witmark, the New York music publisher, wrote a song called "Me Neenyah." The company printed and copywrited it at once. Soon after, copies were sent to Europe, and a music publisher in Germany informed Witmark that the song was an infringement on one which had been copywrited in Germany in 1924. Witmark and his composer compared the two pieces and found them identical, note for note, with the exception of one half-tone. Clearly, it was a coincidence—a composer might steal a few bars but not an entire melody. The German publisher and Witmark agreed on this point, and the matter was dropped.

* * *

Thousands of one-finger piano pieces were written during the 19th century, and served as parlor entertainment. But *Chopsticks* is the only one of these compositions that remains popular today. Published in Glasgow in 1877, this commonplace little tune has been borrowed by such outstanding composers as Liszt and Rimski-Korsakov.

O Say Can You See!

If Benjamin Franklin could see his bifocals now, he'd never recognize them. Not the elaborate rhinestone-encrusted variety sported by some vanity fair. For his invention, Ben just stuck two different lenses—one for distance and one for close-up—on top of each other, and went out into the rain to fly his kite.

Half a millennium earlier, Roger Bacon had invented the first pair of spectacles. His discovery of the powers of convex lenses eased the eyestrain of his literate 13th-century contemporaries.

Although reading glasses improved slowly over the centuries, sufferers of astigmatism had to wait until 1827 for Sir George Airy to invent the cylindrical lens. And grapefruit-eaters had to wait until now for a pair of specs fitted with wind-shield-type wipers. (See the opposite page.)

Aquamate Sunglasses

These sunglasses, designed specifically for boatmen and fishermen, are made of shatter-proof polarized lenses to eliminate glare, and permit gazing beneath the water's surface. A flip-up feature allows the boatman to read his charts or the fisherman to adjust his reel. Featherlight, these glasses will float if dropped overboard. In addition to the standard style, a form of these glasses is made large enough to be worn over prescription glasses. Still another style has side polarized lenses built into the temple pieces to afford protection from wind and glare. Each comes in a case that can be clipped onto a belt. $5.00. Postage 75¢. *Chris Craft.*

Television Glasses

These polished prisms are so arranged that when you are lying down, you can watch your television screen without distortion. Brown frames. Case included. $17.50. Postage $2.10. *Invento.*

Radio Sunglasses

A tiny transistor and an invisible earphone conspire to transform these sunglasses into a radio. Battery included. $9.95. Postage $1.50. *Haverhill's.*

No-Fog Goggles

Can be worn without fogging for up to an hour under the most adverse weather conditions, including sudden temperature changes. Provide eye protection from chemical splatter, dust, sparks, toxic fumes. Shatterproof, lightweight. Fit over all eyeglasses. Adjustable neoprene headboard. $3.50. Postage 75¢. *Brownell's.*

Sunglasses and Telescope

An optical aid with options. Telescopic lenses in the ear pieces will bring an object to twice its size. The larger lenses can be used as a magnifying glass. And the sunglasses are shatterproof. $10.95. Postage 20¢. *Chris Craft.*

Anteojos is the Spanish word for eyeglasses. Anteojos comes from two Spanish words. *Ante* means "in front of" and *ojos* means "eyes." So *ante ojos* means "in front of the eyes," which is exactly where eyeglasses belong.

Sunglasses with Wipers

Powered by a standard battery, these wipers really work. And while this pair cum gadget will probably turn out to be a hilarious party prank, the water skier and snow skier might find these glasses a boon. $8.95. Postage $1.25. *Taylor Gifts.*

Ms-cellany

Sequined Bird

This decorative owl is a fine example of Indian mirror work. Beaded and enamelled by hand. 4½" tall. $10.00. Postage 60¢. *Kenton Collection.*

Papier Poudre

Many leaves of paper are bound in a tiny book. Each leaf contains a fine dusting of white-, rachel-, naturelle-, or sunburn-colored face powder. While the notion of little lengths of paper impregnated with fine face powder is still a novelty in America, the product has been made in England for many years. Specify choice of color. $1.50. Postage 60¢. *Caswell-Massey*

Wear and Tear Apron

A dozen disposable aprons in one package. Twelve layers of soft, strong paper, each printed with a floral design. When the top apron is soiled, you tear it off, and there is a fresh apron underneath. 16½" wide, 17" long. $1.95. Postage 50¢. *Artisan Galleries.*

Ecuadorian Belt

Cotton fajas are woven by the Indians in the Province of Cotopaxi to create this 1½" wide belt. The 4" wooden buckle is handpainted. Specify size. 80¢. Postage $1.00. *Akios.*

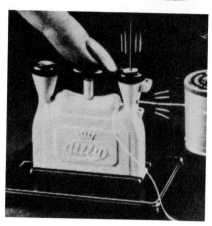

Needle Threader

Do you dread threading a needle? This little device will do the job for you. You insert the needle in the holder, press down, and the needle is instantly threaded. Tiny machine will handle any size needle. Stand, case, needles, and instructions are included. $1.00. Postage 50¢. *Breck's.*

Reversible Kimono

Made of 100% silk. Can be worn on either side. $45.60 postpaid. Air mail delivery. *Hayashi Kimono.*

omander Ball

edolent of Old England, this
harming pomander is almost exactly
ke those used in 17th and 18th
entury England. It is composed of a
ried Seville orange, stuffed with
loves and drenched with perfumed
il. The ball is then carefully dried,
nd then tied with a gold cord.
Ianging in milady's closet or placed in
drawer, this English import will
xude a delightful scent. Gift boxed.
5.50. Postage 80¢. *Downs.*

Leprechaun Hat

Knitted in Ireland, this hat of pure
homespun wool comes from what the
Irish call *bawneen,* or off white. $3.50.
Postage $2.11. *Mairtin Standun.*

DEVICE FOR PRODUCING DIMPLES.

. . . The present invention consists of a device which
serves either to produce dimples on the human body or
to nurture and maintain dimples already existing.

In order to make the body susceptible to the production
of artistic dimples, it is necessary, as has been proved by
numerous experiments, that the cellular tissues surrounding
the spot where the dimple is to be produced should be made
susceptible to its production by means of massage. This
condition is fulfilled by the present process as well as by
the apparatus by which the process is worked, and which is
represented in an enlarged form in the accompanying drawing. . . .

When it is desired to use the device for the production
of dimples, the knob or pearl *c* of the arm *a* must be set on
the selected spot on the body, the extension *d*, together
with the cylinder *f*, put in position, then while holding the
knob *n* with one hand the brace *i* must be made to revolve
on the axis *x*. The cylinder *f* serves to mass and make the
skin surrounding the spot where the dimple is to be produced malleable. . . .

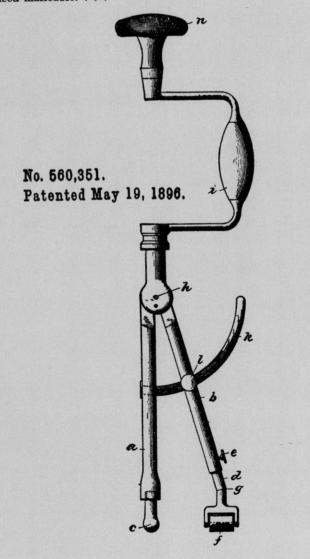

No. 560,351.
Patented May 19, 1896.

Playing Cards

If you've ever sat with a poker hand or a bridge hand so terrible that you've said to yourself, "Where did these cards come from?" you might be interested to know that they probably came from the Chinese, who modeled them after the currency of the T'ang dynasty.

Even before the invention of money, many societies had some form of gambling. One can almost imagine the big loser at an early Chinese all-night card game getting up and telling the boys he'd pay them just as soon as someone got around to inventing coin. It is not certain that the Chinese invented cards; some authorities attribute their origin to the Hindus, others say the Egyptians, and still others point to the Arabs.

However, most authorities agree that the earliest use of cards was as much for divination as for gaming. Hindu playing cards, for instance, used 10 suits representing the 10 incarnations of Vishnu. To this day, cards remain connected with many religious rites.

How were cards introduced to Europe? Some authorities credit the Crusaders, others the Saracens, some the gypsies, and still others point to the Tartars. More than likely, all of these sources are in some part responsible, since cards appeared in many different countries during the late 14th century.

It is the Italians who are credited with the introduction of those picture cards called the Tarot. This deck consists of 22 pictorial representations of material forces, elements, virtues, and vices, one of which was the forerunner of our modern-day joker. For centuries, gypsies have been reputed to foretell the future based on the interpretation of Tarot cards, which use characters and dress strikingly similar to those of the Romany tribe.

At some point the two types of cards—the Tarot and the playing deck—were combined, resulting in a 78-card deck composed of the 56 cards of the oriental variety and the 22 of the tarot. The game derived is still popular in several countries. Further combinations of numbers and pictures resulted in decks of 40 cards (Italy and Spain), 32 cards or 36 cards (Germany), and 52 cards (France). This last deck became the standard in all English-speaking countries. The English retained the French symbols for the suits, but gave them English names. Today, if you want to call a spade a spade in France, you would say *pique.* In German, a spade is a *grun;* and in Italian, a *spada.* The costumes worn by the jack, queen, and king are of the time of Henry VII and Henry VIII.

The Soviet government attempted to substitute revolutionary figures for those of the corrupt monarchy, but the card tradition was so well entrenched that they finally had to give up.

The number of decks in circulation, long limited by the expense of hand-painting, rose dramatically with the invention of wood engraving and block printing. Today, there are more than 70 million decks sold per year in the United States alone.

Even our language is permeated with terms and phrases traceable to cards, like: *double-dealing, dealing from the bottom of the deck, a good deal, ace in the hole,* and *flimsy as a house of cards.*

Solitaire Board
Made of wood. Measures 18" by 14". Included are a 150-page game book and one deck of cards. $4.00. Postage 60¢. *England's.*

Historic Playing Cards

This set of cards imported from Spain presents a full history of America's early discoverers and explorers, in full color. Each suit honors a nation—France, Spain, England, Portugal. Fifty-two cards and jokers. Plastic coated. Gift boxed. $5.00. Two decks, $9.85. Postage $1.00. *Downs.*

Suit Distribution at Bridge

The odds against finding the following distributions are:

4-4-3-2	4 to 1
5-4-3-1	9 to 1
6-4-2-1	about 20 to 1
7-4-1-1	about 249 to 1
8-4-1-0	about 2,499 to 1
13-0-0-0	158,755,357,992 to 1

Playing Cards

Odds at Poker

Hand	Number Possible	Odds Against
Royal Flush	4	649,739 to 1
Other Straight Flushes	36	72,192 to 1
Four of a Kind	624	4,164 to 1
Full House	3,744	693 to 1
Flush	5,108	508 to 1
Straight	10,200	254 to 1
Three of a Kind	54,912	46 to 1
Two Pairs	123,552	20 to 1
One Pair	1,098,240	4 to 3 (1.37 to 1)
Nothing	1,302,540	1 to 1
	2,598,960	

Giant Playing Cards

Compare these 5" by 7" double-sized playing cards with the normal 2½" by 3½" cards. Great for the near-sighted. Book of card tricks included. $5.00. Postage 75¢. *Game Room.*

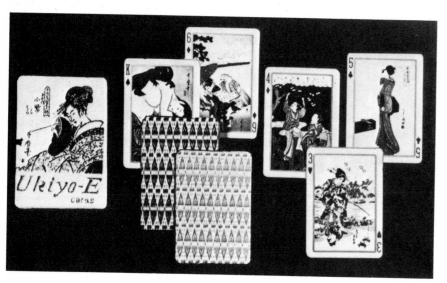

Ukiyo-e Deck

The face cards of this deck are reproductions of the famous Ukiyo-e woodblock prints. Choice of red back or blue back. $7.50. Postage 75¢. *Gump's.*

Magnetized Cards

Perfect for a windy day on the beach, on the patio, or on the deck. Plastic cards are magnetized and hold to the magnetic board. Set consists of two decks of cards, board, and card tray. $12.95. Postage $2.10. *Lewis and Conger.*

Tarotrump

The game of Tarotrump is based upon the original rules of the popular 16th century Italian games of Minchiate and Tarocchi. The deck, printed in Switzerland, contains 78 cards in full color. In addition to King, Queen, and Jack, there is a Cavalier. There are 21 numbered trump cards, and one unnumbered card called the Excuse. Tarotrump is a game played by three to five players. Rules are included. Gift boxed. $6.00. Postage 85¢. *U. S. Games.*

Tiffany Deck

These card designs, created in 1879, have been resurrected by Tiffany and re-introduced with all their amusing pictures. Gold monogrammed, to your order. Comes in blue and red, brown and beige, pink and yellow, aqua blue and apple green, black and white. Set of two decks $8.00. Postage 75¢. *Tiffany.*

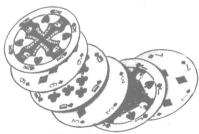

Round Cards

This is a standard deck which can be used at bridge, rummy, or poker. Cards are plastic coated. Can be read no matter how you hold them. Come in red and blue backs. Two decks, $1.85. Postage 49¢. *Lillian Vernon.*

The Jesus Deck

How about it! A set of religious cards! This 52-card deck, printed in full color, shows scenes from the New Testament. Each card is 2 7/8" by 4 7/8". $5.00. Postage 75¢. *U. S. Games.*

Playing Cards

Colonial-Flag Cards

These celutone-finished playing cards are imprinted with two famous colonial flags of 1775. The Pine Tree Flag is green on white; the Gadsden, or Snake Flag, is black on yellow. Decks consist of the standard 52 cards plus jokers. Two decks, box with velvet cover and gold trim. $3.95. Postage 80¢. *Sturbridge Yankee Workshop.*

Pushbutton Card Shuffler

Cards are placed on either side of this gadget, a switch is flipped, and the deck is shuffled, ready for dealing. Battery operated. Made of plastic. 6" by 3". Includes two decks of cards, batteries, and a case. $16.95. Postage $2.00. *Hammacher Schlemmer.*

Tarot Deck

This beautiful 78-card deck with classic designs is complete with 22 major Arcana and 56 minor Arcana cards — 4 3/8" x 2 3/8" in full color. Published in Switzerland, with English titles on the cards. Includes instruction booklet. $5.00. Postage 75¢. *U. S. Games.*

Every Bloomin' Thing for the Garden

One of the most important ingredients for the well-being of all your little green friends is nitrogen. And one of the best sources of this wonder ingredient is compost—organic matter which is decomposed by the action of bacteria, releasing nitrogen as a by-product. Adding compost to the soil will not only make plants and vegetables big and strong, but will make them smile at you and help them resist disease and bugs.

Compost is formed naturally in forests as leaves fall to the ground, building up, layer upon layer, until they gradually decompose, forming new soil. But since it can be rather tedious to sit around in the forest and wait for five years or so, here are some simple instructions for making your very own compost in just five days. Developed by the University of California, the quick-compost method requires the construction of a square-yard framed cube of chicken-wire. The framing is made of 1" x 2"s. Each of the sides is connected with hook and eye assemblies.

Set the box up in a sunny location, and fill it with grass clippings, branch prunings, leaves, and finely chopped organic material. Organic garbage from the kitchen, such as egg shells and fruit and vegetable peelings, are also excellent compostable materials; these have the added advantage of enriching your soil and lessening your garbageman's load. For best results, the pile should be kept moist, but not soaked, and should be turned daily. This is easily accomplished by detaching the sides of your crate, and then refilling the compost box.

Your compost pile will gradually be reduced, until after five days all that will be left is organic material so rich that there's danger of your feet developing roots if you stand in it too long. Spread it generously around your plants and vegetables, and be prepared to have them warmly respond to you.

Blitz Fogger

This insecticide fogger can treat a half-acre in minutes. Simple and safe to use. Comes with propane cartridge, insecticide, and holding stand. $29.95. Postage $1.99. *House of Minnel.*

Every Bloomin' Thing for the Garden

Flower Gatherer and Snippers

This Danish gadget saves pricked and bloody fingers; it permits you to reach through the thorns to your roses. It cuts the bloom with a squeeze of the handle, and then holds the flower firmly in the jaws of the cutter. $4.50. Postage 50¢. *Deluxe Saddlery.*

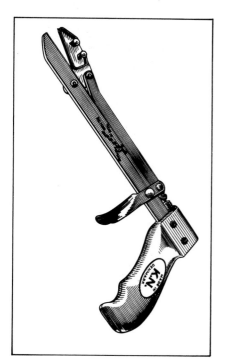

Sunbonnet

Keep that peaches-and-cream complexion out of the sun with this quilted visor. The long ties will make this hat fit almost anyone. Comes in blue, green, red, and yellow. $5.00 postpaid. *Vermont Country Store.*

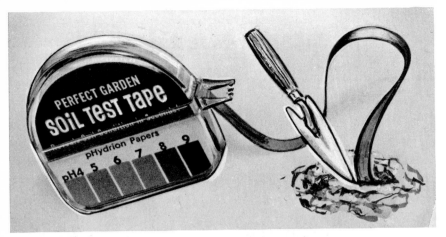

Soil Test Tape

To find out whether your soil is too acid or too alkaline, press this tape into moist soil. In 30 seconds, you'll have the answer. The tape will change color, and you compare the color to a chart that is provided. The instructions, which list 354 house and garden plants, tell you what to do to put your soil into proper condition. Sufficient tape for 100 tests in a plastic dispenser. $1.98. Postage 39¢. *Walter Drake*.

Water Test Kit

All materials to test for pollution—dissolved oxygen, hardness, phosphates, hydrogen sulphides, chlorides— are included in this kit. Can be used to trace the sources of pollution. Enough materials for 25 tests; refills available. $12.00. Postage $1.00. *Orvis*.

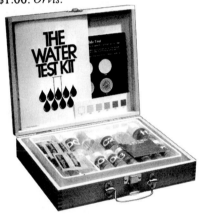

Perhaps the oldest living thing on Earth is the Macrozamia tree, which grows in the Tambourine Mountains of Queensland, Australia. Scientists estimate that these trees are anywhere from 12,000 to 15,000 years old— more than six times as old as the giant redwoods of California and Oregon.

Although there is some controversy over the exact age of these palmlike trees—counting their concentric rings is a very difficult task—everyone agrees that the Macrozamia is unequaled in age. The giant bald cypress of Mexico is definitely known to be 4,000 years old, and is far younger than many of the Australian Macrozamias. These trees were old when David and Goliath were boys.

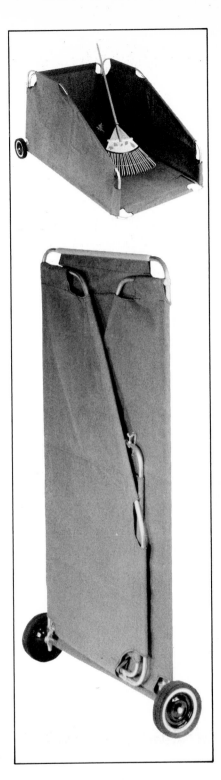

Rake 'n Roll Folding Cart

Holds 24 bushels of leaves. Folds up in a few seconds to 8" wide. Constructed of steel tubing and water-repellent, mildew-resistant green canvas. About 5½' long. Semi-pneumatic rubber tires are 1¾" wide. $49.95. Shipped express collect. *Gallery*.

Every Bloomin'Thing for the Garden

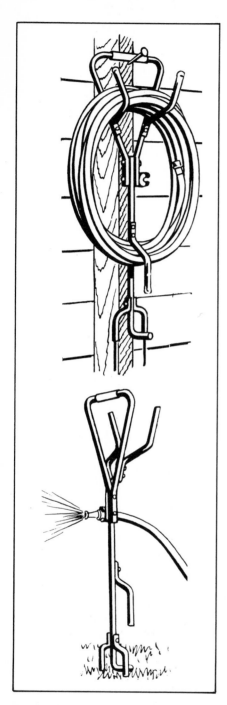

Gardener's Caddy

Soft foam padding cushions your knees while bent over, and a 14" high rail gives you support and helps you to get up and down. A handy compartment holds tools, seeds, gloves. Made of rustproof metal. $6.99. Postage $1.15. *Breck's.*

Stump Remover

When poured into the center of a stump, this chemical saturates the wood so that it can easily be burned and then removed. No need to dig or chop. 16 oz., $1.50. Postage 75¢. *P. & S. Sales.*

Giant Wheelbarrow

Perfectly balanced on two huge wheels, this gargantuan cart will run easily over a lawn or garden carrying up to 400 pounds. $98.50. Shipped express collect. *Garden Way Research.*

Portable Hose Rack

Stick it in the ground on the lawn, and it will hold 100 feet of hose. Or for compact winter storage of hose, this gadget will hang in your garage or basement. The metal clip holds the hose nozzle while you're sprinkling. Made of green steel tubing. $4.27. Postage 80¢. *Walter Drake.*

Lawn Aerators

Lawn aeration, essential for a healthy lawn, is easily accomplished by means of these walking aerators. All you have to do is to strap these contrivances onto your shoes and walk across your lawn. Each aerator holds 13 steel spikes. Adjustable straps will fit any size shoe. $7.95 per set. Postage $1.10. *Walter Drake.*

Natural Insecticide

Each ladybird beetle can eat up to 50 aphids daily; each pint of ladybirds helps protect about 12,000 square feet of ground. The ladybird is the natural enemy of the red spider and the bean thrip, and also thrives on potato beetle eggs, asparagus beetle larvae, scale insects, alfalfa weevils, chinch bugs and the like. This beneficent predator penetrates grass, shrubs, vines, flower beds, tree branches. Live safe delivery guaranteed. ½ pint, $2.98, postage 65¢.; 1 pint, $4.98, postage $1.10; 1 gallon, $25.00, postage $1.25. *Hanover House.*

Garden:
Something that dies if you don't water it and rots if you do.

The smallest flowering plants in the world are Wolffia and Wolffiella which make up the green film seen on fresh-water ponds. These flowering plants, known as the duckweed, run from one-thirtieth to one-fiftieth of an inch in diameter. The duckweed is but one seventy-millionth the size of the mammoth *Amorphophallus titanum*, the world's largest flower.

* * *

The world's tiniest plant seeds are those of the *Epiphytic* orchid. They come 35,000,000 to the ounce!

Final Entries

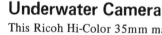

Underwater Camera

This Ricoh Hi-Color 35mm marine camera is waterproof, sandproof, snowproof, and shockproof. Automatic exposure system, with an f 2.8 wide angle lens and shutter speeds up to 1/300th of a second. An automatic film advance lets you click off 15 shots in as many seconds. The protective underwater plastic capsule has an optical glass port, and is watertight down to 100 feet. underwater correction filter. $134.50. Postage $1.20. *Chris Craft.*

Crocus Pot

No hocus-pocus to growing this crocus. Guaranteed to bloom. Will burst out in brilliant purple posies for three or four weeks. The re-usable Delft planter is handmade and hand-painted in Holland. About 5" high and 5" wide, it holds 21 big crocus bulbs. Nothing to add but water. Available for delivery only between December 10 and January 25. $7.95 postpaid. *Harry and David's.*

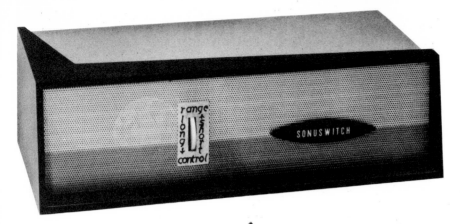

Signal Commander

You clap your hands, snap your fingers, whistle, and the switch will automatically turn on or turn off anything hooked up to this instrument. Black case. 8" by 3" by 2½". $29.95. Postage $2.10. *Hammacher Schlemmer.*

Engraved Pinhead

Any name is engraved on the head of an ordinary sized straight pin. Comes in a flannel pouch on a card inscribed: *This fine pouch of flannel blue/Bears a rare gift especially for you/Upon the pin head, round and shiny,/Your name engraved so very very tiny!* $1.00 postpaid. *Elgin.*

Mini TV

This might well be the world's smallest TV. Weighing less than 2 lbs., it has 1½" diagonal screen with 2" magnifying lens. Fits in the palm of your hand. Solid-state engineered. Complete with earphone, wrist strap, leather carrying case, and two sets of batteries. AC- or rechargeable-battery-operated. 2¼" by 4¾" by 6¾". Silver and black finish. $339.95. Postage $2.00. *Hammacher Schlemmer.*

Wood Skull

From Ecuador. Approximately 3½" high. $14.00. Postage $1.15. *Brooklyn Museum.*

Bosom Pal

This handy white satin secret stuffer snaps onto your bra and saves a lot of cash 'n' carry worries. $2.50. Postage 50¢. *B. Altman.*

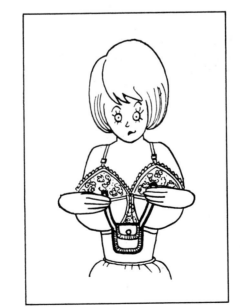

Final Entries

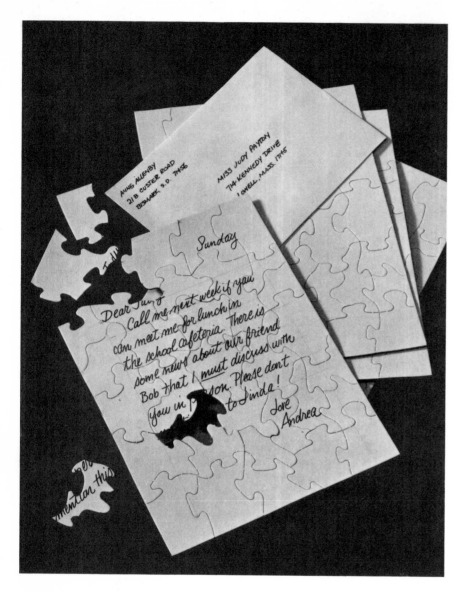

Mini-Bible

The entire Old and New Testaments have been reproduced on 1,245 pages of micro-fiche. Can be read as easily as the family Bible with this viewer which magnifies 100 times. $16.95. Postage $1.50. *Haverhill's.*

Jigsaw Letter

You write a letter on a blank 8½" wide, 11" long white cardboard. You then break up your puzzle board and mail the pieces. Curiosity is likely to get the upper hand, and your correspondent who has travailed over your jigsaw will be sufficiently intrigued to answer—or sufficiently annoyed to answer. Either way you're likely to get a response. Set of six letters, six envelopes. $2.98. Postage 69¢. *Lillian Vernon.*

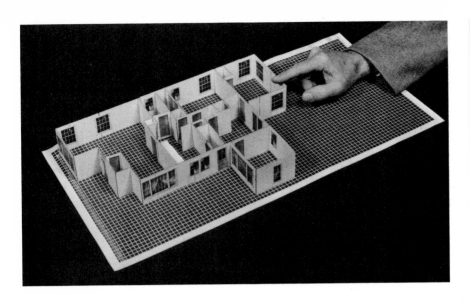

Home Planning Kit

With this kit, you can plan your home and see how your layout will look before you build or remodel. The kit, ¼"=1' scale, comes with dozens of windows, kitchen cabinets, doors, partitions. You can visualize your idea in three-dimensional form. Before you build your dream house, live with it awhile. Included is a 65-page book to help estimate actual costs. $4.95 postpaid. *J.W. Holst, Inc.*

Medical Alert Medallion

Up to eight lines of vital information concerning blood type, allergies, or physical condition are engraved on the back of this medallion. Invaluable in a medical emergency. Caduceus medical symbol is engraved on the front. Silver or 24K gold plate. $4.00 postpaid. *Elgin.*

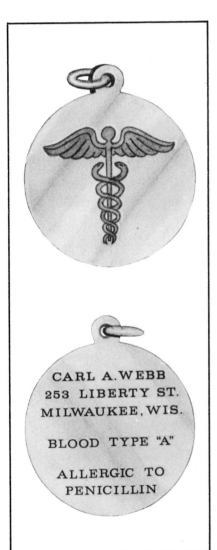

Enameled Boxes

In November of 1970, Bilston and Battersea Enamels of England inaugurated the Great Classical Composers Series with five boxes honoring the immortal composers of the 1700s. Each box was made of wafer-thin copper, delicately hand-enameled in the painstaking Georgian tradition. Each box was issued in a numbered limited edition of 1,000. Two of these boxes, the Mozart and the Handel, second and third in the series, have been sold out. Available in limited quantities: Beethoven box, Haydn box, Bach box, $75.00 each. Postage 70¢. *Kenton Collection.*

Sources

Abelardo Linares, S. A.
Carrera De San Jeronimo, 48
Y Plaza de las Cortas, 11
Madrid 14, Spain

Abercrombie and Fitch Co.
45 St. and Madison Avenue
New York, N.Y. 10017

Acme Hardware Company, Inc.
150 South La Brea Avenue
Los Angeles, Calif. 90036

Adirondack Store
Lake Placid Road
Saranac Lake, New York 12983

Adultrike Manufacturing Co.
1134 Wisconsin Avenue
Youngtown, Arizona 85363

A. E. Kochert
Neuer Markt 15
Wien 1, Austria

Akios Handicrafts
P.O. Box 219
Quito, Ecuador

A Man's World
Village Fair
Sausalito, California 94965

**American Telecommunications
Corp.**
P.O. Box 1041
El Monte, Calif. 91734

Anything Left Handed Limited
65 Beak Street
London W1, England

Appalachian Spring
1655 Wisconsin Avenue, N.W.
Washington, D.C. 20007

Arctic Trading Post
Box 262
Nome, Alaska 99762

Aristera Organization
9 Rice's Lane
Westport, Conn. 06880

Arma Lite
118 East 16th St.
Costa Mesa, Calif. 92627

Arnex Industries Corp.
48 West 48th Street
New York, N.Y. 10036

Art Asia, Inc.
1088 Madison Avenue
New York, N.Y. 10028

Artes Saldana
Sinola #88
Mexico 6, D.F.

Artisan Galleries
2100 N. Haskell
Dallas, Texas 75204

Sources

Artistic Latex
1220 Brook Avenue
Bronx, N.Y. 10456

Asbjorn-Mobler A/S
Bytorvet 29
2620 Albertslund
Denmark

Ashley Furniture Workshops
3a Dawson Place
London W2, England

Astley's Ltd.
109 Jermyn Street
London SW1Y 6HB, England

Aunt Jane's Cupboard
410 South Burdick Street
Kalamazoo, Mich. 49006

Austin Enterprises
2108 Braewick Circle
Akron, Ohio 44313

Bachman Foods Inc.
P.O. Box 898
Reading, Penna. 19603

B. Altman & Co.
361 Fifth Avenue
New York, N.Y. 10016

Bazar de la Cuisine, Inc.
1003 Second Avenue
New York, N.Y. 10022

Bazar Francais
666 Sixth Avenue
New York, N.Y. 10010

Better Sleep, Inc.
New Providence
New Jersey 07974

Bevis Industries Inc.
39 Westmoreland Ave.
White Plains, N.Y. 10606

Bissinger's
205 W. Fourth St.
Cincinnati, Ohio 45202

Bloom & Son
153 New Bond Street
London W1, England

Bloomingdale's
Lexington Avenue at 59th St.
New York, New York 10022

Bluejacket Ship Crafters
145 Water Street
South Norwalk, Conn. 06854

Bonebakker
Rokin 88
Amsterdam-C, Holland

Box Hill Farm
Lebanon, New Jersey 08833

Breck's of Boston
800 Breck Building
Boston, Mass. 02210

Bremen House
200 East 86th Street
New York, N.Y. 10028

Brentano's
586 Fifth Avenue
New York, New York 10036

Brooklyn Museum Gallery Shop
188 Eastern Parkway
Brooklyn, N.Y. 11238

Brownell's, Inc.
Route 2, Box 1
Montezuma, Iowa 50171

Bruce Bolind, Inc.
Bolind Building
Boulder, Colo. 80302

Bryan Robeson
Box 757
Hickory, North Carolina 28601

Cable Car Clothiers
211 Sutter Street
San Francisco, Calif. 94108

C.A. Gordon
17 Church St. Dept. B13
Paterson, New Jersey 07505

Carlo Mario Camusso S.A.
Avenida Mariscal
O.R. Benavides 679
Casilla Postal 650
Lima, Peru

Carriage Shed
29 Labelle Street
West Springfield, Mass. 01089

Casco Bay Trading Post
Freeport Maine 04032

Caswell-Massey Co. Ltd.
320 West 13th Street
New York, N.Y. 10014

Catawba Trader
Box 963
Sandusky, Ohio 44870

Charlotte Horstmann Ltd.
104 Ocean Terminal
Kowloon, Hong Kong

Childcraft
52 Hook Road
Bayonne, N.J. 07002

Chris Craft
Marine Accessories Div.
Algonac, Mich. 48001

Clymer's of Bucks County
Chestnut Street
Nashua, N.H. 03060

Coleman Company, Inc.
250 North St. Francis
Wichita, Kansas 67201

Collier's
P.O. Box 585
4825 Main Street
Skokie, Ill. 60076

Collins Bros.
593 Westminster Dr. N.E.
Atlanta, Georgia 30324

Colonial Garden Kitchens
270 West Merrick Road
Valley Stream,
New York 11582

Country Gourmet
512 South Fulton Ave.
Mt. Vernon, N.Y. 10550

Creation Boutique
Duke Street
Dublin 2, Ireland

Croydon Silvermart Ltd.
625-631 Kings Highway
Brooklyn, N.Y. 11223

Daniel's of Denver
1749 South Broadway
Denver, Colorado 80210

Decor Galore
140 Monument Avenue, HB2
Barrington, Ill. 60010

Deerskin Trading Post
119 Foster Street
Peabody, Mass. 01960

Deluxe Saddlery Co.
1817 Whitehead Road
Baltimore, Md. 21207

Den Permanente
Vesterport
DK-1620 Copenhagen V
Denmark

Desert House
4156 East Grant Road
Tucson, Ariz. 85712

Directional Furniture Showrooms
979 Third Avenue
New York, N.Y. 10022

Dover Scientific Co.
Box 6011
Long Island City, N.Y. 11106

Downs & Co.
Dept. 1072
1014 Davis Street
Evanston, Ill. 60204

Duncraft
25 South Main Street
Penacook, N.H. 03301

Du Say's
P.O. Box 24407
New Orleans, La. 70124

Eastland Co.
P.O. Box 651
West Covina, Calif. 91790

Eddie Bauer
P.O. Box 3700
Seattle, Wash. 98124

Electric Wastebasket Corp.
145 West 45th St.
New York, N.Y. 10036

Electronics International
210 South Desplaines St.
Chicago, Ill. 60606

Elgin Engraving Co.
940 Edwards Avenue
Dundee, Illinois 60118

Elizabeth McCaffrey's
Northport, New York 11768

England's
Pittsfield, Mass. 01207

Ephraim Marsh Company
Box 266
Concord, North Carolina 28025

Ethiopian Tourist Trading Co.
P.O. Box 5640
Addis Ababa, Ethiopia

Ever-Lite Co.
150 Express Street
Plainview, N.Y. 11803

Excalibur, Ltd.
25 Brightside Avenue
East Northport, L.I.,
N.Y. 11731

**Fabrica de Fiancas e
Azulejos Sant'Anna**
Calcada de Boa Hora, 96
Lisbon, Portugal

F.A.O. Schwarz
Dept. M.O.
745 Fifth Avenue
New York, New York 10022

Fioretti & Co.
1470-72 Lexington Ave.
New York, N.Y. 10028

Forslund
122 East Fulton Street
Grand Rapids, Mich. 49502

Fran's Basket House
89 West Main Street
Rockaway, New Jersey 07866

Fritzie Abadi
41 Union Square West
Studio 1101
New York, N.Y. 10003

Gallery
Dept 6792
Amsterdam, N.Y. 12010

Game Room
P.O. Box 1816
Washington, D.C. 20013

Garden Way Research
Charlotte, Vt. 05445

Garrard
112 Regent Street
London W1A 2JJ, England

Garrett Electronics
2814 National Drive
Garland, Texas 75041

Garrett's
P.O. Box 12274
Dallas, Texas 75225

Gaydell Inc.
3030 Wilshire Blvd.
Santa Monica, Calif. 90403

Genada Imports
Dept H-3
P.O. Box 204
Teaneck, N.J. 07666

Sources

Georgetown Tobacco & Pipe Store
3144 M. Street
Washington, D.C. 20007

Gered of London
173-174 Piccadilly
London, W1V OPD
England

Gherardi & Ghilardi
P.O. Box 171
Firenze, Italy

Glit H.F.
Hoefdabakka 9
Reykjavik, Iceland

Gokey Co.
21 W 5th St.
St. Paul, Minn. 55102

Grace Rare Tea
799 Broadway
New York, N.Y. 10003

Greek Island Ltd.
215 East 49 St.
New York, N.Y. 10017

Grey Owl Indian Craft Manufacturing Co.
150-02 Beaver Road
Jamaica, New York 11433

Grove Pet Ranch
P.O. Box 4484
Hialeah Lakes, Florida 33014

Gump's
250 Post Street
San Francisco, Calif. 94108

Hall's
Country Club Plaza
Kansas City, Mo. 64108

Hammacher Schlemmer
147 East 57th Street
New York, N.Y. 10022

Hanover House
Hanover, Penna. 17331

Harriet Carter
Plymouth Meeting,
Penna. 19462

Harrington's
Richmond, Vermont 05477

Harrods
Knightsbridge
London SW1X 7XL England

Harry and David
Bear Creek Orchards
Medford, Oregon 97501

Haverhill's
584 Washington Street
San Francisco, California 94111

Hayashi Kimono
International Arcade
2-4, Yurakucho
Chiyoda-Ku, Tokyo, Japan

Hayim Pinhas
P.O.B. 500
Istanbul, Turkey

Heer's
Springfield, Missouri 65801

Henningham and Hollis
4 Mount Street
Berkeley Square
London W1Y 5AA, England

Herley Imports, Inc.
160 Eileen Way
Syosset, N.Y. 11791

Herter's Inc.
Route 2
Mitchell, South Dakota 57301

Hoffritz
20 Cooper Square
New York, N.Y. 10003

Holiday Gifts
7905 West 44th Street
Wheatridge, Colo. 80033

Holland Handicrafts
Pruimendijk 24
Rijsoord, Holland

Home Industries
330 Athens Street
Jackson, Ohio 45640

Hoover Company
370 Seventh Avenue
New York, N.Y.

House of Minnel
Deerpath Road
Batavia, Illinois 60510

House of Yemen
370 Third Avenue
New York, N.Y. 10016

House of York
63 Oakleaf Lane
Doylestown, Penna. 18901

H. Roth & Son
1577 First Avenue
New York, N.Y. 10028

Hunting World
16 East 53rd Street
New York, N.Y. 10022

Invento
39-25 Skillman Avenue
Long Island City, N.Y. 11104

Intersport
c/o Sport Hintner
Getreidegasse 18
Salzburg, Austria

IPCO, Inc.
541 West 79th Street
Minneapolis, Minn. 55420

Jackson Furniture Corporation
600 Mobile Avenue
P.O. Box 368
Jackson, Tenn. 38301

J. C. Cording of Piccadilly
19 Piccadilly
London W1V OPE England

J.D. Browne
Ghirardelli Square
900 North Point
San Francisco, Calif. 94109

J. F. Day & Company
2810-6th Avenue, South
Birmingham, Ala. 35233

J. Kenneth Zahn & Son, Inc.
225 Fifth Ave.
New York, N.Y. 10010

JLM Products and Design
6805 Boysenberry Way
Colorado Springs, Colo. 80918

Joan Cook
1241 N.E. 8 Avenue
Ft. Lauderdale, Florida 33304

J. W. Holst Inc.
1005 East Bay Street
East Tawas, Mich. 48730

Keene Engineering, Inc.
11479 Vanowen Street
North Hollywood, Calif. 91605

Kenton Collection
P.O. Box 34257
Dallas, Texas 75234

Kreeger & Son Ltd.
30 West 46th St.
New York, N.Y. 10036

Kuja Crafts Ltd.
P.O. Box 49176
Nairobi, Kenya

Kurt Wittmayer
D-8190 Wolfratshausen
West Germany

Laacke & Joys Co.
1432 North Water Street
Milwaukee, Wisc. 53202

Lewis & Conger
39-25 Skillman Ave.
Long Island City, N.Y. 11104

Lew Magram
830 Seventh Avenue
New York, N.Y. 10019

Lillian Vernon
510 South Fulton Avenue
Mt. Vernon, N.Y. 10550

L. L. Bean, Inc.
Freeport, Maine 04032

Lynchburg Hardware
& General Store
Box 239
Lynchburg, Tenn. 37352

Magnolia Hall
726 Andover
Atlanta, Georgia

Mairtin Standun
An Spideal
Co. Galway
Ireland

Maison Glass
52 East 58th Street
New York, N.Y. 10022

Manganaro's
488 Ninth Avenue
New York, N.Y. 10018

Martha M. House
1022 South Decatur Street
Montgomery, Ala. 36104

Martin Sylvester Furniture
Little Clarendon Street
Oxford, England

Maryland Gourmet
441 Amsterdam Avenue
New York, N.Y. 10024

Mayors
Coral Gables,
Florida 33134

McArthur's Smokehouse
Millerton, New York 12546

McNulty's Tea & Coffee Co.
109 Christopher Street
New York, N.Y. 10014

Mexican Art Annex
23 W. 56th Street
New York, N.Y. 10019

Morsan
810 Route 17
Paramus, New Jersey 07652

Netcraft
3101 Sylvaniz Avenue
Toledo, Ohio 43613

New Hampton General Store
Box 872
Hampton, N.J. 08827

Nichols Garden Nursery
1190 North Pacific Highway
Albany, Oregon 97321

1984 Store
Brownstone Court
Avon, Connecticut 06001

Norwegian Silver Corp.
114 East 57 St.
New York, N.Y. 10022

Old Guilford Forge
Boston Post Road
Guilford, Conn. 06437

Old Mexico Shop
Patio 10
Santa Fe, New Mexico 87501

Orvis Company, Inc.
Manchester, Vermont 05254

P & S Sales
P.O. Box 45095
Tulsa, Oklahoma 74145

PAM Products
299 Heath Terr.
Buffalo, N.Y. 14223

Pappagallo Shop
#7 Jefferson Sq.
Austin, Tex. 78731

Paprikas Weiss
1546 Second Avenue
New York, N.Y. 10028

Patio
550 Powell Street
San Francisco, California 94108

Sources

Patrice, Unlimited
Box 212
Chester, N.J.

Pearson's
2260 North Walnut Street
Muncie, Indiana 47305

Pennsylvania Dutchman
520 Fifth Avenue
New York, N.Y. 10036

Peterson's Ltd.
70 E. 42 St.
New York, N.Y. 10017

Pipe & Pouch
311 Madison Avenue
New York, New York 10017

Pipe Dan
13 Vestergade
1456 Copenhagen K
Denmark

Plan-It-Kit
Box 429
Westport, Connecticut 06880

Plume Trading and Sales Co., Inc.
P.O. Box 585
Monroe, New York 10950

Plumlea Peddler
HB2, Box 22232
Lyndon, Kentucky 40222

Plummer's Ltd.
145 East 57th Street
New York, New York 10022

Pohlson Galleries
Pawtucket, Rhode Island 02863

Pollock's Toy Theaters, Ltd.
1 Scala Street
London W1, England

Popular Archaeology
Box 18365
Wichita, Kansas 67218

Postamatic Company, Inc.
Lafayette Hill,
Pennsylvania 19444

Preston's
Main Street Wharf
Greenport, Long Island,
New York 11944

Projects Unlimited, Inc.
3680 Wyse Road
P.O. Box 1426
Dayton, Ohio 45414

Rainbow Wood Products, Inc.
40-35 21st Street
Long Island City, N.Y. 11101

Recreational Equipment Inc.
1525-11th Avenue
Seattle, Washington 98122

Ritchie Bros.,
37 Watergate
Rothesay, Bute.
Scotland

Robert Lawrie Ltd.
54 Seymour Street
Marble Arch
London, W1H 5WE, England

Rosalind Light Ltd.
499 Central Avenue
Cedarhurst, N.Y. 11516

Saltwater Farm
York Harbor
Maine 03911

Seymour Mann Inc.
225 Fifth Avenue
New York, New York 10010

Sherle Wagner
125 East 57th Street
New York, New York 10022

Ship's Wheel
Nottingham Sq. Rd.
Epping, New Hampshire 03042

Shuttle Hill Herb Shop
256B Delaware Avenue
Delaware, N.Y. 12054

Sleepy Hollow Gifts
6651 Arlington Blvd.
P.O. Box 2327
Falls Church, Virginia 22042

Spinning Fool Top
P.O. Box 158
Sparta, Tenn. 38583

Stadry
6th Avenue Department 1
Whitestone, New York 11357

Stern's, Inc.
1248 West Paces Ferry Road, N.W
Atlanta, Georgia 30327

Storehouse
3106 Early Street NW
Atlanta, Georgia 30305

Sturbridge Yankee Workshop
Brimfield Turnpike
Sturbridge, Mass. 01566

Suburbia Inc.
Finch Building
366 Wacouta
St. Paul, Minn. 55101

Sundials and More
New Ipswich, N.H. 03071

Sun Gold Marketing
230 Central Park South
New York, N.Y. 10019

Sunset House
188 Sunset Building
Beverly Hills, Calif. 90213

Superlux Ltd.
79 Madison Avenue
Suite 1503
New York, N.Y. 10016

Svenskt Glas
Birger Jarlsgatan 8
S-114 34 Stockholm
Sweden

Swiss Colony
1112 Seventh Avenue
Monroe, Wisconsin 53566

Tartan Gift Shop
96 & 96A Princes Street
Edinburgh EH2 2EX Scotland

Taylor Gifts
Conestoga Road &
Lancaster Avenue
Strafford, Wayne, Penna. 19087

Templeton Colonial Furniture
Jct. Scenic Route 2
Baldwinville Road Exit
Templeton, Mass. 01468

Three New Yorkers
39-25 Skillman Avenue
Long Island City, N.Y. 11104

Tibetan Arts & Crafts Ltd.
693 Madison Ave.
New York, N.Y. 10021

Tiffany & Co.
Fifth Avenue and 57th Street
New York, New York 10022

Trails End Zoo Co.
St. Stephen, S.C. 29479

Treasures of the Universe
230 Fifth Avenue
New York, New York 10001

Trencherman's Ltd.
The Town Mill
Alresford, Hampshire, England

Triangle Stores
182-4-6 Flatbush Ave.
Brooklyn, N.Y. 11217

Unicorn Leather Co. Ltd.
Burlington Arcade
Piccadilly
London W.1 England

U. S. Games Systems, Inc.
468 Park Avenue South
New York, New York 10016

Vassilios Rallis Co.
34-41 85th Street
Jackson Heights, N.Y. 11372

Vermont Country Store
Weston, Vermont 05161

Vroubel, Inc.
303 Babylon Turnpike
Roosevelt, L.I., N.Y. 11575

Walter Drake
HP02 Drake Building
Colorado Springs, Colo. 80940

Western Brands
P.O. Box 1880
129-139 East Elkhorn Avenue
Estes Park, Colo. 80517

Windfall
Main Street
Sharon Springs,
New York 13459

World Wide Games, Inc.
Box 450
Delaware, Ohio 43015

Yield House
Dept. 262
North Conway,
New Hampshire 03860

Yorkraft, Inc.
550 South Pine Street
York, Penna 17405

FINIS.

Index